THE BOOK OF WEBMIN
. . . Or How I Learned to Stop Worrying and Love UNIX

THE BOOK OF WEBMIN

WEBMIN

. . . Or How I Learned to Stop Worrying and Love UNIX

by Joe Cooper

NO STARCH PRESS

San Francisco

THE BOOK OF WEBMIN. Copyright © 2003 by R. Joe Cooper.

 Printed on recycled paper in the United States of America

1 2 3 4 5 6 7 8 9 10 – 06 05 04 03

Publisher: William Pollock
Managing Editor: Karol Jurado
Cover and Interior Design: Octopod Studios
Copyeditor: Kenyon Brown
Compositor: Wedobooks
Proofreader: Stephanie Provines

Distributed to the book trade in the United States by Publishers Group West, 1700 Fourth Street, Berkeley, CA 94710; phone: 800-788-3123; fax: 510-658-1834.

Distributed to the book trade in Canada by Jacqueline Gross & Associates, Inc., One Atlantic Avenue, Suite 105, Toronto, Ontario M6K 3E7 Canada; phone: 416-531-6737; fax 416-531- 4259.

For information on translations or book distributors outside the United States, please contact No Starch Press, Inc. directly:

No Starch Press, Inc.
555 De Haro Street, Suite 250, San Francisco, CA 94107
phone: 415-863-9900; fax: 415-863-9950; info@nostarch.com; http://www.nostarch.com

Library of Congress Cataloguing-in-Publication Data

Cooper, R. Joe.
      The book of Webmin, or how I learned to stop worrying and love UNIX / R. Joe Cooper.
          p. cm.
Includes index.
        ISBN 1-886411-92-1
1. User interfaces (Computer systems) 2. UNIX (Computer file) I. Title: How I learned to stop
worrying and love UNIX. II. Title.
        QA76.9.U83C6597 2003
        005.4'37--dc21
                                                              2003000469

BRIEF CONTENTS

CONTENTS IN DETAIL

PREFACE

1
OBTAINING AND INSTALLING WEBMIN

2
LOGGING IN

3
WEBMIN CONFIGURATION

4

USERMIN: A WEBMIN FOR USERS

5
GENERAL SYSTEM CONFIGURATION

6
SERVER AND DAEMON CONFIGURATION

7
APACHE WEBSERVER

8
BIND

9
FTP SERVER

10
POSTFIX

11

SENDMAIL

12
SQUID

13
NETWORKING CONFIGURATION

14
HARDWARE CONFIGURATION

15
OTHERS CATEGORY

INDEX
273

PREFACE

Webmin is a web-based graphical UNIX system administration tool written by Jamie Cameron in the Perl programming language that is designed to be lightweight, functional, and easily extensible. Webmin has been translated to over 20 languages and dialects at the time of this writing, and it has been embraced by a number of hardware and operating system vendors as their default system administration tool. It is extremely portable, offering support for more than 35 different UNIX-like operating systems and Linux distributions. And it is very easily extended to support new features and options, due to an open and well documented API.

Webmin also happens to be a fast and easy to use tool for general UNIX system administration. This document attempts to introduce to you many of the concepts you will need to maintain a UNIX system using Webmin. While no single volume can address every aspect of UNIX system administration, a real effort has been made to provide both a solid introduction to many important tasks and a nearly comprehensive reference to a typical UNIX server and its parts. It is my hope that with nothing more than this book, a copy of Webmin, and the documentation that accompanies your server, you will be able to configure the system to provide the most popular services, create a reasonable security policy, and manage your users and normal system maintenance tasks. Advanced topics are often covered, but I hope that it will not be at the expense of preventing you from seeing the forest for the trees.

Conventions Used in This Book

This book is divided into chapters, with each one being devoted to a particular module or section of Webmin. Often, a short introductory section is included at the start of a chapter that explains the purpose and design of the module and also the function of the underlying software package that is configured by the module. Also, in most cases, one or more tutorials are provided at the end of a chapter to introduce the user to some common functions of the software and how to perform those functions with the Webmin interface.

Type faces have been chosen to indicate the purpose of a word or value. The following type faces have been used in the described manner. Note that some type faces are used for multiple purposes, but context will generally clarify the intention.

Type Faces

Italics Indicates an emphasized word or concept. Also used to indicate the first use of a term in a given context.

Boldface Used to specify a module name or an individual option within a module. The full path to a given module will be represented by separating each level in the hierarchy separated by colons in a bold face. For example, the Squid Access Controls module, located under the Servers tab, can be specified with **Servers:Squid Proxy Server:Access Control**. This form will be used throughout the book.

`Fixed width` Indicates an option value, or a directive within a text configuration file. This type face is also used for filenames and directory pathnames, as well as example input on the command line. When text console examples are used, they will also be in this font and set off from the rest of the text on the page.

When an item is of particular interest, or is of importance for security or compatibility reasons, it will be set off from the rest of the text. A small icon will indicate the type of information and why it has been separated from the normal text. Those icons are used as follows:

NOTE *This is a note, used to indicate some item of interest or a reference to additional documentation on a subject. Notes may be informational, anecdotal, or referential; i.e., they might make a suggestion, tell a story, or refer you to more extensive documentation on the subject.*

CAUTION *This is a warning, used to denote important security information or stability, compatibility, or other information on options that could lead to improper functioning of your server if configured incorrectly. Hopefully, the hammer will remind you that something could get broken if care is not taken.*

TIP *This indicates a helpful tip. Usually a short recommendation for how to best use a feature or option to make your system easier to administer.*

Who Webmin Is For

While it is probably clear by now that the author of this book is a big fan of Webmin, it is worthwhile to discuss who else Webmin is good for and why. Webmin is unique in the UNIX world, in that it provides a one-to-one graphical interface to nearly every service and action needed to maintain a UNIX system. It is universally accessible, because it only requires a web browser. It can potentially be accessed from anywhere in the world via a network connection. It is simple, concise, and consistent in its presentation across a wide array of differing services, functions, and operating systems. It is predictable, in that it does not modify files unnecessarily or in incompatible ways. Configuration with Webmin does not preclude configuration via other tools or via the command line. Equally importantly, Webmin will not damage files if it doesn't understand a particular option or directive in your existing configuration. If Webmin does not understand a portion of your configuration, it will simply ignore it and leave it untouched in the configuration file. Webmin is also accessible, in the sense that it can be used successfully from nearly any browser. Text-mode browsers, small screen displays, and nearly anything else can be accommodated through the appropriate use of themes and numerous configurable display parameters.

Webmin is an excellent tool for both novice and experienced system administrators. As a tool for novices, it can provide a means of getting involved in system administration in a very visual way. All of the options available are presented in a clear and complete fashion. For new users, seeing the possibilities laid out so plainly can be a very effective teaching tool, as well as a helpful safety net to avoid many common pitfalls. It is possible to explore the possibilities of a system, without wading through obscure man pages (you only need wade through the pages in this book, which are perhaps less obscure).

For experienced admins, the advantages are less obvious but no less real. An administrator cannot possibly remember every option to every system function that he or she must configure and maintain. With Webmin, an administrator no longer needs to remember complex syntax or the exact directive needed to accomplish some task. Using Webmin may not be as quick or flexible for some tasks and some users as the command line, and it should not be viewed as a complete replacement for study of traditional system administration tools and techniques. But it is an excellent helper for getting your job done without having to experiment with weird configuration file syntax.

I often tell people that Webmin doesn't make being a good system administrator easy; it just makes the problems more visible and the solutions more consistent. That fact will be a focal point of this book. We will cover precisely how the Webmin interface maps to the traditional configuration files that actually control your UNIX system. UNIX, like any sufficiently powerful and flexible system, is complex, and Webmin doesn't remove that complexity, though it can make the complexity easier to manage by presenting it in the form of a consistent interface.

Who This Book is For

This book is targeted at intermediate UNIX users as an introductory text to many complex topics and as a reference guide for experienced system administrators who must maintain a wide array of services and operating systems. It can also be a valuable companion volume to a beginning UNIX text, for beginners who would like to learn the *Webmin Way* alongside more traditional methods and practices. There is no substitute for learning and understanding your operating system. But this book attempts to bring the two worlds together, so that time spent with a book covering traditional methods will map directly onto your Webmin experience, with the hope of making both more valuable and comprehensible.

If you have a desire to learn more about your system and Webmin, no matter your current level of knowledge, this book can be valuable to you. I make no assumptions of the level of experience of the user. I do assume a reader willing to read not just this book and not just approach the system from the Webmin perspective. The reader who will gain the most from this book will be the one who reads the man page for a software package while working through the chapter on that subject. Links to other sources of information are often provided, as are notes to help you locate where on your system the actual configuration files are located. Finally, every single option in Webmin maps to some configuration file directive, command-line option, or system variable value. Each of these directives, options, and values for the modules covered is pointed out and described. If Webmin has turned your system into a black box in your mind, this book seeks to pull the top from the box so you can look inside. There is nothing wrong with allowing Webmin to make your job easier, but ignorance of how it relates to the underlying system can only lead to confusion and problems.

Because Webmin itself predates the writing of this book by a couple of years, Jamie Cameron has a significant head start on this author. I'd love to cover every module in the core Webmin and a few of the better third-party modules, but deadlines must be met. The book has to be called *finished* at some point, and I believe I've made a valiant first effort to document the *core* modules. This book covers all of the general system modules and functions, the Webmin configuration modules, and the modules for the Apache web server, the Sendmail mail server, the Postfix mail server, the WU-FTPD ftp server, the BIND domain name server, and the Squid proxy server. I believe these are the most common services being configured with Webmin, and therefore I considered them the most important to document completely and accurately for the first published edition of this book. At any rate, they are the most common source of questions on the Webmin mailing list, and thus those are the modules that are covered here.

NOTE *Perhaps you've noticed that there are two mail servers in the above list of topics covered, Sendmail and Postfix, while all other services are covered by one module and chapter only. The reason is simple: I prefer Postfix to Sendmail. However, the last time I saw any data regarding the subject of mail server usage Sendmail was moving over 65 percent of the world's email, while Postfix was merely a small but growing blip on the radar. So, while Postfix is an easier mail server to configure and maintain in most environments, and functionally equivalent to Sendmail in most ways, I felt compelled to address both.*

Why a Webmin Book?

Though the question is perhaps of little relevance to some readers, I've come to the conclusion that every technical book ought to be able to convincingly answer the question of why it was written. If an author can't answer that simple question it is quite likely the book should have never come to be, and given the alarming number of fat, empty books in the technical section at my local bookseller I'd guess that too few authors ever attempt to answer it. So, for the next few paragraphs I'm going to answer the question by explaining why a Webmin book, and more specifically a Webmin book written by me, should be on the bookshelves at your local bookseller and on the web for all to read.

I started writing the Webmin book in late 2000 for entirely selfish reasons, though reasons unrelated to making money on the book in any direct way. Some time before that in 1999 I co-founded a company to build appliance servers based on the Linux operating system and a number of other Open Source software packages. Starting Linux-based technology companies was very much the thing for nerds like me to do at the time, just as two years later it was equally popular for Linux-based technology companies to fold into bankruptcy and oblivion just as enthusiastically as they had started, if with somewhat less fanfare and revolutionary talk. The company, Swell Technology, was founded on a lot of high ideals about how a hardware vendor ought to behave toward customers and toward the Open Source community, plus a little money that I had made in the stock market before the Internet bubble burst. After all, no matter how high the ideals or how vibrant the Linux server market potential appears at the time it still takes a little money to start a company. But, unlike a lot of other Linux-based technology startups, Swell Technology still exists three years later, possibly partly because we didn't bother with venture capital or a hyped IPO, as was the standard operating procedure for most Linux-based technology companies of the time.

In 1999 when we founded Swell, we focused on one small niche market and developed a web caching appliance product based on the previously mentioned Linux, Squid, and a still young but rapidly developing Webmin. The choice of Webmin was mostly an easy one, because at the time it was either Webmin or text editing of configuration files with vi or emacs. Luckily, Webmin was already an exceedingly solid piece of work with a quite wide feature set. So I built the product, packaged the product, marketed the product (with some help on all counts), and even sold a few of the product by the middle of 2000. I also wrote a lot of documentation, to the tune of a few hundred pages — first in LinuxDoc and then in the far more capable and flexible DocBook. However, most of this documentation was mostly written for users of our products. It contained a large amount of information that would be useful to a general reader using Webmin and not just our clients, but that information was interspersed with occasional information that was only useful to a user logged in to one of our servers. Thus, no one was reading it except our customers who, at the time, did not make an exceedingly large audience.

Also during this time, I was reading and answering questions on the Webmin mailing lists whenever I knew the answer. As on all technical mailing lists, there are questions that come up every few days or weeks no matter how many times they are answered. On some lists this is particularly annoying, because the documentation for a project usually answers those sorts of questions in vivid detail. Perhaps there is a FAQ with the answers or a nice man page. Webmin, however, had very little in the way of documentation. At the time, the Webmin FAQ consisted of about five questions and answers and online help only existed for a few modules (I had already written the online help for the Squid module and still maintain those help files today). So the questioners couldn't simply be referred to the documentation, because there was none that answered their question. So, out of a profound desire to be lazy, I started writing a book. I'm sure there is an apparent contradiction in that statement to many readers, but probably not to anyone who regularly contributes to an Open Source project mailing list. Answering the same question half-heartedly several times is far more tiring than answering it once with the thoroughness it deserves.

So I set out to answer some of those questions with a thoroughness that I hoped would severely reduce the number of repetitive questions on the mailing list, as well as answer some of the questions I found my clients often asked about Webmin on our servers. According to my revision information I posted the first 0.01 draft on October 6, 2000 on a back corner of my personal website. It contained four chapters, none of which was more than ten pages. It covered Apache, Squid, and most of the Webmin-related configuration options. I had taken off a long weekend from Friday to Monday to write it and another couple days to figure out how to process DocBook SGML. Within three days of mentioning it on the Webmin list my book, if it could be called that in its diminutive early form, was receiving 1,000 hits and a few hundred unique visitors each day. Our company web server, where my home page is hosted, had never seen that much traffic in its entire existence. Interesting. Free stuff draws visitors, and free, *useful* stuff draws a *lot* of visitors. This discovery was very exciting for me because, as a devout capitalist and businessman, I like to give stuff away. Or maybe I'm merely a little less than humble and enjoy knowing folks have read my book and find it useful. Either way, I enjoyed the popularity my book was gaining among Webmin users.

A lot of people seemed to like the early versions of the book, and I was enjoying writing it because it gave me a structured way to learn a lot of things that I didn't already know and reinforced things I did. Thus, the book grew whenever I had a weekend to spare and a subject that I wanted to write about. Somewhere along the way, I began to receive requests to buy the book, and as the book grew these requests came more frequently. So in a fit of brilliance unmatched by any of my previous intellectual revelations (which number in the hundreds on a good day), I decided to publish the book myself.

I began the process of preparing it for printing via a print-on-demand publisher and trying to figure out all of the complexities of transferring digital words onto paper cost-effectively and with a high-quality resulting product. Luckily, this madness was interrupted by a phone call from Bill Pollock of No Starch Press, a *real* book publisher with a well-earned reputation for quality production, who was interested in publishing a book about Webmin. He had spoken to Jamie Cameron who referred him to me as a possible choice for doing the writing. After a brief discussion about licensing (because I insisted on being able to offer a free version on my website) we came to an agreement. Several months later by way of magic and editors and printers this book has found its way to your local bookseller with an attractive cover and in a nice binding. Or I suppose I should say I *think* it will find its way to your local bookseller with an attractive cover and nice binding . . . one can never be sure about the future. It was a brief discussion, because I've been a fan of No Starch since reading *The Book of JavaScript* by Thau! with its brilliant cover design and very nice presentation overall. Also, the terms of the boilerplate contract were quite fair and more generous than most similar agreements from other publishers. Adding Bill's immediate agreement to allow me to publish a free version online, it was a quick and painless process. If all publishers were this nice to work with, I would probably become a full-time writer and rid myself of the complexities and uncertainties of running a business in a highly volatile market.

Now that the story of the book and how it came to be is out, I will wrap up by saying I hope you enjoy my first book and find it a valuable addition to your bookshelf. I've attempted, with possibly varying degrees of success, to strike a balance between a comprehensive reference to the options found in Webmin and a valuable learning tool for UNIX and Webmin users who may not have extensive system administration experience. More succinctly, I hope this book answers your questions.

How to Contact the Author and Errata

I've done my best to make this book a useful and accurate desktop reference guide for administering a UNIX system with Webmin. If you have ideas about what would make this a more useful guide in future editions, or if you find an error in the text, please feel free to contact me. Email is the preferred method of contact: webmin-book@swelltech.com. I will maintain a list of errata online at The Book of Webmin home page [http://www.swelltech.com/support/webminguide].

How to Contact No Starch Press

Visit No Starch Press online at [http://www.nostarch.com/webmin.html] for book updates, errata, and other information.

Acknowledgments

This book could not have been completed without the extreme patience and helpfulness of Jamie Cameron, the author of Webmin. Not only did he go to the trouble to create Webmin to start with, but he managed to fix every bug this author could find and explain every detail I could not figure out on my own during the course of writing the book. He also maintains a breakneck pace of development, which has only accelerated in the time that I've been using Webmin. The Webmin community could not hope for a more benevolent or productive leader.

Thanks also are due to the regulars on the Webmin users' and Webmin developers' mailing lists. Many patient individuals helped me learn the ropes of Webmin long ago. The fine users of Webmin have continued to provide support and assistance to me throughout the writing of this book by spotting the problems and complaining loudly. It is surely a better book because of the criticisms of every person who sent emails detailing my failings. It could be said that this book has been continuously edited by the Webmin community from the day of its first publication on the web. Of particular note for sharing their in-depth knowledge of Webmin, Perl, and Linux systems in general, are Ryan W. Maple and Tim Niemuller.

Much thanks are also due to members of the docbook-apps mailing list, where all of my SGML and DocBook questions were answered. The book would not be as nice to look at or read without the guidance of the kind individuals there. In particular, Norman Walsh deserves praise for his modular DocBook stylesheets and the prompt attention to my questions regarding them, and Sebastian Rahtz is due thanks for his JadeTeX and PDFJadeTeX macro package, as well as the great work he does in helping to compile the TeXLive CD, all of which were instrumental in producing the HTML, PostScript, and PDF variants of the book. There seems to be a small revolution in the world of open tools for publishing, and the folks involved in making all of these technologies possible are due my highest praise and appreciation. I couldn't have prepared a book for publication without their hard work on PDFJadeTeX, Jade and OpenJade, teTeX, and probably others that I don't even realize are involved in the process. My next book will be in XML DocBook, so I'm hopeful they will still be around to help me through the process.

Finally, the screenshots within this text have been made using the Swell Technology Webmin theme. The icons in this theme were created primarily by me, but with early assistance and guidance by Youngjin Hahn (aka Artwiz), a very talented young artist who is perhaps best known for his excellent icon and themes work at Themes.org [http://www.themes.org]. Other design elements, including the theme colors and titles, were created with the assistance from Charity Baessell, the webmistress and graphic designer at Swell Technology and of the PenguinFeet project. Thanks also go to Jamie for making Webmin themeable to start with. Not to say the original theme was ugly or anything . . . well, I'm just happy Webmin is themeable.

NOTE   *The latest version of the Swell Technology Webmin theme can be downloaded from the Open Source Projects page [http://www.swelltech.com/projects] at swelltech.com.*

1

OBTAINING AND INSTALLING WEBMIN

Obtaining Webmin is easy. In fact, it may be installed on your system already. Several Linux distributions now include Webmin as either its primary system administration interface or as an optional package. Also, a large number of Linux hardware vendors use Webmin or a modified version of Webmin as their graphical administration interface. Best of all, because Webmin is free software, even if you don't have Webmin already, it is only a download away.

Where to Download Webmin

It is often best to obtain Webmin from your OS vendor if it provides a package for it. In this way, you can be sure it is automatically configured suitably for your particular OS and version. Executable and configuration file locations vary somewhat from OS version to version and from vendor to vendor, so getting Webmin from your vendor ensures consistency.

CAUTION *It is necessary to temper the advice to get Webmin from your vendor with the warning that some vendors lag behind the release schedule of the official Webmin by a month or more. In recent months at least two exploitable conditions have been found in older versions of Webmin. If you are obtaining Webmin from your vendor, it is imperative that you check to be sure it is a recent version, which does not have exploitable bugs. Good vendors will of course update their packages immediately with a secured version, but being cautious is wise when the security of your server is at stake.*

If your OS or system vendor does not provide a package of Webmin, then you can go to the Webmin home page at [http://www.webmin.com/]. Here you will find the latest version of Webmin in a tarball package, a Solaris pkg, and an RPM package. The tarball will work on nearly any UNIX version that has Perl, while the RPM package is known to work directly on at least Red Hat, Mandrake, SuSE, MSC, and Caldera versions of Linux.

Installing Webmin

Installation of Webmin differs slightly depending on which type of package you choose to install. Note that Webmin requires a relatively recent Perl for any of these installation methods to work. Nearly all, if not all, modern UNIX and UNIX-like OS variants now include Perl as a standard component of the OS, so this should not be an issue.

Installing from a tar.gz

First you must untar and unzip the archive in the directory where you would like Webmin to be installed. The most common location for installation from tarballs is /usr/local. Some sites prefer /opt. If you're using GNU tar, you can do this all on one command line:

```
# tar zxvf webmin-0.87.tar.gz
```

If you have a less capable version of tar, you must unzip the file first and then untar it:

```
# gunzip webmin-0.87.tar.gz
# tar xvf webmin-0.87.tar
```

Next, you need to change to the directory that was created when you untarred the archive, and execute the setup.sh script, as shown in the following example. The script will ask several questions about your system and your preferences for the installation. Generally, accepting the default values will work. An example installation might look like this:

```
[root@delilah webmin-1.050]# ./setup.sh
********************************************************************
*          Welcome to the Webmin setup script, version 1.050          *
********************************************************************
Webmin is a web-based interface that allows Unix-like operating
systems and common Unix services to be easily administered.

Installing Webmin in /usr/local/webmin-1.050 ...


********************************************************************
Webmin uses separate directories for configuration files and log
files.  Unless you want to run multiple versions of Webmin at the
same time you can just accept the defaults.

Config file directory [/etc/webmin]: /usr/local/etc/webmin
Log file directory [/var/webmin]: /usr/local/var/webmin


********************************************************************
Webmin is written entirely in Perl. Please enter the full path to
the Perl 5 interpreter on your system.

Full path to perl (default /usr/bin/perl):

Testing Perl ...
Perl seems to be installed ok


********************************************************************
Operating system name:    Redhat Linux
Operating system version: 8.0


********************************************************************
Webmin uses its own password protected web server to provide
access to the administration programs. The setup script needs to
know :
- What port to run the web server on. There must not be another
web server already using this port.
- The login name required to access the web server.
- The password required to access the web server.
- If the webserver should use SSL (if your system supports it).
- Whether to start webmin at boot time.

Web server port (default 10000):
Login name (default admin): root
```

```
Login password:
Password again:
The Perl SSLeay library is not installed. SSL not available.
Start Webmin at boot time (y/n): n
****************************************************************
Creating web server config files..
..done

Creating access control file..
..done

Inserting path to perl into scripts..
..done

Creating start and stop scripts..
..done

Copying config files..
..done

Creating uninstall script /usr/local/etc/webmin/uninstall.sh ..
..done

Changing ownership and permissions ..
..done

Running postinstall scripts ..
..done

Attempting to start Webmin mini web server..
Starting Webmin server in /usr/local/webmin-1.050
..done


****************************************************************
Webmin has been installed and started successfully. Use your web
browser to go to

http://delilah.swell:10000/

and login with the name and password you entered previously.


[root@delilah webmin-1.050]#
```

Here you can see that I've chosen the default in some locations and deviated from the default in others. The most likely changes you may want to make include changing the default installation directories and altering the port on which Webmin will listen. Webmin also politely generates an uninstall.sh script that allows you to easily remove Webmin from your system.

Installing from an RPM

Installing from an RPM is even easier. You only need to run one command:

```
[root@delilah root]# rpm -Uvh webmin-1.050-1.noarch.rpm
```

This will copy all of the Webmin files to the appropriate locations and run the install script with appropriate default values. For example, on my Red Hat system, the Webmin perl files will be installed in /usr/libexec/webmin while the configuration files will end up in /etc/webmin. Webmin will then be started on port 10000. You may log in using root as the login name and your system root password as the password. It's unlikely you will need to change any of these items from the command line, because they can all be modified using Webmin. If you do need to make any changes, you can do so in miniserv.conf in /etc/webmin.

Installing from a pkg

To install on a Solaris machine using the pkg file, the steps are almost as simple as using the RPM. First, unzip the file using gzip and then use pkgadd to install the package:

```
root# gunzip webmin-1.050.pkg.gz
root# pkgadd -d webmin-1.050.pkg
```

This will install Webmin into /usr/opt and run the install script with appropriate default values.

After Installation

After installation, your Webmin install will behave nearly identically, regardless of operating system vendor or version, location of installation, or method of installation. The only apparent differences between systems will be that some have more or fewer modules because some are specific to one OS. Others will feature slightly different versions of modules to take into account different functioning of the underlying system. For example, the package manager module may behave differently, or be missing from the available options entirely, depending on your OS.

NOTE *A common problem after installing Webmin is that some modules do not work or do not seem to work completely. This can be caused by some of the software being installed in non-standard locations on your system. By default, when Webmin is installed, it creates a configuration for each module based on the standard filesystem structure and configuration file locations for your selected OS. If you have installed software from source tarballs instead of packages, or packages from a different source than your OS vendor, Webmin may not be able to find the files it needs to function correctly. Correcting these problems is usually a simple matter of modifying the configuration for the individual modules to match the actual locations of your configuration files.*

Changing Webmin Passwords from the Command Line

Generally, once Webmin is installed all configuration of Webmin can be performed from within Webmin. However, there are a few things that can lead to being unable to log in. A common question is how to log in if you've forgotten the Webmin administrator password. If you have root access to the machine in question (i.e., you haven't also forgotten your system password), you can use the changepass.pl tool, that is found in the same directory as all of the other Webmin executable files (this is the directory in which you installed Webmin). For example, to use changepass.pl to change the root password, you could use the following command:

```
# ./changepass.pl /etc/webmin root newpassword
```

In the preceding example, the first option should be the directory where your Webmin configuration files are located. The second is the login name of the user whose password you'd like to change. The third is what you'd like the password to be changed to. Note that this script only works if you are logged in as the system root user and can change any Webmin user's password.

Changing the Webmin Port from the Command Line

Another problem after installation may be that a firewall prevents access to the Webmin port from across a WAN link (if, for example, you are remotely maintaining your Webmin server). If this is the case, you will want to consult with the firewall administrator to find out whether port 10000 can be opened, or if not, what port you can use for your Webmin installation. Changing the port on which Webmin runs after installation is also a pretty simple process. Simply edit the file miniserv.conf in the /etc directory where your Webmin configuration files were installed (this is likely one of the following: /etc/webmin, /usr/local/webmin/etc, or /opt/webmin/etc). You'll find a port directive. Change this to whatever port you need Webmin to listen on, and then restart the Webmin web server.

Restarting Webmin from the Command Line

Restarting the Webmin server is usually required when making changes to the miniserv.conf file. Some OS versions provide a standard method to stop, start, and restart services, which Webmin often supports. But all versions of Webmin on all OS versions will have start and stop scripts, usually located in the configuration file directory of Webmin.

Restarting the Webmin server can be accomplished in a few different ways depending the OS and version. Under Red Hat Linux and its derivatives, for example, you would use the standard service command:

```
[root@delilah /root]# /sbin/service webmin stop
[root@delilah /root]# /sbin/service webmin start
```

If your OS does not have a standardized service control tool like service, you may use the standard Webmin stop and start scripts located in the Webmin etc directory:

```
[root@delilah /root]# /etc/webmin/stop; /etc/webmin/start
```

The miniserv.conf file contains many other options, but you will only need to edit a few manually. Other common problems that users run into include restricting their access by IP. This can cause them a problem if their service provider changes the IP. Simply mistyping an IP can also lead to the same trouble. The remedy for this problem is to add the correct IP to the allow= directive and then restart the Webmin server.

2

LOGGING IN

Logging In with Netscape or Internet Explorer

Logging in to Webmin is easy. Open a web browser, such as Netscape or Internet Explorer, on any machine that has network access to the server on which you wish to log in. Browse to port 10000 on the IP or host name of the server, as shown here.

```
http://delilah:10000/
```

Webmin will then respond with either an authentication window or an authentication web form, in which you can enter the administrator username (usually "root" or "admin") and password. After successful authentication, you will be greeted with the Webmin index page. The type of login form you receive (either on a web page or in a popup window) depends on the configuration of the Webmin server. The differences between session authentication (Figure 2-1) and standard HTTP authentication are discussed later in the book.

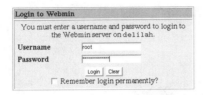

Figure 2-1: Session authentication

NOTE *Many systems are configured with Webmin running in SSL encrypted mode. On these systems, you will log in using a URL beginning with* https:// *rather than* http://. *Also, at least one Linux distribution that includes Webmin, specifically Caldera, installs it on port 1000 rather than 10000. This is theoretically a more secure arrangement, however, be aware that some firewalls will prevent you from accessing your Webmin-enabled server from outside of the local network if Webmin runs on a port below 1024.*

Logging In with Lynx

Sometimes, it may be desirable or necessary to administer your system from the command line without the benefit of a GUI. Luckily, one does not have to give up Webmin entirely in these circumstances. Using Lynx, or a similarly capable text-mode web browser, one can log in and use most of the Webmin modules much the same as using a graphical browser. Logging in when Webmin is using session authentication is identical to logging in with a graphical browser, but logging in when Webmin is configured to use traditional HTTP authentication is slightly different. Lynx requires that authentication information be included on the command line when starting up:

```
[joe@delilah joe]$ lynx -auth root:passwd http://delilah:10000
```

CAUTION *If you plan to administer your system via a text-mode browser, you will want to choose an alternate theme rather than the new default MSC.Linux theme. The old default theme, or the Swell Technology theme has a simpler icon and table layout, allowing Lynx and other text-mode browsers to display them more effectively. The MSC.Linux theme, while attractive in a GUI browser, uses a complex layout that leads many areas of Webmin to be difficult to read and impossible to use in a text-mode browser.*

Another limitation of using a command line client is that SSL is not well supported by all versions of Lynx and other text-mode browsers. This means you may need to run your Webmin server without encryption; therefore, more extreme measures should be taken to ensure the security of your server. Securing a Webmin installation will be discussed in detail in later chapters.

A First Look

Webmin is divided into a number of modules that each allow you to administer a single aspect of your system. Modules exist for most common, and many uncommon, system administration tasks. The standard modules provide a graphical interface for: *Apache, Squid, Bind, NFS, man pages, Sendmail, Postfix,*

Samba, and much more. There also exists a wide array of third-party modules that provide even more extensive functionality. This book focuses on the standard modules, but may expand to encompass other modules in time.

Upon first logging in, you'll see a row of tabs and a number of icons (Figure 2-2). The tabs are labeled **Webmin**, **System**, **Servers**, **Hardware**, **Cluster**, and **Others**. You may also have, depending on your OS and version, one or two additional tabs. The selected tab when first logging in is always **Webmin**. This category is where all of the Webmin-related configuration details are located.

Figure 2-2: A first look

The view from Lynx is actually pretty similar if using one of the traditional themes (Figure 2-3). The MSC.Linux theme makes many links inaccessible when using Lynx; overall usage is quite difficult when you're working in a text-mode browser, so be sure to switch to a more conventional theme if you'll be administering your system from the command line. On my server using the Swell Technology theme, Webmin is quite usable entirely from a text console, making Webmin useful even when no browser is available. The MSC.Linux theme can also be rather heavyweight when administering a server across a WAN link with a graphical browser. This is because the number and size of images makes browsing the pages rather slow even via a fast connection.

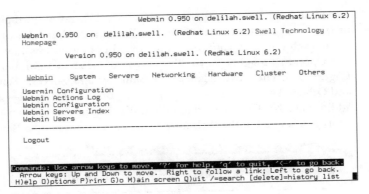

Figure 2-3: A first look from Lynx

Because Webmin is web-based, interacting with the GUI will probably be immediately comfortable, though for beginners it may take a few minutes to locate specific modules or features. In the following chapters, the discussion will focus on specific Webmin modules and the services that the modules configure. It proceeds through the category tabs from left to right, beginning with **Webmin** and ending with **Others**.

3

WEBMIN CONFIGURATION

Webmin provides a number of configurable options and access control features, as well as flexible action logging that provides you with the maximum flexibility and security of the Webmin server and the various Webmin system administration modules.

These features are accessed through the **Webmin** tab on the index page of Webmin. When you display the **Webmin** tab, you see icons for **Usermin Configuration**, **Webmin Actions Log**, **Webmin Configuration**, **Webmin Servers Index**, and **Webmin Users**. Keep in mind that the modules located under the **Webmin** tab are for configuring *Webmin itself*, not the underlying system.

So, for example, creating a user in the **Webmin Users** module will not create a system user, only a Webmin user. Likewise, the **Webmin Actions Log** module allows you to search and view the Webmin log, not any system or service log that might exist. We'll get to those kinds of options later. For the moment, we're going to skip over **Usermin Configuration** because Usermin receives full coverage in the next chapter.

Webmin Actions Log

The Webmin Actions Log page provides access to the Webmin log. You can configure this log for each module and individual users. This module does not configure the logs, but provides you with a means to search the logs for actions performed by particular logged users or actions performed in given logged modules. Configuration of Webmin logging capabilities is covered in the **Webmin Configuration** section.

With this module it is possible to search for actions by specific users, within specific modules, for a given range of dates, or any combination of those qualifications. For example, if you manage a number of junior system administrators and you'd like to find out if one of them has edited an Apache virtual server configuration in the past week, this module makes those kinds of questions easy to answer (assuming logging to that degree is enabled, of course).

Webmin Configuration

The **Webmin Configuration** module (Figure 3-1) allows you to configure most of the important aspects of Webmin itself, as well as install new modules, upgrade existing modules, and upgrade Webmin itself. It also provides a means to change the port and address where the Webmin miniserv.pl web server listens for connections, select different languages, enable or disable SSL encryption, and configure the Webmin built-in logging features.

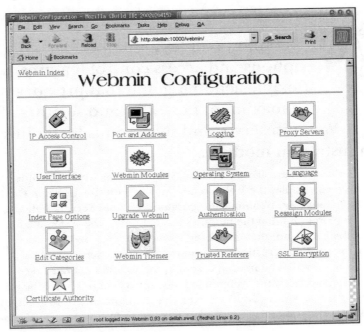

Figure 3-1: Webmin Configuration

IP Access Control

Webmin has its own web server, called `miniserv.pl`, which provides a simple IP access control feature. This page allows you to configure this option. You may enter IP networks (such as `192.168.1.0`), IP host addresses (such as `192.168.1.79`), and host names (such as `joesbox.penguinfeet.org`). It is wise to limit access to the Webmin server to just those addresses that are trusted. While Webmin has no known exploits in versions greater than 0.970, if someone were to obtain your password, this would provide an additional level of protection from unauthorized access. This option configures the `accept` and `deny` directives in the `miniserv.conf` file. The default is to allow any address to access Webmin.

CAUTION *Be aware that using IP access controls within Webmin is an application-level security feature. In other words, if ever an exploitable problem were discovered in the Webmin `miniserv.pl` web server, it would still be accessible from an IP not permitted to use Webmin. So it is still theoretically possible to attack the web server even if the user isn't offered a login page. However, this is a pretty unlikely scenario, requiring a bug in `miniserv.pl` that is exposed even when an authentication page is not provided.*

Port and Address

The Webmin server will, by default, listen on every active IP address on the system. But if you have multiple addresses and would prefer Webmin to only listen on one of them, you may use this option. So, for example, if you have one network interface connected directly to your local network and a second network interface connected to the Internet, you could improve security by causing Webmin to only listen on the local network. In this case, any requests from the Internet at large would be ignored, but it would still be possible to connect from local computers. This can be a very effective first line of defense. After all, if the bad guys can't even talk to the Webmin server, they certainly can't try anything funny to break into it.

The **Listen on Port** option specifies the network port on which Webmin will listen. In a standard Webmin install this will be port 10000, although Caldera installs it on port 1000. Some firewalls may restrict access to ports below 1024, and some may restrict even ports above 1024. If your network has strict proxy restrictions that prevent connecting on port 10000, you may wish to try port 553 or 443 (assuming these ports are not already in use on your Webmin server for normal SSL service). These ports will nearly always be usable through a proxy, even when using an SSL enabled Webmin.

NOTE *In a proxied environment, your client browser must use a `CONNECT` method to construct a tunnel through the proxy device. Because of the potential for abusing `CONNECT` requests most proxies prevent this method on all but a few ports. The standard port for SSL web connections is 443, and so it is the most likely port to be available for `CONNECT` requests. If your proxy is running Squid and you have administrator privileges, you may wish to add Webmins default port to the allowed SSL ports as documented in the Squid chapter of this book.*

As mentioned briefly in the installation chapter, it is possible to alter these configuration settings in the `miniserv.conf` configuration file in addition to graphical configuration with the Webmin Configuration module. This may be necessary if a firewall prevents you from accessing port 10000 and you only have console or SSH access to the machine. In this case, editing the port option will alter the port, and the bind directive configures the address on which Webmin listens. Whenever editing the miniserv.conf file, Webmin must be restarted for changes to take effect.

Logging

As mentioned earlier, Webmin provides very flexible logging features. With these features, you can very easily monitor what actions those users with administrator privileges are performing on the server. It is also possible to log actions based on the module where the actions are performed. The option **Log resolved host names** will cause Webmin to provide a host name rather than just an IP address for the client computer that performed an action. And **Clear logfiles every...hours** causes Webmin to rotate its own logs and keep them from over-filling the disk with old logs. If long-term logs are needed for security auditing purposes, it may be wise to include the Webmin log in your normal system backup rotation.

The decisions regarding what to log, whose actions to log, and how long to store those logs should be carefully considered for your situation. In some cases, a log is unnecessary, while in others it may be required by company policy or useful in addressing the security needs of your environment. If logging is enabled, care should be taken to ensure Webmin will have plenty of disk space in the Webmin log directory, as some options can lead to quite verbose logging (**Log changes made to files by each action**, for example). Remember that Webmin action logging has nothing to do with the logging features of other parts of the system. Syslog is configured separately in the **System:System Logs** module, while application-specific logging is usually configured within the application module.

Proxy Servers

Webmin provides several tools that must connect to the Internet to operate correctly. These include the **Webmin Update** feature, the **Software Packages** module and others. If your local network uses a proxy to access Web or FTP sites on the Internet, you may configure those settings here. If your proxy requires authentication, the username Webmin will use to log-in can also be configured on this page in the **Username for proxy** and **Password for proxy** fields.

User Interface

The Webmin user interface is configurable in a number of ways. In this module you may configure the colors of your Webmin pages. The colors are expected to be in standard hex triplets, as used in HTML markup on the Internet. You may also choose to use the standard fonts of your browser to display page titles, rather than the font provided by the theme you are using. Finally, you may configure where on the page Webmin will display the login name and host name of the server. This page does not configure Webmin themes, which are configured on their own page, and the changes that can be made here are mild by comparison to the possibilities when using themes. Be aware also that these changes may not take effect when using a theme other than the old standard Webmin theme. For example, the new MSC.Linux theme overrides all of these options with its own standard values.

Webmin Modules

As previously mentioned, one of the best things about Webmin is that it is completely modular. Every server daemon, every system feature, every Webmin feature, has its own module that connects to the core Webmin libraries and answers to the Webmin miniserv.pl web server. Because of the elaborate, but still easily comprehensible, modular framework that Webmin provides, it is very easy to write full-featured modules that integrate seamlessly into Webmin and your operating system.

Install Module

From this page, you can install new modules, either from a local file, an uploaded file, or a file downloaded from an FTP site or website. Webmin module packages are simply tar archive files that contain the complete directory structure of the module. These modules end in the suffix .wbm.

NOTE *A great resource for additional Webmin modules is the Third Party Modules for Webmin [http://www.thirdpartymodules.com/webmin] page, run by Richard Teachout. Richard is a longtime fan and supporter of Webmin and a regular contributor to the Webmin discussion lists. After spending some time on the list, he perceived a need for a comprehensive resource for modules that work with Webmin. At the time of this writing, there are over 200 modules listed at his site, though it should be mentioned that the site also lists the modules included in the standard Webmin distribution. If you've written a Webmin module, you should post it to this site, so others will be able to easily find and benefit from your efforts. It is also a great place to find example code to help you when writing your own modules (in addition to the standard modules, of course!). Beware, however, that as with any group of free software the modules vary wildly in quality. Some are excellent and on par with any of the best standard Webmin modules, while others are in such an early stage of development that they are not useful.*

Clone Module

The **Clone Module** feature provides an impressive amount of flexibility for administrators who must provide limited administration access for several instances of the same software on the same machine. If, for example, you have two different Apache configurations running on your system, you could clone the Apache module to allow different users to access the different Apache configurations.

CAUTION *While this feature does allow interesting and powerful options for multiple users configuring similar services, Webmin should not yet be viewed as an ideal tool for administering a virtual hosting server, where many users configure the Apache virtual servers, Sendmail aliases, and DNS entries. There are a number of commercial and Open Source efforts underway to provide such services within the framework of Webmin. At the time of this writing none are production-ready, but with the number of people pursuing the goal, it is likely that such a tool is not far off.*

To clone a module, select the module to clone from the drop-down menu, then enter a new name for the module. To avoid the problem of the new module interfering with the original module, you will want to carefully consider the service being administered by the cloned module. Usually, you will need to set up the new clone with a wholly separate installation of the service being configured. So, for example, if you have cloned Squid so that you may run two different Squid processes you *must* configure them to use separate configuration files, cache directories, log files, and process IDs. If this precaution is not taken, one or both of the processes will behave erratically or fail to work at all.

Example: Cloning the Squid Module

To take the example further, let's create a clone of the Squid module and configure two Squid processes to run on the same server without stepping on each other. First, copy the squid.conf configuration file from the command line or the Webmin File Manager to a file named squid2.conf.

```
[root@delilah /]# cp /etc/squid/squid.conf /etc/squid/squid2.conf
```

Next, create your module clone of the Squid module (referred to as **Squid2** from here on). Browse to the newly created clone module, and edit the module configuration by clicking the **Module Config** link in the upper left corner of the Squid2 index page. Here you should change the **Full path to squid config file** to point to the newly created configuration file. You will also need to change the **Command to start squid** and **Command to stop squid** to point to another file name as well; let's call it /etc/rc.d/init.d/squid2. We'll have to actually create these files before trying to start up our new Squid process.

We will also need to alter the **Full path to PID file** to point to squid2.pid rather than squid.pid and change the log directory name. I usually use /var/log/ squid2 for a cloned Squid process. This is all that is required within the module configuration for the moment. Click **Save** to save your changes and return to the **Squid2** index page.

Now that we've told Webmin the file to edit, we can actually edit it to configure Squid2 to operate independently of Squid. First we'll need to change Squid2 to operate on a different port or IP than Squid, because no two processes can listen on the same IP:port combination. 8080 is a good secondary cache port to use. This option is configured in **Squid2:Ports and Networking**. Next alter the cache directories to something different than the **Squid** cache directories, because they cannot be shared. The same must be done for the access.log, `cache.log`, and `store.log`. As mentioned previously, I usually place my Squid2 logs into `/var/log/squid2`, so this directory must be created with ownership by the same user and group names that Squid runs under (`squid:squid` on Red Hat Linux).

Finally, copy your Squid start-up script to a new location and modify it to call Squid with the new configuration file and check against the new PID file. For example, on my Red Hat system I would copy `/etc/rc.d/init.d/squid` to `/etc/rc.d/init.d/squid2`. You can now configure access controls in Webmin to allow access to separate administrators for each Squid process or further modify the Squid2 configuration to provide different functionality than the primary Squid process.

Delete Modules

In this section, you may select any modules that you'd like to delete from your Webmin installation. Beware that using this form will delete the selected modules entirely from the system. If you decide later to use a deleted module, you will have to download the module again and reinstall it. It is usually a better idea to simply remove the module from each users access list (possibly even including root), rather than deleting the module here. However, if disk space is a concern, you can use this to delete all unneeded modules from your system.

Operating System

Webmin knows how to interact with your system based on configuration files for each module that are selected based on the operating system configured here. If your system has Webmin preinstalled, you usually will not need to concern yourself with this. But if you upgrade your system, and the new version moves some configuration files to new locations, updating this may be necessary. On this page you may also set the search path for both programs (like system commands) and for libraries (such as for the password encryption library). Again, these options rarely need to be changed unless you have installed system tools and configuration files in odd locations on your system.

NOTE   *In current versions of Webmin, at least up to 1.020, changing the OS does not alter existing module configuration files and will only apply to newly installed modules. A future version will likely alter this behavior to modify the already installed module configurations only if they have not been altered by the user.*

Language

Webmin supports a large number of languages for titles and module text. This page allows you to choose the language of your Webmin. New languages are being added regularly. Users of languages that are not supported are encouraged to write a translation and send it to the author of Webmin. He's always happy to receive new translations, and users are always happy to find that their native language is one that is provided with the distribution.

Index Page Options

This page allows you to configure the layout of the Webmin index pages. You may choose the number of icons to display per row using the **Number of Columns** field. The **Categorize modules?** selects whether modules will be grouped under category tabs based on the type of function they perform. The **Default category** is the category that will be displayed when first logging in to Webmin. An alternative header can be used by selecting the **Use alternative header** option, which provides a somewhat different appearance by placing the host information on the upper right side of the display rather than below the Webmin title. Finally, selecting **Go direct to module if user only has one?** will cause a user to see *only* the module they have access to, rather than the Webmin index page when logging in.

Upgrade Webmin

Using this page, you may upgrade your Webmin to the latest version automatically from the Webmin home page or from a local or uploaded file. This module will use a package management system to perform the update if one is available on your system. If, for example, you have an RPM-based system like Caldera, Red Hat, or Mandrake, this feature will upgrade from an RPM package (it even knows how to find the correct package type for your system on the Webmin home page!).

Authentication

Webmin provides some nice features for preventing brute force password-cracking attacks on your server, as well as protection against "forgetful users." If your Webmin server is widely accessible and provides service to many users, it is probably wise to make use of these features to maximize the security of your system. Security policy in your company may even require usage of some or all of these features.

Password timeouts provide a means to prevent brute force password attacks by limiting the frequency of login attempts by a given user. If enabled, Webmin will block hosts that have a given number of failed login attempts. The time to block the host is configurable in seconds. Webmin will expand the delay on continuing failed login attempts from the same host. Logging of blocked logins can also be enabled.

The next option, **Log blocked hosts, logins and authentication failures to syslog** configures Webmin to log authentication failures and blocked addresses attempting to log in to syslog. These logs will usually appear in the secure or auth file in your system log directory.

Session authentication provides a means of logging users out after a specified time of inactivity. This can help prevent unauthorized users from accessing the server by simply using the computer of someone who does have access. This isn't fool-proof, as many browsers now have password management features and authorized users may store their passwords on the local computer, making them accessible to anyone with access to the computer. If security is a concern, you should strongly discourage users from saving login information for the server on their local machine, as well as discouraging leaving open browser sessions when away from their desk or office.

Finally, you may choose to allow logins from users on the same machine where Webmin is running based on the username. This feature should only be used for single-user machines, where security is not a major concern. If enabled, anyone with access to the local machine will easily be able to gain root access to your system.

CAUTION *As any complete system administration tool must, the Webmin web server runs with root privileges. Security should always be a first priority for any publicly accessible Webmin-enabled system. A weak security policy, or no security policy at all, is an invitation for disaster. A comprehensive security policy will include a good firewall, an intrusion detection system, vigilance with regard to software updates and errata from your OS vendors, and perhaps most importantly education of users and administrators of your network.*

Reassign Modules

As mentioned earlier, Webmin categorizes modules based on the function they perform, by default. This page provides a simple means for moving modules to new categories if you find the default categorization is confusing to you. Some third-party modules, written before the categorization features were added to Webmin, are miscategorized into the **Others** category by default, so you may wish to manually move them to their more sensible locations using this module.

Edit Categories

Instead of moving modules within existing categories it may be most sensible to create a *new* category for your favorite modules or for custom modules written just for your organization. This page allows you to create new module categories, as well as rename or relabel old ones.

Webmin Themes

One of the more fun additions to the Webmin feature set is that of "theme-ability." Themes in Webmin are very flexible, allowing a theme developer to modify nearly every single aspect of the appearance and layout of the Webmin pages. For example, in the screenshots throughout this guide, you may have noticed that the icons and titles are not the same as the standard Webmin appearance. These screenshots were taken on a Webmin using the *Swell Technology* theme, which is a custom theme designed by the author of this book with some help and pointers from Youngjin Hahn (aka Artwiz of Themes.org fame), and Charity Baessell (the webmistress and designer at Swell Technology).

TIP *For information on making your own themes for Webmin, you can consult the Creating Themes [http://www.webmin.com/modules.html#theme] section of the Webmin module developers guide.*

Switching amongst installed themes is simply a matter of selecting the preferred theme and then clicking the **Change** button. Installing a new theme requires you to choose the location of the file (Webmin themes have a suffix of .wbt) and then clicking **Install Theme**. Changing themes will require a forced refresh of your browser display in order for all new icons and title images to be displayed because browsers often cache images and pages. To force a refresh in Netscape, Mozilla, and related browsers, press and hold the SHIFT key, while clicking the Refresh button. Similarly, in Internet Explorer, press and hold the CTRL key while clicking the Refresh button. Themes can be chosen systemwide or for an individual user in both Webmin and Usermin.

Trusted Referers

Because Webmin is web-based, it is accessed from your browser. Browsers often store authentication information and will automatically resend it on demand from the Webmin server. Because of this, it *could* be possible for remote websites to trigger dangerous actions on your Webmin server (assuming the website owner has malicious intentions—it would not happen accidentally!). This page allows you to configure which hosts may refer to actions on your Webmin server.

Anonymous Module Access

In some circumstances it may be useful to have one or more Webmin modules accessible to any user, without requiring authentication. For example, it may be useful to allow users to view some read-only statistics about the server, or allow a user to mount or unmount a device using a custom command, or similar. Extreme caution should be taken when using this feature of Webmin, as giving users access to the wrong module can easily lead to an exploitable condition. To be more explicit, very few standard modules are harmless enough to be safely usable with this feature.

SSL Encryption

If your system has the OpenSSL libraries installed, as well as the Net::SSLeay Perl module, you will be able to use SSL-encrypted connections to your Webmin server. This increases the security of your server by allowing password and user information to be sent in an encrypted form. If you will be accessing your Webmin server from across the Internet, it is strongly suggested that you use SSL-encrypted sessions. Now that both the export restrictions on encryption have been relaxed and the RSA patent has expired, it is becoming more common for Linux and UNIX versions to always ship with the necessary libraries and Perl module for this to be enabled out of the box. But if you do need some help setting this option up, there is a nice tutorial on the Using SSL With Webmin [http://www.webmin.com/webmin/ssl.html] page.

Certificate Authority

This page allows you to configure the SSL certificate for this server. Using this, you may configure your system to allow logins without a user name and password. If configured, clients may request a personal certificate in the **Webmin Users** module, and from then on the browser will authenticate itself via the certificate provided. If your users are located in controlled and secured environments, this feature can make using Webmin simpler.

To create a certificate, simply fill in the authority information (this can be any information you'd like to include, such as the name of the administrator of the Webmin server), and click **Setup certificate authority**.

CAUTION *If using this authentication method, users should be made aware of the potential security issues involved. Anyone who has access to a machine with such a certificate will be able to access the Webmin server with the same privileges as the primary user of the machine. This prevents the use of the login timeouts that are normally possible with Webmin, and so should be used with caution in environments where a logged-in machine may be left unattended.*

Webmin Servers

This page provides access to every Webmin server on your local network (Figure 3-2). Clicking any icon will direct your browser to the login page of the server clicked. Clicking **Broadcast for servers** will cause Webmin to send out a broadcast request to port 10000 over your local network. Every Webmin server on your network will reply and identify itself. Webmin will then add those servers to the list of servers. You may also scan specific networks for servers, if you manage Webmin servers remotely. Simply enter the subnet to search and click **Scan for servers**.

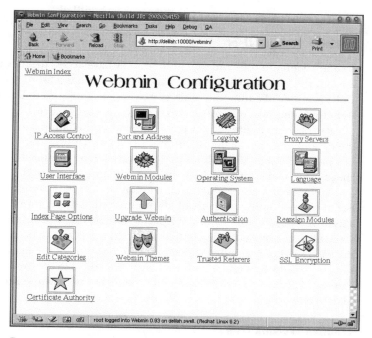

Figure 3-2: Webmin servers

Clicking a server icon will simply direct your browser to the Webmin port on the selected server, allowing you to log in. You may also configure Webmin to connect you to the server through a proxied connection, if you provide a user name and password for the other server. This can be useful when connecting remotely to a front-end Webmin server on the routable Internet that also connects to a non-routable private network, allowing an administrator outside of the private network to tunnel through to administer systems inside the private network.

Versions of Webmin beyond 0.85 provide support for some functions to be executable via remote procedure calls, if login information is provided for the remote server. This allows a single Webmin server to directly configure or monitor other Webmin servers. Currently this functionality is limited to the **System and Server Status** module and some of the modules in the **Cluster** category. It is likely that many of the other modules will expand to take advantage of this new functionality in the future.

Webmin Users

This page allows you to configure any number of users and give each some specified subset of the system to maintain. It would allow you, for example, to create a mail administrator who only had access to the Sendmail module, a DNS administrator who could only modify the DNS records, and a Squid administrator who only had permission to edit the Squid configuration. In this way, delegation of authority is very simply and securely handled.

Editing a Webmin User

To edit a Webmin user and the modules they have access to, click the name of the user on the **Webmin Users** index page. Each user has a list of accessible modules and a number of additional options that can be configured. From the **Edit Webmin User** page, it is possible to change the user's password: Select an SSL certificate for them to use for authentication, alter the language and theme from the default and specify the IP addresses from which this user can log in. Also on this page is a list of all modules that are installed on the machine, each with a check box beside it. If checked, the user will have access to the module.

Webmin also allows finer grained control over many modules, and this functionality is becoming more flexible with every release (Figure 3-3). For example, a user with permission to use the **Apache module** can be denied the ability to edit some specific aspects of the configuration. In the example below you can see that the user is being granted permission to edit only one of the many available virtual servers. To edit fine grained access controls, browse to the **Webmin Users** index page, and click the module name link beside the user whose access controls you wish to edit.

Creating Webmin Users

Creating new users is also easy. Click the **Create a new Webmin User** link and choose a user name or use one of an existing user on the system (Figure 3-4). Choose between using the user's UNIX password or using a new one. Select which modules the user will have access to and click **Save**. Now you can edit the fine grained access controls for the user, or accept the defaults. Adding or deleting modules from the users access list can be performed by clicking the username from the **Webmin Users** page, and then editing the user in whatever manner is required.

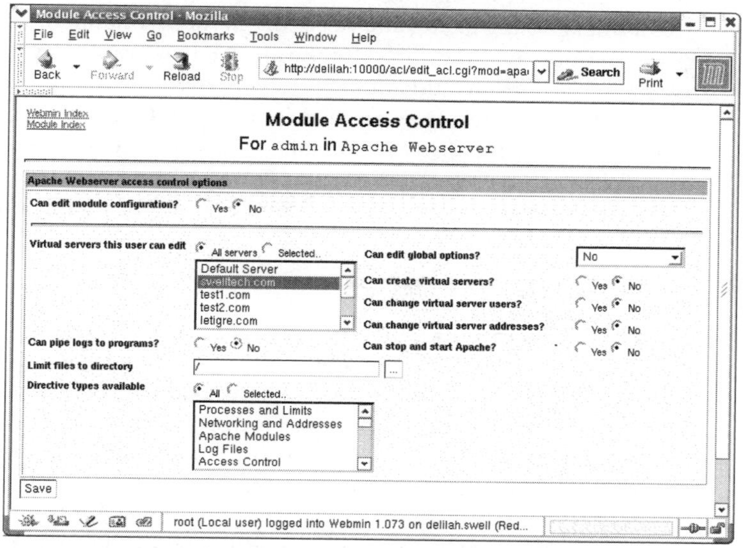

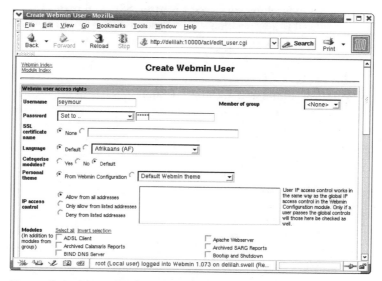

Figure 3-3: Editing user access controls

Figure 3-4: Create Webmin user

Webmin Groups

Webmin, like UNIX, understands the concept of groups. Groups in Webmin are similar to UNIX groups in that they ease administration of heavily populated servers by allowing easy creation of any number of users with the same set of permissions and access controls. To create a group click the **Create a new Webmin group** link, give it a name, and select the modules that members of the new group should have access to. After saving the new group, any user can be assigned to the group and automatically receive the module access of the group, plus whatever modules are specified for the user. Currently users can only be a member of one group, so the Webmin groups feature is somewhat less flexible than that of most modern UNIX variants and Linux where users can be members of a primary group in addition to a number of supplemental groups.

Tutorial: Securing Webmin

Because Webmin runs with the privileges of the root user, it is vitally important that Webmin be locked down tightly before allowing remote Internet access. Historically, Webmin is pretty secure, but there have been exploits discovered in the past, and there will probably be exploits discovered in the future. Any tool that runs as root has the potential to be an entry point for a malicious cracker to unlimited access to the machine.

So in order to prevent all of the woes that can result from an exploited machine, we're going to take a few steps to limit our risk and minimize the damage that can be done without us noticing. We will briefly discuss password policy, application-level network access control, SSL, and firewall configuration. The tutorial will wrap up with a survey of some other techniques and technologies that can be used to help maintain a secure system.

Password Policy

Countless studies and anecdotes from both sides of the security issue (crackers on one side and those who implement systems to protect against crackers on the other) have told us that cracking weak passwords is nearly always a reliable, if time-consuming way to obtain illicit entry into a system. Because many users, and even system administrators use weak, easily guessed passwords, it is quite common for a determined hacker to run an automated password hunt on a target system. Another, perhaps even more frightening, technique crackers use is what is known as *Social Engineering*.

Social Engineering is a technique as old as malicious cracking itself, which plays on human nature to overcome technical barriers to entry by going the easier path of getting through a human's line of defense. One common technique is for a cracker to pose as tech support staff and simply ask for the user's password so they can "test" something or other on the network. This works disturbingly often, even among technically savvy users. This type of attack can happen via any communications medium, including telephone, IRC, email, and so on, and its continued success relies on the human desire to be helpful. This technique is often enhanced through the use of other subtle additions to further lower the guard of the person answering the phone or email. The cracker may mention that there is a "problem" on the network, of some sort, which taps into another fundamental aspect of human nature: complaining about the state of the network. Everyone complains about the state of the network in an office at one point or another, and when a "tech" calls to say he is going to fix it, it further establishes his credibility with the victim. In the user's mind, it seems obvious that no outsider would know about the "network problems" he has been experiencing lately, so this caller must be legitimate.

In my time of supporting UNIX servers I've noticed another aspect of human nature that is sometimes exploited by crackers. When asked to type in their password, some users spell it out quietly under their breath while entering the letters. Experienced typists are far less likely to speak the text they are entering in this way, but it may be a last-resort trick used by a Social Engineering cracker to simply ask the user to type in their password a few times (because by the second or third time, the user is either excited enough to be taking part in "solving a network problem" to begin talking or singing along with their text input or be frustrated enough at being kept away from his real work to start muttering along with what he is typing). Users should be cautioned against this habit. This may all sound like a rather silly way to break into a network, when Hollywood movies always show us a lone cracker in a basement filled with computer junk, but it is likely that the most determined, and thus the most dangerous, crackers will use these techniques before attempting more time-consuming technical attacks like brute force password searches. These techniques work, if users are not aware of the danger.

This only scratches the surface of how crackers operate. But it does begin to make it clear that good passwords and educated users are a core part of any successful security policy. Insist upon quality passwords, and notify your users of the policy. A good password policy might include the following requirements:

Minimum Length

A good password should be a minimum of six or eight characters. All other things being equal, longer passwords are more secure than shorter passwords, simply because a brute force attack has more possibilities to go through to find a password that works.

No Dictionary Words

It is generally recommended to avoid plain dictionary words, or even dictionary words at all. The reason for this is that brute force attacks usually involve attempting all of the words in a word list, or in a dictionary file. Real words are simply easier to guess and easier to obtain through brute force attacks. Weird spellings, odd capitalizations, and combinations of word fragments can all be used to create less easily guessed passwords without making them much less memorable for the user. After all, if the user has a drawer full of their passwords on sticky notes because they can't remember them, the cure is worse than the disease.

Include Numbers

Another good possibility is to enforce the inclusion of at least one number in all passwords. This automatically increases the pool of possible passwords by an order of magnitude, even if dictionary words are allowed. Again, this doesn't make passwords significantly less memorable for the user, but does increase the security of the password. However, use of birthdays, anniversaries, and so on should be discouraged, as these are easily guessable and more prone to Social Engineering attacks.

Scheduled Password Changes

In environments where security is important, it is wise to implement a mandatory password change after some specified period of time. The inconvenience to users of this choice should be carefully balanced against the security needs of the environment. It is less useful if frustrated users alternate between two passwords because they are being forced to change them every two weeks, or even worse, if they write them down somewhere in their desk because they don't want to take the effort to remember a new password every week. Once every six months is probably frequent enough for all but the most extreme circumstances.

Failed Login Timeouts

In the event that a cracker attempts a brute force attack on your server, password timeouts can be very effective at making the process extremely time-consuming, or even impossible. Going on the assumption that a user usually will not mistype their password more than a few times, many authenticators can timeout and refuse to allow any login for that user for a specified period of time after that number of failed logins is reached. With this feature enabled, it becomes a daunting task to use brute force password searches to break into a system that has password timeouts of this sort. It can potentially increase the time it takes by months or years, and the likelihood of detection of the scans considerably because one or more users will begin to complain of being unable to log in (because their password is in a state of timeout most of the time).

Education

This is perhaps the most important in light of the prevalence of Social Engineering. Users of the network, both new and old, should receive training about the password policy, why the policy has been implemented, and how to use the tools required to take part in the new policy. This training doesn't have to be a large investment in time, effort, or money. In high-tech environments, a simple email reminder with the policy and instructions sent out every month to old users and immediately to new users could be enough. In traditional business, education, or government environments it may be better to schedule a one-hour group lecture the first time in order to explain both the whys and the hows, followed by a question and answer period. It is also vitally important that users understand that *no one* should ever ask for their password, and they should never give out their password to anyone, no matter who they claim to be. It might also be appropriate to make clear that the real system administrator doesn't need a password to log in as any user, and thus would never need a user's password to test or fix anything.

CAUTION   *Some of these policy choices cannot currently be enforced with Webmin. As of version 0.970, only password timeouts are available. Even so, encouraging users to use secure passwords, and more importantly for you as an administrator, using good password policy can achieve the same goals without enforcing them. It is likely that Webmin will have all of these features in some form or another in future revisions. Your underlying OS variant probably supports some or all of them, as well, for system passwords. Educating users about these issues becomes more important when policy cannot be enforced via technical measures.*

Setting Authentication Policy

As discussed above, a carefully considered password policy can be very helpful in defending against crackers. Webmin provides a simple means to enforce some aspects of password policy for Webmin users in the **Webmin:Webmin Configuration:Authentication** module. Here you may choose to enable password timeouts and automatically block hosts that appear to be running brute force attacks on the Webmin server.

Also, enabling logging of failed login attempts is an excellent idea, assuming someone will read those logs on occasion. It is possible using tools like logwatch to automatically be notified via email of some types of logged data. While logwatch is not currently configurable within Webmin, it is well worth your time to read up on this utility or any similar tool provided by your OS vendor and to make use of it to help ease the burden of administering a system. To enable logging of authentication failures, browse to the **Webmin:Webmin Configuration:Authentication** module and select **Log blocked hosts, logins and authentication failures to syslog Disable session authentication**. Then you may configure any log analysis tools you use to flag these authentication failures so that a human administrator can watch for signs of cracker activity.

NOTE   *The logwatch utility is Open Source software, available from [http://www.logwatch.org]. The program is maintained by Kirk Bauer and is included with many Linux distributions. Other OS variants often provide similar functionality.*

Setting Network Access Controls

As discussed earlier in this chapter, Webmin provides a few mechanisms to provide network-level security to your Webmin installation. Utilizing some or all of them can increase security immensely, without adding complexity to the deployment. The primary purpose of these features is to allow Webmin to refuse to even talk to someone on an address that is not allowed to log in.

To begin, take a look at your network topology diagram, or write down your local network information if your network isn't large enough to justify a full diagram. Then write down the network information for every user that must be able to access your Webmin server. This may get complicated rather quickly, if you have dial-up or other remote users who need to log in from dynamically assigned IP addresses, but even in such cases it may be possible to reach a viable compromise.

Setting the Listen Address and Port

The first step is to decide if you can restrict access to one particular network interface on your server. If your Webmin server has a non-routable local address and a routable Internet address, you should decide whether anyone will ever need to be able to access the Webmin server from outside of your local network. If not, simply configure Webmin to listen on the local interface. This can be configured using the **Webmin:Webmin Configuration:Port and Address** module by selecting the radio button beside the **Listen on IP Address** option and entering your internal IP in the Entry field.

Before moving on to other items, it may be worthwhile to consider moving Webmin to another port. Webmin being on port 10000 leads to one additional type of possible exploit that would be difficult for a cracker to take advantage of, but is probably not impossible for a local user. Because port 10000 is a non-privileged port, any user with login permission on the server could start an arbitrary server that listened on that port, if Webmin were not currently running on the port. Once a local user is able to start a server on port 10000, it is trivial to set up a web server that *looks* like the Webmin login page, but in fact is just a simple CGI script in the users home directory. If the system administrator then attempts to login, his password can be grabbed and stored for the user to pick up later (or worse, mailed out automatically as soon as it has been grabbed). A particularly clever script of this sort could delete itself after its job is done and even restart Webmin so the administrator will believe they simply entered the wrong password when they attempted to log in the first time. One solution to this problem is to simply run Webmin on a port below 1024, as these ports require root permission to bind to, so a malicious user would not be able to run a password-grabbing Trojan on the same port, and thus would not be able to fool anyone into entering their authentication information.

NOTE *In some OS variants and versions, it is possible to control which users can bind to any port, whether above or below 1024. This feature is sometimes known as* capabilities *or* ACLs. *A proposed, but then withdrawn, specification labeled POSIX.1e provided some of the capabilities that are supported by some Linux versions. With features of this sort it may be possible to make port 10000 behave just like a sub-1024 port, but availability of this kind of feature varies wildly, so it will not be covered here. In the vast majority of environments, it makes sense to run Webmin on port 1000, or if connectivity through very restrictive proxy firewalls is required, port 553.*

IP Access Control

The next step is to set up application-level IP access control to your Webmin installation. If you have only static or local addresses that should have access to Webmin, then your job is simple. Just open the **Webmin:Webmin Configuration:IP Access Control** module, and select the **Only allow from listed addresses** radio button, and then enter all of the addresses or host names that must have Webmin access.

If, however, you have users who will be accessing Webmin from dial-up connections or some other form of dynamic link, you cannot know in advance what IP address they will need to log in from. In some cases this can be mostly worked around, if you have a friendly ISP who will provide a list of their IP blocks. With the list of all *possible* addresses on which your dial-up users may come in on, you can severely limit the percentage of Internet users who can access your Webmin installation, simply because a single ISP only represents a tiny number of the total addresses on the Internet. This is, for lack of a better term, *Good Enough*. Obviously, large nationwide ISPs are not generally helpful enough to provide this information for you, but if you are lucky enough to have a service-oriented local or regional ISP, you will likely find the technicians to be quite helpful.

If address-based access control is not feasible due to needing nationwide dial-up access or similar, it isn't the end of the world. Assuming systems are kept up to date and other security policies followed, it is highly unlikely that your Webmin server will ever expose an exploitable condition to crackers.

NOTE   *Webmin version 1.000 and above provides the option to do a host name lookup for every user access. The result of this will be that a dynamically assigned IP with a DNS entry with DynDNS, or a similar service, will be able to be checked against the IP Access Control list, just like a fixed address. This is not efficient if you have more than a few domain names entered in the IP Access Control list, due to the high overhead of performing a name lookup for every host name in the list on every request. But it can be very useful if you have one or two administrators or users who travel or simply don't have a fixed address at their normal location, because they can have a domain name that follows them wherever they go, and this name can be used to allow them access. I use this feature for the swelltech.com web server, because it is remotely located and I often access it from my dynamically assigned home ADSL link.*

Enabling SSL

Webmin is a web-based application, thus it operates using the standard protocols of the Internet and specifically the HTTP or HTTPS protocol. In a default installation from tarball or package, Webmin operates via the standard unencrypted HTTP protocol. In some environments this presents no major security threat, but in most situations this is a quite large hole in the security of a Webmin installation. If you only access Webmin across a local network of only trusted clients, and have a firewall closing your local network to outsiders, then you may feel safe in using Webmin over an unencrypted link. Otherwise, if you ever access your Webmin across the Internet or an intranet that may have untrusted clients (for example, a laptop owned by an outside consultant, temporary employees, etc.) encryption should be considered mandatory.

Luckily, setting up Webmin for use with SSL connections is pretty simple, and requires only installation of two other packages: OpenSSL and the Perl Net::SSLeay module. Here we'll briefly discuss installing these tools from source, though it is even easier if your OS vendor provides binary packages. Documenting the actual installation process will be left for the included documentation of these packages.

Install OpenSSL

OpenSSL is an Open Source implementation of the Secure Sockets Layer (SSL) protocol, as well as the Transport Layer Security (TLS) protocol. It provides strong encryption library routines that are easy to integrate into other software, and is thus used quite frequently in Open Source projects requiring encryption. Because of this, if you are using any modern Open Source operating system, like Linux or FreeBSD, you probably already have OpenSSL installed on your system or can get a package for your OS that is simpler to install.

OpenSSL is free software and can be downloaded from the [http://www.openssl.org] home page or one of its many mirrors. Download it to the server running Webmin. If you don't have a graphical browser installed or are accessing your server remotely you can use lynx or wget to fetch it from the website. If no text mode HTTP client is available, you can get the file from the [ftp://ftp.openssl.org] FTP site instead. I've never seen any Internet-capable operating system that does not have at least one text-mode FTP client available. Even Windows includes a simple FTP client for use in the MS-DOS shell! To install simply follow the instructions found in the INSTALL document included in the source distribution.

Getting the Net::SSLeay Perl Module

Because Webmin is written in Perl, it needs a Perl interface to the OpenSSL libraries. The standard choice for this is the Net::SSLeay module, which can be downloaded for free from CPAN or one of its mirrors. You may also be able to download a packaged binary version from your OS vendor.

Webmin itself offers a module for managing and installing Perl modules on your system. Using this module, documented later in this book, you may be able to install the Net::SSLeay module using this module. On my test systems (mostly Red Hat Linux of varying versions) I could only successfully install using the Webmin module if I left out the make test option, selecting only make and install. No additional arguments were required, however.

If a package is not provided by your vendor and installation via Webmin fails for some reason (and there are several reasons why it might), simply visit the Comprehensive Perl Archive Network (CPAN) and search for "SSLeay" to get the latest version. After downloading the tarball, unzip and untar it:

```
[joe@grover /joe]$ tar zxvf Net_SSLeay.pm-1.15.tar.gz
```

Or, if your OS doesn't use GNU tar you may have to unzip and untar in two steps:

```
[joe@grover /joe]$ gunzip Net_SSLeay.pm-1.15.tar.gz
[joe@grover /joe]$ tar xvf Net_SSLeay.pm-1.15.tar
```

Change the directory to the newly created Net_SSLeay directory. Run the Makefile.PL using Perl, like so:

```
[joe@grover Net_SSLeay.pm-1.15]# perl Makefile.PL
```

Assuming no problems arise, this will generate a standard makefile suitable for your system. If OpenSSL was installed from an RPM, you may need to explicitly specify the /usr directory on the command line, though it appears to be unnecessary in new versions of the module. But if it complains about being unable to find an OpenSSL installation you can try the following:

```
[joe@grover Net_SSLeay.pm-1.15]# perl Makefile.PL /usr
```

Next, use make to build, test, and install the module into the correct location. The command sequence is as follows (don't forget to switch user to root before the install phase):

```
[joe@grover Net_SSLeay.pm-1.15]# make
[joe@grover Net_SSLeay.pm-1.15]# make test
[joe@grover Net_SSLeay.pm-1.15]# su
Password:
[root@grover Net_SSLeay.pm-1.15]# make install
```

Finally, test to be sure the module is installed, using the following command line:

```
[root@grover Net_SSLeay.pm-1.15]# perl -e 'use Net::SSLeay; print "Success!\n"'
Success!
```

If the result is only the word Success!, then the module has been successfully installed. Otherwise, if you see an error regarding Perl's inability to find the module, it is not installed correctly.

Turning it on

Now that the correct additional tools are installed, all that is left is to turn on SSL connections in the Webmin configuration. This can be done from within Webmin itself, or if you're particularly paranoid and don't even want to log in once over an unencrypted connection you can edit the configuration file manually.

To enable SSL connections using Webmin, browse to the **Webmin:Webmin Configuration:SSL Encryption** page, and click the radio button labeled **Enable SSL support, if available**. Click Save, and you will automatically be redirected to the https port and connected via an SSL link.

To enable from the command line, for example from an SSH login or a direct console login, edit the `miniserv.conf` file, usually located in `/etc/webmin` or possibly `/usr/local/webmin-0.980/etc`, where `0.980` is replaced by the version of Webmin you have installed. The option to modify is `ssl=`, which defaults to `0` (off). Changing it to a `1` and restarting the Webmin server will enable SSL connections. You can then log in on the HTTPS port as documented earlier.

Firewall Configuration

As in the earlier discussion of IP Access Controls, the goal when constructing a set of firewall rules is to prevent access to sensitive ports by unknown persons. If, for example, you can restrict the external network addresses that can talk to your server on port 10000 (or 1000, depending on the port you choose to run Webmin on) you can very easily make it impossible to exploit your Webmin installation via most types of attack. This is perhaps a bold claim, but it is easily provable assuming one can trust the firewall to do its job.

Unfortunately, the Internet is a world of trade-offs and constantly changing conditions. Sometimes, you simply cannot lock down your machine using a firewall without locking out all of the people who need to use it. If you remotely manage your server via a dial-up connection, the firewall clearly cannot be restricted to allowing only one IP. So compromises are required. As in the IP Access Controls, an ideal world would allow you to restrict access to only one or two external IP addresses (and some or all of the IP addresses within your own local network), but most likely you'll have to allow large blocks of IP addresses to account for dynamically assigned addresses on dial-up, DSL, and cable Internet connections. As before, if you have a helpful ISP, you'll be able to obtain a list of the network blocks that may be assigned to you.

Firewall configuration is outside the scope of this book, but adding protection for Webmin to an existing firewall is usually trivial. If your network does not yet have a firewall of some sort, it is well worth your time to research the options and implement a reasonable firewall. If you are using a free UNIX-like system like FreeBSD, Linux, OpenBSD, NetBSD, and so on you already have access to a very flexible firewall system. All that will be needed is a few hours or days to study the implementation of such firewalls and a few minutes to construct an appropriate ruleset (just don't forget to protect the Webmin port!). Users of other UNIX OS variants may need to purchase a firewall package from your vendor, or a free firewall system may be available for download.

Other Security Techniques and Tools

Security is a many-sided problem, and as such, a number of tools have been developed to help an administrator implement a highly secure system. In the preceding four sections, I've addressed the first-line defensive techniques and how they can be applied to Webmin. Those techniques are designed to prevent intrusion in the first place. They do nothing to let you know an intrusion has taken place, nor do they respond proactively to an attack that is underway. Therefore, it is worth taking a brief tangential look at some intrusion detection tools, and attack response tools.

Intrusion Detection

There are a large number of free and commercial intrusion detection systems (IDSs) available for all of the major UNIX variants. An IDS provides an easy method of auditing one or more systems to ensure that they have not been exploited. Most such systems create a database of file identifier keys (usually an MD5 hash or similar strongly encrypted key), which is also encrypted with a passphrase known only to the system administrator. Some systems provide an easy means to store the database on another machine, or it can be written to a floppy or CD for use in a read-only mode, so that even if the machine is violated tampering with the file key database is impossible rather than merely extremely difficult.

Perhaps the most popular IDS for free UNIX systems is Tripwire, which is available in both an Open Source and proprietary version. It is available in package form from many Linux distribution vendors and source downloads for all supported operating systems. Tripwire uses a database of MD5 keys, which is generated on a known secure system. Using a simple cron job, Tripwire can then be run periodically to ensure no unexpected changes have occurred on the system since the last database generation. Using two passphrases, it is possible for Tripwire to prevent unauthorized tampering with the database (for example, a cracker regenerating the database after having modified all of the files needed for future entry).

NOTE *The Open Source variant of Tripwire can be downloaded from [http://www.tripwire.org]. A thorough reading of the documentation is recommended before attempting to use it, because though it is relatively simple to use, the required steps for initial setup and database generation are not at all obvious.*

Another simple but effective intrusion detection method for systems that use RPM or any other package manager that keeps a database and can verify file integrity is to keep a copy of the package database on another system or stored on read-only media. With this database and a known good installation of the package manager, one can verify all of the system files quickly and easily. The drawback of this method is that it cannot detect new files and modification of files that were not installed from packages. If no proper intrusion detection system is available, this can be a lifesaver in the event of an intrusion on a system that has no complete IDS installed.

Some pitfalls to watch for in the event of an intrusion is that once a cracker has gained access to your system with root privileges, there is nothing to prevent him from modifying the Tripwire or package manager binaries to prevent them from reporting good results even after all of their changes. Such a modification is usually obvious to an experienced administrator, because normal file changes should show up in such checks, and over time those changes will probably not be accurately reported by the cracked IDS or package manager. This problem is most easily worked around by installing secondary versions of these tools and running them against a database stored on read-only media, like a CD or floppy disk with writing disabled. While a cracker with the knowledge to make these changes is rare, it is likely that such ideas will eventually be included in rootkits, making it easy for even the most brain-damaged cracker to thoroughly cover his tracks pretty effectively.

Proactive Attack Response Tools

There are several new tools designed to recognize common types of attack and respond to them quickly enough to diffuse the attack. There is no single name for such systems, and the way in which they work varies depending on their particular focus. Two such tools are PortSentry and Hogwash.

PortSentry is the most mature of these types of tool and takes a more basic approach to the problem. PortSentry keeps an eye on network connections and watches for a rapid series of abnormal connections that is usually indicative of a network scan. When such a scan is detected the host from which the attack originates is simply blocked using the normal packet filter on the system. PortSentry is made more attractive by the fact that a Webmin module exists to easily administer and configure a PortSentry installation.

NOTE *PortSentry, like Tripwire, is available in both commercial and Open Source versions. The Open Source release is available for download from [http://www.psionic.com/products/ portsentry.html].*

A newer entry into the field, Hogwash uses a rule-based system to detect hundreds of known exploit types and can drop those packets without disturbing any other kind of traffic from the host. Hogwash is based on the rule engine of the Snort network intrusion detection system, but adds the ability to respond to the intrusion by dropping or disarming the troublemaking packet by rewriting it to a harmless form.

4

USERMIN: A WEBMIN FOR USERS

This chapter is a short detour away from Webmin to cover a closely related tool called Usermin. The two tools have a lot in common and are often used together to provide a multi-tiered GUI for users and administrators. The commonalities begin with the fact that both were written and are maintained by Jamie Cameron. They share much of the same code base, and the operation of Usermin closely parallels that of Webmin.

Because the Usermin modules are so closely related to the modules in Webmin, it would be pointless to cover them in detail here. What the chapter will cover is the Usermin Configuration module in Webmin, document the modules that do diverge from similar Webmin modules or simply do not exist in Webmin, and provide some discussions about using Webmin and Usermin in real environments with examples to help make the best use of them. Compared to Webmin, Usermin is severely limited, but it is just those limitations that make it ideal for a certain class of problem, and so those will be the problems that will be discussed along with how Usermin can help solve them.

Introduction to Usermin

The differences begin with the intention of each. Webmin is used primarily by system administrators, and it provides unlimited power to the logged-in administrator unless permissions are explicitly restricted. Usermin, on the other hand, is used primarily by system users, and the powers of a logged-in Usermin user are by default limited to only the permissions of a normal user. Specifically, Usermin provides access to a web-based mail client, a Java file manager applet, SSH configuration and client modules, GnuPG encryption and decryption, mail forwarding, changing passwords, cron jobs, and a simplified web-based command shell.

CAUTION *Usermin prefers to use the PAM authentication mechanism used by most Linux distributions and Solaris. Unfortunately, PAM is not well supported on many UNIX variants, or even all Linux versions. For this reason, Usermin will attempt to fall back to directly using the shadow password file if PAM cannot be used for some reason.*

NOTE *PAM is an acronym for Pluggable Authentication Modules. It allows easier integration of a variety of authentication technologies without requiring all authenticating software to be modified to support each authentication type. Modules are available for a vast array of authentication methods, including LDAP, Kerberos, RSA, and UNIX* passwd *and* shadow *files. It is widely deployed on most major Linux distributions and Solaris versions 2.6 and above, and is available as packages or in source form for FreeBSD and HP-UX.*

Usermin Installation

Before you can use Usermin, you will have to install it. Unlike Webmin, at the time of this writing no major Linux distribution or UNIX vendor is including Usermin in its standard installation or offering it as an optional package. This will certainly change in time, and OS vendors may be installing it by the time you read this. Check with your vendor for packages, or simply download it from the Usermin website.

Checking for the Authen-PAM Perl Module

Installing Usermin is just about like installing Webmin, with the one exception that it is recommended to install the Authen-PAM Perl module before installation of Usermin. So first it will be necessary to check for, and possibly install, this Perl module. The easiest way to check for a Perl module is to use a command like the following:

```
[root@grover root]# perl -e 'use Authen::PAM; print "Success!\n"'
```

If this module is available, you will see only the word "Success!" printed on the next line. If the module is not installed, a number of errors will result instead. If you have success with the module check, proceed to the next section. If not, visit the Comprehensive Perl Archive Network (CPAN for short) at [http://www.cpan.org]. Use the search function to find the latest version of **Authen-PAM**, download it, and follow the instructions in the README file that is included. Briefly, all CPAN Perl modules are installed in the same simple way.

First generate a makefile by running the Makefile.PL file, as follows:

```
[root@grover Authen-PAM-0.13]# perl Makefile.PL
```

If successful, run make and make install.

```
[root@grover Authen-PAM-0.13]# make
[root@grover Authen-PAM-0.13]# make install
```

Next, use the Perl command suggested at the beginning of this section to test for the availability of the module. Then add a PAM service called usermin in the appropriate location. Under many Linux distributions, this involves creating a file named /etc/pam.d/usermin that contains the following:

```
#%PAM-1.0
auth       required      pam_unix.so    shadow nullok
account    required      pam_unix.so
password   required      pam_unix.so    shadow nullok use_authtok
session    required      pam_unix.so
```

Now the installation of Usermin should proceed smoothly.

NOTE *You may be able to download a package of Authen-PAM for your operating system, which is usually preferable from a system maintenance perspective. Also, if you use an RPM-based Linux distribution, you may be able to use cpanflute or cpanflute2 to automatically generate a package from the Perl module, if your vendor doesn't provide a package for you. The use of cpanflute is not discussed in this book. However, it is worth looking into if you frequently install Perl modules, because it makes generating Perl module RPMs a simple and painless process.*

Obtaining Usermin

Lucky for us, Usermin is free under a BSD-style license, just like its more powerful sibling. It can be downloaded for free from the Usermin site or one of its mirrors. For reference the primary Usermin site is [http://www. usermin. com]. Like Webmin, Usermin is available in a tarball, as well as an RPM for Red Hat, MSC Linux, Caldera, Mandrake, and SuSE. Unlike Webmin, there is currently no Solaris package of Usermin. Choose the most appropriate option for your system.

Installing the Package or Tarball

Depending on the installation method, you follow similar steps as you did for installing Webmin. For the tarball, copy it to the desired installation location (usually /usr/local), unzip it, untar it, and run the setup.sh script:

```
[root@delilah /root]# cp usermin-0.6.tar.gz /usr/local
[root@delilah /root]# cd /usr/local
[root@delilah local]# gunzip usermin-0.6.tar.gz
[root@delilah local]# tar xf usermin-0.6.tar
[root@delilah local]# cd usermin-0.6
[root@delilah local]# ./setup.sh
```

The install script will ask a series of questions, for most of which you should accept the default values. After the installation script finishes running, you will be able to log in to the Usermin server on port 20000.

Installing Usermin from an RPM

Installing from an RPM package is, just like with Webmin, even easier than installation from the tarball. When installing from a package, it is still necessary to insure you have the PAM Perl module as documented previously (if you will be using it). Then use the following command for an RPM installation:

```
[root@delilah /extra]# rpm -Uvh usermin-0.6-1.noarch.rpm
```

The RPM will automatically run the installation script with sensible defaults and start the Usermin server on port 20000.

Usermin Configuration

You configure Usermin, perhaps paradoxically, from within Webmin. Clicking the **Usermin Configuration** icon under the **Webmin** tab displays a few rows of icons of Usermin options, which are very similar in form and function to those of the **Webmin Configuration** module (Figure 4-1). There are far fewer configurable options, of course, but because Usermin is based on the same web server framework as Webmin (miniserv.pl, specifically), it provides all of the same access control and security mechanisms.

Usermin Module Configuration

On first entering this module, all that is displayed is a page listing all of the Usermin modules that have configurable options. Clicking a module name will open a page that contains the configuration options for the selected module.

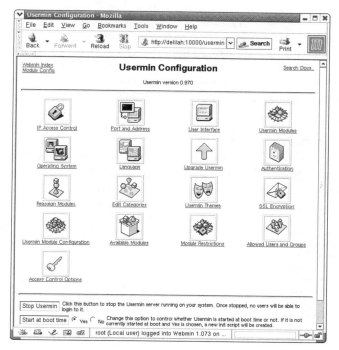

Figure 4-1: Usermin Configuration index

GnuPG Encryption

GnuPG (Gnu Privacy Guard, or gpg for short) is a complete and Free Software implementation of the encryption standards originally provided by PGP (Pretty Good Privacy, a commercial product). It does not rely on the patent-encumbered IDEA algorithm, so it can be used with no restrictions for commercial or non-commercial purposes. GnuPG provides strong encryption and digital signatures of several types for email and files. Using GnuPG strong encryption it is possible to send a private email with confidence that only the recipient can decrypt the message. Additionally, a message may be digitally signed, allowing confirmation of sender identity and verification of the contents of the message (i.e., it confirms this actually is the message as it was composed by the sender and it hasn't been modified in some way during transit).

This module only has one configurable option, the keyserver which is used for sending and receiving key files. If you use GnuPG to confirm signatures, it is necessary to use central keyservers so that identities can be looked up in a centralized database. In this way, a *web of trust* can be woven between individuals who can confirm the identity of others. Because there is a large number of public key-servers available all over the world and they synchronize their data, it is a good idea to choose one near you.

Configurable Options for Mail Forwarding

Webmin and Usermin support a number of different mail transfer agents (MTAs), namely Sendmail, Postfix, and Qmail. This option should be set to the mail transfer agent that your server uses. Postfix is not listed as an option, however, because Postfix is entirely Sendmail-compatible from a user perspective. Simply select Sendmail if Postfix is the MTA, and everything will work as expected.

Configurable Options for Read Mail

The Usermin **Read Mail** module offers users a complete, if basic, web-based mail client. It allows the user to send and receive mail, as well as keep a simple address book and digitally sign or encrypt messages. For this module there are a number of configurable options, as shown in Figure 4-2 and Figure 4-3.

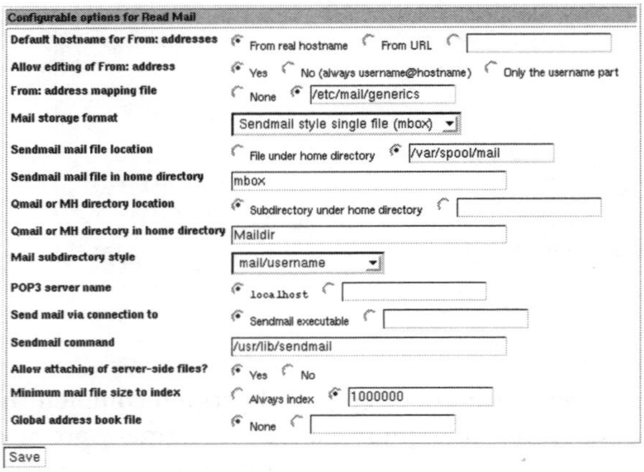

Figure 4-2: Configurable options for Read Mail

Default hostname for From: addresses

This is the host name that will be included in the mail headers in the From field. If you wish all mail from your domain to be addressed from just the domain name (rather than, for example, mail.domain.com) you may enter it here. Entering domain.com will cause all mail sent from this machine using the Usermin mail client to appear to be from domain.com.

Allow editing of From: address

If Yes the user can enter any address they choose in the From field. If No, all mail will be marked as originating from the domain you chose in the previous option. It may be appropriate to permit this change, if clients have their own domain names or would like to be able to primarily use another address and do not want to keep up with replies to another mailbox.

From: address mapping file

When hosting virtual domains, it may be useful to have the From: address set to the appropriate user@virtualdomain.com address rather than that of the real username and the domain of the system. This option sets Usermin to choose the correct address from a domain mapping file, usually the generics table.

Mail storage format

Like that of the **Mail Forwarding** configuration above, this selection should match that of the MTA that is running on your server. You can choose Sendmail style single file if Postfix is the installed MTA.

Sendmail mail file location

Here you select the location of your mail storage directories. This is usually located in /var/spool/mail, and another common option is to deliver it to the user's home directory into mbox. This depends on the configuration of your mail delivery system (which may or may not actually be Sendmail). Postfix can use Sendmail-compatible mail delivery options and so requires no special configuration here.

Sendmail file in home directory

If mail is stored in the user's home directory, specify the file name for the inbox here. Often this is mbox, but some mail servers or mail clients may choose something different. Often the inbox is not in the user's home directory at all, and so this option isn't always necessary.

Qmail or MH directory location

If using Qmail of MH, specify the location of the system mail storage directory here. QMail and MH use custom mail storage formats that are implemented as one-mail-per-file, as opposed to the traditional mbox format which puts all emails into a single file. This is thought to provide better performance and better reliability by some administrators and developers.

Qmail or MH directory in home directory

If mail is stored in the users home directory rather than in the system mail spool directory, you may specify the location here. Often, this will be the Maildir directory, though it could be something else.

Mail subdirectory style

Some mail delivery agents allow the mail spool directory to be divided into multiple subdirectories in order to ease management and accommodate limitations of some UNIX filesystems. If your delivery agent does not deliver all mail to a single mail spool directory, and instead delivers to users spread across many subdirectories, you may configure that here.

POP3 or IMAP server name

In addition to reading local mail, Usermin can retrieve email from a POP3 or IMAP server. If your mail spool is located on a remote server, you can specify it here.

Send mail via connection to

Selects how Usermin will send mail. It can be sent to any local mail transport agent or a remote SMTP server. By default this is the sendmail executable, but several alternatives exist.

Sendmail command

The location of your MTA executable. This is the command that will be called when Usermin sends mail, unless configured to send via a remote SMTP server.

Allow attaching of server-side files?

This allows users to attach files that are located on the local machine (on which Usermin is running). This could potentially be a minor security risk, because the user could then attach any file for which they have read permissions. This setting applies to all users, and is not configurable by the user.

Minimum mail file size to index

For performance reasons, Usermin can be configured to create an index file of email in a users mailbox. It is usually unnecessary unless the mailbox is rather large, so you may configure the minimum size of a mailbox that Usermin will index.

Global address book file

Usermin provides a simple address book for users to store email addresses. If specified here, a global address book can be created that can be shared among all Usermin users on the system. This can be useful for companies that have a lot of employees, and require frequent email interactions.

The lower portion of the Read Mail page (Figure 4-3) is devoted to configuring the default user preferences for the module.

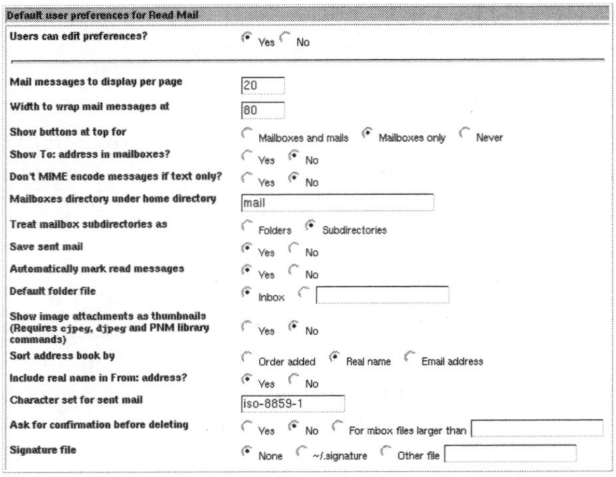

Figure 4-3: Default user preferences for Read Mail

Users can edit preferences

If you would like to prevent users from modifying their preferences for the Read Mail module, you may specify No here. By default, the user will have the preferences you specify here, but they can change any of them. Some options, like line-wrap widths and number of mail messages to display at once, allow changes that would make the mail client more suitable for different environments, such as palm-sized access devices. Others are merely matters of personal preference.

Mail messages to display per page

This option is pretty much self-explanatory. You may choose to display more or fewer messages, which can be useful if clients are using small display devices for using the web mail client and too many lines makes browsing messages in the inbox cumbersome. You are configuring the system-wide default here. Users can alter this setting, and all of the following **Read Mail** display-related options for their own account.

Width to wrap mail messages at

Again, your users may find this option useful for small displays, such as handheld computing devices. The default is 80 characters per line.

Show buttons at top for

Selects on which pages the **Delete**, **Mark message as**, and **Forward** buttons will be displayed at the top of the page. By default, these buttons appear at the top and bottom of the mailbox pages and only at the bottom on the view mail page. If large mails are common, your users may find it convenient to display buttons at the top of both. If your users don't have a lot of screen real estate (such as with a palm-sized device, for example) you might not want to display buttons at the top of any page.

Show To: address in mailboxes?

This option allows you to select whether the mailbox page will display the To: field. It's useful if a mailbox receives messages with different email addresses via mail aliases.

Don't MIME encode messages if text only?

If set to Yes, messages that contain no binary files will not be MIME encoded. MIME encoding is a means to transmit data and text that falls outside of the 7-bit ASCII that is permitted in plain-text emails.

Mailboxes directory under home directory

Mail folders will be created by Usermin for storage of sent mail, drafts, and custom folders. These folders will be created in the user's home directory within the subdirectory specified here.

Treat mailbox subdirectories as

If there exist other subdirectories within the directory specified above, Usermin can consider them as folders, or as subdirectories, as specified here.

Save sent mail

If selected, mail sent by users via the Read Mail module will be saved in a sent mail folder in the user's home directory.

Automatically mark read messages

Messages that have been read will be marked with a check mark if this option is set to Yes.

Default folder file

This selects the folder that will be displayed when the user first opens the Read Mail module. By default this is the inbox for the user.

Show image attachments as thumbnails

If selected, and the appropriate libraries are available, image attachments will be displayed as thumbnails. Clicking the thumbnail will display the full-sized image.

Sort address book by

Address book entries can be sorted alphabetically by the real name or the email address, or they can be sorted chronologically by the order in which they have been added.

Include real name in From: address?

If available, the user's real name can be included in the From field of messages being sent using the Read Mail module.

Character set for sent mail

MIME mail messages may contain characters from several character sets. This option specifies the default character set for sent mail. Locations with native languages other than English and other romance languages may wish to change this to a different character set.

Ask for confirmation before deleting

This option configures the level of confirmation required when deleting emails and folders. If set to Yes, every delete request will have to be confirmed. If set to No, email deletions will not require confirmation.

Signature file

If specified, the user may have a signature file that will be automatically appended to every email composed. Traditionally, the file name for signature files is .signature in the users home directory, but any file name may be specified.

Running Processes

The **Running Processes** module in Usermin allows users to view all of the processes they are running. There are a couple of configurable options here.

Default process list style

The options correlate to the modes of the ps command. Therefore, it allows output forms, such as a process tree (where parent/child relationships are clear) as well as simpler process lists.

PS command output style

This option should match the OS on which Usermin is running, as it chooses how to parse the output of the ps command. However, if your system uses a custom variant of this command, you may need to modify this to an OS that provides a similar ps.

Cron Jobs

The **Cron Jobs** module allows users to create their own scheduled tasks to be performed automatically by the system at a specific time. The commands are performed with the permissions of the user that configured them.

Crontab Directory

This should be set to the directory where cron looks for its crontab files.

Command to read a user's cron job

Some crontab versions may use slightly different command line options, or you may use a special-purpose wrapper for cron. Here you can select the command and options for reading a user's crontab.

Command to edit a user's cron job

Similar to the above **Command to read a user's cron job**, except it configures the command to edit a user's crontab.

Command to accept a user's cron job on stdin

crontab can usually accept input from the standard input also, if the - pseudo-file name is given on the command line.

Command to delete a user's cron jobs

This option sets the command Usermin will use to delete a user's crontab entries.

Cron supports input to cron jobs

This option configures whether Usermin will provide a text entry box so that the user can provide data to the command being run via standard input. The command being run must accept data from standard input.

Path to Vixie-Cron system crontab file

This should be the path to your system-wide crontab. Generally, it would be /etc/ crontab.

Path to extra cron files directory

Many systems make use of an extra cron directory for program specific cron jobs to execute when cron runs. This is likely /etc/cron.d.

run-parts command

The run-parts command is often run in the system crontab file, and is used to specify other directories to run at specified times. For example, on a Red Hat Linux system the crontab contains:

```
SHELL=/bin/bash
PATH=/sbin:/bin:/usr/sbin:/usr/bin
MAILTO=root
HOME=/

# run-parts
01 * * * * root run-parts /etc/cron.hourly
02 4 * * * root run-parts /etc/cron.daily
22 4 * * 0 root run-parts /etc/cron.weekly
42 4 1 * * root run-parts /etc/cron.monthly
```

The previous example sets a few defaults in the cron environment and executes run-parts at a few specified times. Specifically, the /etc/cron.hourly file is executed at one minute after every hour. run-parts is simply the program that processes the specified directory and executes all of the commands in it.

Available Modules

Much like the Webmin module selection page, this page allows you to select which modules will be available to users. If, for example, you do not want users to have any direct filesystem access, you could disable the **Command Shell**, **File Manager**, and **SSH/Telnet Login**. The **SSH Configuration** and **Login Script** are then useless, so may be disabled as well.

When to Use Usermin

It has probably become quite clear that Usermin and Webmin are strikingly similar in many ways, and Usermin has very little that Webmin does not. So, why use it? Why not simply give everyone access to Webmin and simplify life for everyone? There is no way to answer that question fully without analyzing the environment in which the system is deployed. Under some circumstances, Usermin would be useless while requiring additional resources to install and run it. But in other circumstances, Usermin can be a valuable addition to an administrator's toolkit.

Usermin is at its most useful when the server is being used by a large number of unprivileged users, and administration of those users needs to be simplified. Before Usermin, it was possible to grant users access to Webmin to read their mail, change passwords, and perform a few normal user functions, and that functionality is still there. One *could* use Webmin for the same purposes by constructing elaborate ACLs and groups and being careful to configure those new users with just those permissions. However, this leaves some room for administrator error, which could have dramatic consequences. Usermin, on the other hand, leaves no room for error. A Usermin user has the permissions of the user that is logged in and no more. The user can't accidentally receive additional rights, and so a careful selection of available modules is not needed to ensure security and ease of use (because, let's face it, many users can become quite confused by too many complicated options).

Another good use for Usermin is to provide an easy method for users who travel to read their mail and retrieve files from their own home directories. By providing a web interface to the local machine (and via network file servers, potentially all of a user's data) telecommuters can do all of these things from any web-enabled device in the world. In other words, users can log in to the local network from an Internet cafe, an Internet kiosk at trade shows, or a wireless web device. Doing so requires no specialized software to be installed on the client system.

Another interesting use for Usermin would be in a shared-hosting environment, allowing users the ability to view their own directory, upload files via a web browser, edit many of the basic features of their shell account, read mail, and so forth. It wouldn't be difficult to implement a few nifty extras such as running a web log analysis tool and allowing users to view the results from within Usermin.

5

GENERAL SYSTEM CONFIGURATION

The second category on the Webmin tab bar is System. Clicking it will allow you to edit such system features as: Bootup and Shutdown behavior, Disk Quotas, Filesystems, Manual Pages, NFS Exports, Processes, Cron Jobs, System Logs, and more. Figure 5-1 shows the options available on a Linux system (specifically, a server that's running Red Hat Linux).

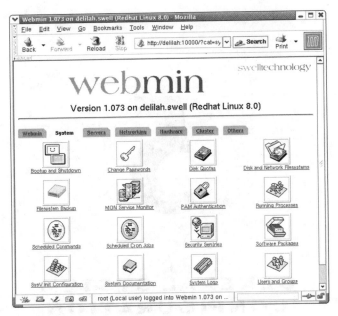

Figure 5-1: System category

Bootup and Shutdown

Clicking Bootup and Shutdown brings you to a page of bootup options. In the case of a Red Hat system, it provides access to all of the init scripts found in /etc/rc.d/init.d. Similarly, on a Solaris system the scripts are located in /etc/init.d. Clicking on any of the script names will provide the ability to edit, start, stop, and delete the init script. Usually, each init script provides functions to start, stop, and restart system services such as Sendmail, named, and Apache, as well as perform basic system initializations such as setting up network devices and routing tables. An easy way to add a new service or command to the system start-up routine, if it does not have an init script, is to add it in /etc/rc.d/rc.local or /etc/rc.local.

Also on this page you'll see the **Reboot** and **Shutdown** buttons. They do just what you would assume, after a confirmation screen.

Disk and Network Filesystems

The **Disk and Network Filesystems** page provides a detailed view of the filesystems listed in /etc/fstab. From this page you can edit mount points, create new mount points, umount and mount partitions, and add execute and setuid restrictions to specific mount points for security (Figure 5-2). This module configures the /etc/fstab file.

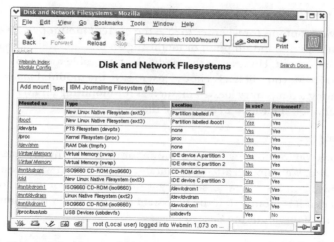

Figure 5-2: Mounted filesystems

To edit one of the listed filesystems, simply click it. From there you'll be able to mount and unmount the filesystem and adjust several filesystem options. The available options may vary depending on the operating system and the media. Linux and Solaris have large differences and so will be documented separately. Irix and FreeBSD are nearly identical to Linux and so are not given their own section.

Linux Native Filesystem Mount Details

In the upper table on the **Edit Mount** page, Webmin offers access to several general options that are applicable for all filesystems (Figure 5-3).

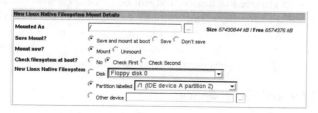

Figure 5-3: Linux Native Filesystem Mount Details

Mounted As

This is the *mount point* on which the filesystem will be located in your system's directory hierarchy. A mount point is a directory, made like any other directory using the mkdir command. When mounting a filesystem, the OS checks this value to decide where the contents of the filesystem should be located in the hierarchy. Some mount points, such as /usr and /, have a specific meaning for the OS and must not be changed. While several other mount points are so named because of long-standing UNIX tradition, such as /home and /usr/local. Nevertheless, most mount points can be named in any way that suits your environment; just be careful when you diverge from the historically accepted names.

Save mount?

Provides options for whether to save the current mount point. Generally, when creating a new mount point or modifying an old one, you will want to save and mount at boot. However, if the media is a removable media, like a floppy disk or a CD-ROM, you will likely choose just to save the mount. Finally, if you are only creating a temporary filesystem, such as for mounting an ISO image as a filesystem, you'll have no need to save the mount point.

Mount now?

Allows you to choose whether to mount or unmount the filesystem now. If Mount is selected, Webmin will attempt to mount the filesystem when you click the **Create** or **Save** buttons. Likewise, selecting Unmount will attempt to unmount the filesystem if it is mounted. If the filesystem is in use by any programs, the OS will refuse to unmount the filesystem.

Check filesystem at boot

Selects whether the filesystem will be checked using fsck on system boot, and if so, what priority the check should receive. Note that some filesystem types, such as journaled filesystems like ReiserFS and XFS, do not usually need to be checked. Also, read-only filesystems, such as those of CD-ROMs, should not be checked. Under Linux, the ext3 filesystem will quietly skip the fsck, even when the fstab entry specifies a priority here, unless the user specifies otherwise manually during a boot after an unclean shutdown. As it is a journaling filesystem, this is reasonable behavior, but may not be immediately obvious from the documentation.

Linux Native Filesystem

Allows you to choose the device that will be associated with the mount point. Some modern Linux distributions use labeled devices for this, while others simply identify the device directly. The drop-down menu provides access to all of the known disk devices. You may also enter a device or ISO file name directly in the text entry field by clicking the Other devices radio button.

Linux Advanced Mount Options

The lower table on this page displays the advanced mount options for Linux filesystems and indicates which are currently enabled (Figure 5-4).

Figure 5-4: Advanced Mount Options

Read-only?

Sets the read-only flag for the filesystem. If Yes, the filesystem will not allow writing, even by the root user. CD-ROM drives, floppy disks mounted with the write protect tab enabled, and some other media will always have this flag enabled, regardless of the setting in fstab. This option correlates to the ro mount option.

Buffer writes to filesystem?

Allows you to disable write buffering for this device. By default, disk I/O is buffered in UNIX, to improve responsiveness and increase overall disk throughput. In some circumstances, buffering can be detrimental to the reliability of a system. Some database or email server software may be more reliable on a filesystem that has buffering disabled. Ordinarily, this change is unnecessary, as most software that requires this behavior forces a flush to disk after every transaction, thus disabling buffering for only the application that requires it. In most situations, altering this will only slow down the system without providing any tangible benefit. This option enables the sync mount option switch.

Allow device files?

This option dictates whether a file can be treated as a device on this filesystem. Device files are a special type of file that does not map to a portion of the disk, but instead directs I/O to another physical or virtual device, such as a printer, a modem, or a console display. In general, only the root user should be allowed to mount filesystems containing device files. This option enables the nodev switch.

Allow execution of binaries?

When this option is enabled, no file contained on the filesystem will be treated as an executable file. It could be useful when mounting a filesystem that contains binary executables for another architecture, such as PPC executables from Yellow Dog Linux on an x86 system running FreeBSD. This option correlates to the noexec switch.

Disallow setuid programs?

A program that is setuid will be treated by the system as though it were executed by the user to which it has been set to. For example, a program that has been setuid root will be executed with the permissions of the root user, thus it can be very dangerous. Since a program that is setuid root could be very dangerous, there must be a means to prevent users from being able to introduce setuid programs into the system from outside sources such as CD-ROM or floppy disks. This option correlates to the nosuid directive.

Allow users to mount this filesystem?

If users need to be able to mount the filesystem, this option can be selected. In general, most filesystems will be mounted at boot time and will thus always be available to users. But in the case of removable media like floppy disks, USB drives, and CD-ROM disks, the user is likely to need to access their own disks on occasion. This option corresponds to the user mount switch.

Action on error

When mounting the filesystem, errors may occur. This option allows you to choose how the system should behave in response to mount errors. The default is set in the filesystem super block, and can be configured using the tune2fs utility. When set to Continue the filesystem will be mounted and the filesystem will be marked as being in an erroneous condition. When set to Remount read-only, the system will attempt to remount the filesystem as a read-only filesystem. This can provide some safety and help maintain the ability to recover data from the disk if the errors were due to a failing disk. The Panic option halts the system with a filesystem mount error. This option corresponds to the errors mount option.

CAUTION *When attempting to recover data from a damaged disk, or a disk with data that has been accidentally deleted, it is vital that no additional data be written to the disk. Because of the design of most UNIX filesystems in use today, including Linux ext2 and the BSD system's UFS, a file's contents are not usually removed from disk until the space is required by the OS for new storing new data. Thus, if you immediately remount your filesystem read-only, your ability to restore deleted data is greatly improved. A better choice, of course, is to make good use of a reliable backup utility and a regular backup schedule. It is impossible to guarantee recovery of deleted files or files lost due to a failing drive without a recent backup of the files.*

Files inherit parent directory GID?

When new files are created on a UNIX filesystem, they usually have user and group ownership matching the creator of the file. If a directory must be shared by a number of users, it may be desirable to have the group membership of the files set to a specific GID. When this option is enabled, new files will have group membership set to the GID specified by the containing directory. This option corresponds to the grpid or bsdgroups mount options and defaults to no.

Use Quotas?

If quotas should be used to manage disk usage for this filesystem, you may select the type of quotas to be applied. This option corresponds to the grpquota, noquota, quota, and usrquota option switches and defaults to applying no quotas.

Reserve space for user, Reserve space for group

Most UNIX filesystems implicitly set aside a small amount of space for emergency use by an administrator. This space will remain available even if the normal users of the system have filled the rest of the disk. By default this user will be the root user, however, in ext2 and ext3 filesystems the reserved space may be used by the user or group specified here. This option configures the resuid and resgid options.

Solaris Filesystem Options

Solaris has a few of its own additional options beyond the traditional UFS options. This section will cover the options that diverge from the Linux options discussed already.

UFS Disk

This option is only moderately different from the similar option on Linux and other systems. Disks are identified by type, SCSI or IDE, system device numbers, and the partition number. RAID devices may be specified by Unit number, and other devices may be specified by pathname.

Solaris Advanced Mount Options

The Solaris UFS implementation provides a few special features differentiating it from the previously documented Linux advanced mount options, specifically, **Repair Delay, Update access times?, Force direct IO?, Allow large files?,** and **Enabled logging?** are available, while **Allow execution of binaries?, Allow device files?, Allow users to mount this filesystem?, File inherit parent GID?,** and the reserved space options that were available in Linux are not.

Allow user interrupt?

This option configures whether a user will be permitted to interrupt a process that is blocked waiting for a disk operation on this filesystem. This option corresponds to intr and nointr, and defaults to yes (intr).

Repair Delay

Because it is possible for the server to reboot on a failed mount attempt, the system needs a protective mechanism to prevent it from going into a repair/reboot cycle, which might do more harm to an already damaged filesystem. This option specifies the minimum amount of time between repair attempts. If the system reboots within this time frame and attempts to repair the disk a second time within the time specified, it will simply halt. This option correlates to the toosoon mount directive, and is only available in Solaris versions older than 7. It is unnecessary and ignored on later Solaris revisions.

Update access times?

This option specifies whether the access time, or atime, value of a file will be updated when accessed. Immediately means that a files access time will be updated immediately every time the file is accessed. Deferred means the access time will be updated, but only during the course of other filesystem activity. Finally, No means that access time will never be updated on a file. On ordinary filesystems, it is desirable to leave atime enabled. Alternatively, when using a filesystem exclusively for an application that does not require access time updates, like an NNTP news spool or a web cache, disabling atime updates can provide a small performance boost as the number of disk transactions required is reduced. This option correlates to the noatime, and dfratime and nodfratime switches.

Force direct IO?

This option is functionally the same as the **Buffer writes to filesystem?** described previously. In its simplest terms it disables buffering between processes and the filesystem. For programs that use very large contiguous files without frequent random access, forcing direct I/O can improve overall throughput. This option correlates to the `forcedirectio` and `noforcedirectio`. By default, direct I/O is not enabled, and all disk I/O will be buffered.

Allow large files?

Maximum file size on Solaris, as on most operating systems, has throughout its history gone through changes. In simple terms, this option dictates whether a filesystem will permit files over the size of 2GB (currently). Because there are a number of programs, operating systems, and other filesystems that cannot support files larger than 2GB, this limit can be imposed to maintain reliable operation between those differing parts. For example, if a filesystem is to be exported via NFS to operating systems that cannot handle large files, it is wise to enforce this limit on the exporting machine as well. This option corresponds to the `largefiles` and `nolargefiles` mount switches.

Enabled logging?

Logging, when enabled, stores filesystem transactions in a log before applying the transaction to the filesystem. In other words, before making an I/O transaction permanent, it must successfully complete. The result of this is that in the event of a unclean shutdown of the system, the filesystem will remain in a consistent state, eliminating the necessity of running `fsck` on the filesystem. This option correlates to the `logging` and `nologging` mount switches.

System Documentation

This page (Figure 5-5) provides access to the extensive help that is available on most UNIX systems through man pages, in addition to the Webmin help files, installed package documentation files, Perl module documentation, as well as results from the Google search engine.

Figure 5-5: System documentation

System Documentation Search

Using the module is as simple as entering a search term and clicking **Search**. If you choose to **Match any** in your search, the module will return a list of all pages that it can find that match your query. You may specify which types of documentation you'd like to search, including man pages, Webmin help files, documentation for installed packages, Perl module documentation, and *The Book of Webmin* either locally or remotely. It will also provide a simple gateway to a Google search.

Man pages are divided into numbered sections, in order to clearly distinguish programming documentation from user command documentation, and the like. When performing a search of the man pages, you will likely see multiple results matching your search term. In some cases, there will be more than one entry precisely matching the command or term you're looking for, in different manual sections. The sections are roughly divided as described below:

- User commands that may be run by all users:
- System calls, or functions provided by the kernel.
- Library Functions.
- Devices or special files in the /dev directory.
- File format descriptions, for such files as /etc/passwd and **Sendmail's** /etc/ aliases file.
- Games.
- Miscellaneous, macro packages, and conventions. Examples include bootparam and unicode.
- System administration tools that only root can execute. Examples include **ifconfig** and **halt**.
- OS Specific kernel routine documentation. Not always available on all systems.

Also available on some systems are a few lettered sections. They are: **n** for New documentation, which may be moved in the future to a new location, **o** for Old documentation, which will likely be phased out, and **l** for Local documentation specific to this particular system.

Searching Documentation from Another Module

This page also provides the configuration for searching from within the other modules. In most Webmin modules, there will be a **Search docs** link in the upper right corner of the page. When clicked, Webmin will search all of the available documentation that has been selected and present links and short excerpts from the documents. If your system will be disconnected from the Internet, you may wish to disable Google searches. Likewise, if you do not want package documentation or similar types of documentation to be searched you may unselect them here.

TIP *In recent versions of Webmin, it is possible to search the contents of this book, if the corresponding module is installed. To obtain the Webmin module for this book, visit the Projects [http://www.swelltech.com/projects] page at Swell Technology for downloads in .wbm and .rpm packages. It is not included in the base Webmin package, due to its large size.*

Process Manager

The **Process Manager** is accessed by clicking the **Running Processes** icon (Figure 5-6). This page provides a list of all running processes grouped by lineage. Clicking a **Process ID** will provide more complete information about the process, including the command that was run, the parent process, the CPU usage, runtime, size, niceness level, and more.

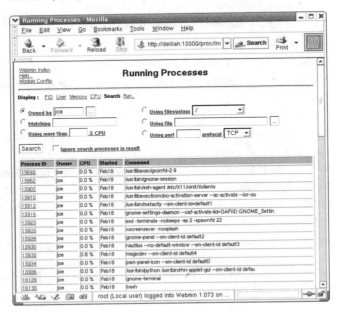

Figure 5-6: Running Processes

Niceness level is configurable. Niceness is a measure of how much processor time the process will be allowed compared to other processes on the system, and its values go from -20 (highest priority) to +20 (lowest priority).

Clicking the **Files and Connections** button provides a list of the files that are being used by the process, as well as a list of open file descriptors and details about each. The open files will often contain a number of shared libraries, configuration files, and possibly user files that have been open by the user of the process if it is a user application. Open network connections will provide information about what network connections exist for this process. In many cases, this list will only contain local loopback connections from 127.0.0.1, or this section of the page may not be present if the application has no network connections.

The module also offers several alternative views of the data, including sorting by user, memory usage, and CPU usage. Clicking the **Search** link provides the ability to filter on a given aspect of the process. Finally, the **Run** link provides a simple method of running a command, with optional arbitrary command-line input.

Similar information can be gained from the standard UNIX command ps on the command line. Niceness level of a process can be set from the command line using the nice command. Sending a signal to a process or terminating a process is achieved using the kill command. The list of files and connections is gathered using the lsof command.

Scheduled Commands

The at command provides a simple means to execute a specified command at a specified time. Its usage is simple, made even simpler by the Webmin interface. It can be very useful for a number of tasks, such as running one-time CPU intensive tasks at off-hours, notifying you of appointments, and so on.

To create a new at job, simply fill in the details. Specifically, the **Run as user** option dictates the user under which the command will be run. **Run on date** and **Run at time** specifies the date and time at which the command will run. The **Run in directory** option specifies where the at command will be run from, as a change directory command will be run before the command is executed. This directory must be accessible by the user under which the command is run. Finally, **Commands to execute** is where you may enter the commands to be run by at at the specified time. Any number of linefeed separated commands may be entered and they will be executed in sequence.

NOTE   *If you have a repetitive task that needs to be executed at a specified time daily, or weekly, or monthly,* at *is not the best tool for the job. There is another command called* cron *that is more appropriate.* cron *is covered in the next section.*

Scheduled Cron Jobs

The **Cron Jobs** module is used for editing the crontab on your system. Cron is a daemon that runs constantly on most UNIX systems and allows users and the administrator to run specified tasks automatically at selected times. Ordinarily, crond is configured from the system-wide crontab as well one or more configuration directories in /etc/cron.d, and on Red Hat Linux systems and some other Linux distributions. crond draws its configuration from /etc/cron.hourly, /etc/cron.daily, /etc/cron.weekly, and /etc/cron.monthly. Note that even on Red Hat and similar systems, /etc/cron.d and /etc/crontab still exist and can be used just as on any other UNIX system.

Configuration of crond is much simplified by use of the Webmin module. To create a new cron job, click **Create a new cron job**. The **Create Cron Job** page (Figure 5-7) allows you to select the user that the cron job will run as, thereby limiting its permissions to those of the selected user. As in all permissions situations, it is best to choose a user with the least permissions required to actually accomplish the task needed. There are fields for entering the **Command** you want to be executed, as well as for any **Input to command** you might have. The **Active** option dictates whether the command is enabled or disabled by commenting it out with a hash mark at the beginning of the line.

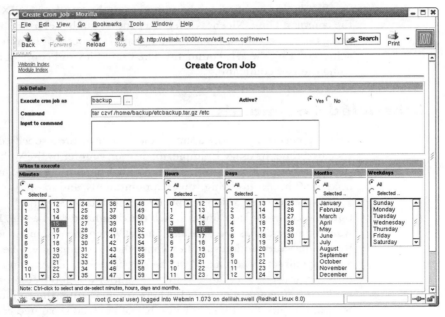

Figure 5-7: Create Cron Job

In Figure 5-7, I've created a cron job that is run as a user named backup (a user I've created just for such tasks). The job is **Active**, so it will run at the specified times. The command that is being run is a simple tar command line to back up my complete /etc directory to a tarball in /home/backup. While this is not a terribly sophisticated backup system, it gets the job done without much complexity. Furthermore, a simple periodic backup of important files is far better than no backup at all. In this case, it is made slightly more effective by the fact that /etc and /home are partitions on two different hard disks.

Software Packages

The **Software Packages** module allows an administrator to perform software upgrades and package maintenance via a quite friendly interface. Although the actual implementation can vary quite a lot depending on which software packaging system your operating environment uses, Webmin masks most differences, and the overall usage of each is very similar.

Introduction to Package Managers

Most modern UNIX systems feature a package manager. The concept of a package manager may be foreign to new users migrating from Windows operating systems, in which software is installed by one of a number of installation processes. There is usually no record kept of the locations of installed files and no easy way to remove all of them if the software is no longer needed. While some installation utilities are more effective and reliable than others, all of them have difficulty making wise decisions about software dependencies and available library versions. The lack of a unified package manager has led to an entire product category devoted to removing old software installations because of these problems.

A package manager solves this problem, and quite a few other problems that aren't obvious until you've lived with one for a while. With a package managed system, you never have to wonder where a given file originated, or whether a given library or system component is installed. Finding the version of any installed package is quick and easy, and upgrading old packages to new versions can usually be done without fear of overwriting configuration details. So, now that it is clear why package managers are great, it is a good time to talk about how you can use your package manager from Webmin.

Supported Operating Systems

Webmin provides a mostly consistent frontend to most major OS package managers. The supported operating systems include RPM-based Linux distributions, like Red Hat, SuSE, and Mandrake; deb-based systems like Debian; systems using the pkg-style tools like Solaris, Slackware Linux, and SCO Unixware and OpenServer; and the HP/UX and IBM AIX package managers. A notable exception to the list of supported operating systems is Irix. Though it has a package manager, it is not currently supported by Webmin.

Using the Package Manager

Webmin presents a simple interface that provides the ability to install packages, search currently installed packages, view the installed packages, and remove packages (Figure 5-8). Additionally, it is possible to identify the package from which a specified file was installed.

Installed Packages

To search for a package, enter the package name here. A package name is the name of the file that was installed, without the version number or file name extension. For example, on a Red Hat system, the Postfix mail server package is simply called postfix. When searching, Webmin will return all packages that have the search term as part of the package name or as part of the package description. This usually makes it easy to find what you're looking for even if you don't know the exact package name.

To view a list of all installed packages, click the **Package Tree** button. When applicable, packages will be divided into their appropriate categories as designated by the packager.

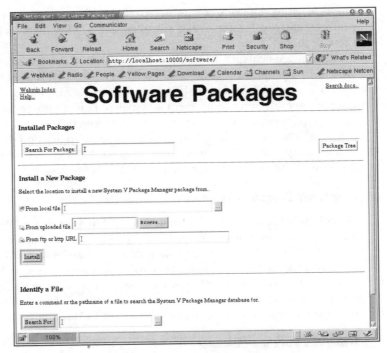

Figure 5-8: Software package management on Solaris

Install a New Package

To install a new package (Figure 5-9), specify its location, either a local file path or a URL, or by uploading it from your local machine using the **Browse** option. The package will be identified, the title and description will be displayed, and the installation path may be specified for relocatable packages.

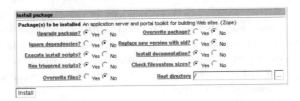

Figure 5-9: Install package

It may also be possible to specify options regarding dependencies, installation scripts, documentation, filesystem size, and so on. Generally, the default options will work fine.

Identify a File

Often it is useful to know which package provided a particular file on the filesystem. Simply enter the path to the file you would like to find information about into the text field and click the **Search for** button.

Edit Package

Clicking a package name provides access to the **Edit Package** page (Figure 5-10). This page includes package details such as the description, the category or class of the package, the date of installation, and so on. Here you can list the files contained in the package as well as uninstall the package.

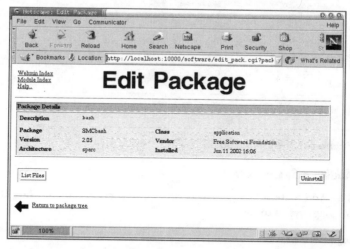

Figure 5-10: Edit Package

System Logs

System Logs provides a method for controlling the syslogd daemon used on most UNIX system to provide standard logging functions. The module opens with a list of all currently existing logs. By clicking the **Log destination** of a log file, you can edit the logging properties, as shown in Figure 5-11. On the editing page there is also a **View log** button that allows you to view a configurable number of lines from the end of the log file. It also allows a constantly refreshing log view if selected.

This module edits the /etc/syslog.conf file and provides a pretty easy way to check up on your logs remotely. And even though the module is designed primarily for syslogd logs only, it is flexible enough to allow you to view other types of logs as well. For example, the web-caching proxy Squid doesn't use standard **syslog** facilities, so doesn't fall under the control of syslogd. Nonetheless, I like to be able to check up on a running Squid, so I add an entry on all of the boxes I administer to allow me to watch those logs in Webmin. To create a new syslog entry, click the **Add a new system log** link.

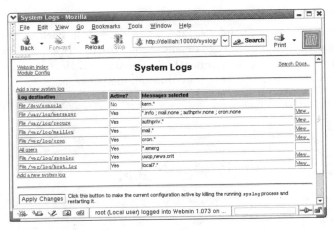

Figure 5-11: System Logs

Adding a System Log

The Add System Log page is divided into sections labeled **Log Destination** and **Message types to log**.

Log Destination

The log destination options below specify where log entries will be written, and whether a particular log is active.

Log to

This option configures the destination of the log file. Syslog can log to a file, a named pipe, a remote syslog server, or the console of some or all local users.

File

The log entries will be appended to the file name specified. A complete path should be given. Historically, system logs are stored in /var/log. The **Sync after each message?** option will cause the syslog daemon to flush to disk after every entry, therefore overriding the disk I/O buffering provided by the operating system. This can be detrimental to performance in circumstances in which logging occurs at a very rapid rate, such as the mail log on a very busy mail server. In most circumstances, the integrity of the log is far more important than avoiding the small amount of disk activity system logs generate.

Named pipe

The concept of pipes is fundamental to the UNIX Way, or the philosophy of combining small tools to perform large jobs efficiently and flexibly. Most UNIX users are familiar with the standard command-line pipe, which allows the output of one command to be the input of another command. A named pipe expands upon that and allows output to be sent to a pipe that is located within the normal filesystem under a normal file name. Or, to put it another way, the output of syslog will go to whatever program is accepting input from the named pipe. While named pipes and their usage is beyond the scope of this book, I will point out a few resources to get you started on the subject. Many modern UNIX systems, including Linux systems, include a command called `mkfifo`, which creates the FIFO special file connected to a named pipe. Reading the man page, as well as reading about named pipes in your favorite general UNIX reference should give you a good overview of the topic.

Syslog server on

The `syslogd` daemon can log to local files, pipes, and users, as well as direct its output to a remote server running `syslogd`. However, the remote server must be configured to permit remote logging from your server. When using remote logging, the address of the server is entered here.

Local users, All logged-in users

When one or more users, or all users, are specified here, the log entries that match the description will be written to all open consoles of the users specified. For example, on most systems, all messages of priority `.emerg`, or emergency, are sent to all user consoles. Most systems are configured to send shutdown and reboot messages at this priority.

Logging active?

This is a simple yes or no question, with obvious meaning. However, what may not be obvious is that a disabled log is simply commented out in the `/etc/syslog.conf` file with a hash mark, and so the configuration details remain in the file even though it is no longer an active logging entry.

Message Types to Log

Here the types of messages to log to the configured log destination can be specified. Any given log entry has two identifiers: its facility and its priority. The facility specifies the type of program generating the log, such as `mail`, `daemon`, `cron`, or locally definable facilities, named `local0` through `local7` on many Linux systems and similarly defined on other UNIX variants. The priority is the level of message on a scale of `debug` to `emergency`. The priority level used by any given program for any given message is somewhat arbitrary, as it is chosen by the author(s) of the program. However, it is safe to say that `debug` level messages will be incredibly verbose and unnecessary in all but the most complicated trouble-shooting situation, while `emergency` is reserved for messages of the utmost importance. Generally, you'll want to configure the priority of logs somewhere in the middle of this, somewhere around `warning` or `err`.

Users and Groups

UNIX is, at its very core, a multi-user operating system. It was built from the ground up to provide services to a number of simultaneous users. Because of these features, UNIX provides a simple, but effective, method for restricting users to only the parts of the system in which they should have access. The **Users and Groups** module in Webmin attempts to provide a nice front end for those features of the system. Each version of UNIX has differences in how users and groups are implemented. However, Webmin hides those details quite effectively so that you never have to think about it. The Webmin **Users and Groups** module edits several system files, depending on your OS. Usually, the files are /etc/passwd and /etc/shadow, for usernames and passwords, and /etc/group and /etc/gshadow, for groups and group passwords. Note that the shadow versions of the preceding files are far more secure than standard passwd files because they are only accessible by the root user. Shadow passwords are standard on most Linux distributions today, and many other systems as well.

Clicking a username or group name will take you to an **Edit User** page, allowing you to edit all facets of the account. Note that changing the user or group ID at some point in time after the account is created is risky, as permissions are set by ID, not username/group name. While the module will change these for you on the home directory, there may be user programs or even system programs that rely on the UID to remain the same. Also note that on some systems (Red Hat and probably other Linux distributions) the user and the user's primary group are always the same name by default. Red Hat Linux includes the adduser command, which will create a group of the same name and ID as the user, and therefore Webmin can do the same. You should not change this behavior, unless you really know what you're doing, as the system relies on this for much of its access control flexibility. Unlike some traditional UNIX variants, Linux users can have many secondary groups active at all times, which can be set to any group(s) you need.

Users and Groups Module Configuration

Unlike most module configuration pages, the **Users and Groups** module configuration contains a number of options that impact the usage and usefulness of the module significantly. While most other modules only use the module configuration to specify paths to files, display characteristics, etc., the **Users and Groups** module specifies many defaults that are used when creating new users.

Before and After Commands

This section includes fields for specifying commands you want to run before and after changes are made. This option allows things like a NIS make to be run after adding a user. If more than one command needs to be run, it is trivial to write a simple shell script to execute any commands that you need to run.

Webmin provides access to a number of variables within the local environment in which the command is run. This allows you to construct a command that includes the username, UID, generated password, and so on. For example, to email a notice to the system administrator when a new user is created, which contains the username and password, you could use the following:

```
[ "$USERADMIN_ACTION" = "CREATE_USER" ] && echo "Created user $USERADMIN_USER with
password $USERADMIN_PASS" | mail -s "New User" root
```

While shell scripting is beyond the scope of this book, I will point out a few things about how this script works. Using the environment variables set by Webmin when the user is created, the comparison within the test operators ([and]) checks to see if the command is being executed after a user creation, rather than a change to an existing user. If it is a newly created user, an email will be sent to root and contain the contents of the variables for the username and password. Below is a list of the variables exported and what they contain:

Environment Variables Exported When Saving a User

The following environment variables are always set whenever a user is created or modified:

USERADMIN_USER

The username of the user being edited. A user must have a username, and it must be unique.

USERADMIN_UID

The user ID of the user being edited. Every user must have a UID. The UID is not required to be unique, but there is rarely any reason for it not to be unique. Permissions are applied to files based on UID rather than username, so changing this will effectively change a user's permissions to that of the new UID.

USERADMIN_REAL

The real name of the user. This is not a necessary field in the passwd file, and so may be empty.

USERADMIN_SHELL

This variable contains the path and name of the shell for this user.

USERADMIN_HOME

The path to the user's home directory.

USERADMIN_GID

This variable will contain the primary GID of the user.

USERADMIN_SECONDARY

This variable will contain a comma-separated list of secondary groups the user belongs to.

USERADMIN_PASS

If the password has been changed by entering a plain text password into the password field, the new password will be contained in this variable. If the password is unchanged or pre-encrypted, the variable will be empty.

USERADMIN_ACTION

This variable contains the Webmin action being run that led to a user change. If the user is a new user being created, the variable will contain "CREATE_USER," while if it is an existing user being altered the value will be "MODIFY_USER."

Home Directory Options

When creating a new home directory for a user, or when modifying an existing user's home directory, Webmin can be customized to suit many different environments. The following options specify details about home directory creation and modification:

Permissions on new home directories

New directories for users will be created with the permissions specified here. The default is 0755, which means the owner of the file can read, write, and execute files in the directory assuming permission on the file itself, while the group and all other users on the system, can read and execute within the directory. In a web-hosting environment, this looseness is often necessary to permit the web server to have access to a users document root. However, in most business environments, these permissions are unacceptably lax. A better choice would be 0700 or 0711. The former disallows all users, other than UID 0, from being able to list the contents of the directory or read anything within the directory, while the latter permits other users to change directory into the directory, but not necessarily to read or execute files within it. It is useful to permit other users to pass through the current directory to a directory within which is intended to be shared with other users.

Copy files into new home directories from

When creating new UNIX users, it is customary to provide a base set of configuration files to set up sensible defaults for the shell, desktop settings, path and other environment variables, and any local configuration details that would make the user's life more convenient. For example, on a machine used primarily for development, it is likely that the CVSROOT environment variable will be set on login. Similarly, a desktop machine will have icons to make it easier for the user to locate the files they need to use in day-to-day work. This file is usually called /etc/skel, where skel is short for *skeleton*, but it can be any directory name.

Automatic home directory base

Webmin can automatically set the home directory path for you if automatic directory creation is selected. This option allows you to specify the location of the home directory. There is rarely a good reason to stray from the tradition of using /home for this purpose.

Automatic home directory style

In most environments, the traditional home directory naming scheme of /home/username is perfectly acceptable, but in some large-scale networks, the number of users would make managing such a directory cumbersome. So administrators have resorted to breaking down the username distribution in various ways to permit easier home directory maintenance. Webmin supports several such alternate name distributions, specifically: /home/u/username, /home/u/us/username, and /home/us/username.

New User Options

The following options specify the defaults and restrictions Webmin will use when creating new users:

Lowest UID for new users, Lowest GID for new groups

Most UNIX systems use lower-numbered user ID and group ID numbers to specify special system users like the root user, syslog, and nobody. Because these users usually have special permissions it would be dangerous to assign a new user to one of the special UID numbers accidentally. Many older UNIX systems use UID and GID numbers from 0 to 100 for the system user and group IDs. Most modern Linux distributions use 0 through 500 for this purpose. Specifying the appropriate number here makes it impossible to accidentally specify a special UID or GID for a new normal user. Some environments may have other numbering schemes for which this feature can also be helpful.

Create new group for new users?

Many modern UNIX systems use a groups system wherein every user has primary group named after themselves. In a system that supports a large number of simultaneous secondary users, this makes it possible to use permissions in very flexible ways. If your system supports this, it is useful to select Yes here, and Webmin will automatically create the new group for you. Older-style UNIX systems may use a generic users group for this purpose. In which case this option should be set to No.

Don't use MD5 passwords if missing perl MD5 module?

If MD5 passwords are the default on your system, Webmin can use them for both authentication and when creating new users or changing passwords. If this is set to Yes, Webmin will not use MD5 passwords for users if the MD5 perl module is not installed. It will use instead the older, less secure, crypt function to encrypt the passwords.

Check for sendmail alias clashes?

When creating a new user, it is possible that there might already be an alias for the new username in the sendmail aliases file. The result of this clash would be that the new user would not receive mail; instead, the mail would be delivered to whatever user or program to which the alias pointed to. If this option is selected, Webmin will warn about any clashes that exist.

Only delete files owned by user?

When removing a user, Webmin can remove the user's home directory and all of its contents. If this option is enabled, it will remove only those files that are owned by the user. If any files exist in the user's home directory that are owned by another user on the system, it will not be removed, and the home directory and any subdirectories containing the files not owned by the user will be retained. This option may be useful if the user shares a portion of his or her home directory for use by others in group projects.

Maximum user and group name length

Here you may specify the longest a user and group name may be. If usernames must be exportable to a system with strict length requirements, you may have to place a limit here. For example, some old UNIX systems and legacy print- and file-sharing systems had eight- or even six- character username limits. Most modern systems have much larger hard limits, and so this is rarely necessary.

New User Defaults

The following are new user defaults:

Default primary group for new users

Normally, Webmin will create a user with a primary group appropriate for your system and based on the configuration of the earlier option **Create new group for new users?**. But if this is specified, Webmin will set the group specified as the primary group for the user. It may be appropriate to use this feature in some web-hosting environments. Usually, however, if your system supports flexible secondary groups, you shouldn't need to use this option.

Default secondary groups for new users

You may add any number of secondary groups here, separated by spaces. Modern UNIX systems support multiple simultaneous secondary groups, although some older systems have more primitive support for secondary groups.

NOTE *Secondary groups are a very flexible way to utilize UNIX filesystem permissions to provide limited access to parts of the system. For example, if I needed to provide access to a shared* ftp *directory to all users, so everyone could drop off files in the directory but couldn't delete or modify each other's files, I could create an* ftpusers *group. Then I would set the public FTP directory to be owned by* ftp:ftpusers, *with write access by both the owner and the group and world read access. Finally, any user who needed to be able to drop files into the directory could be added to the* ftpusers *group. Each user would be able to write and delete their own files but no one else's files.*

Default shell for new users

Most UNIX systems usually have at least two user shells available. The most common are bash, Bourne sh, cshell, ash, and kshell. While experienced users always have a preference, for most users any reasonably functional shell will be fine. The system default is probably what your users will expect, so it is the best choice in most cases. On Linux systems bash is usually the standard shell, while on Solaris the Bourne sh is the default. Because most shells are available on most operating systems, you have much flexibility in your choice if you need it.

Default minimum days for new users, Default maximum days for new users

If password timeouts are supported on your system, this option allows you to specify the default minimum and maximum number of days between password changes. As discussed earlier, a policy enforcing password timeouts is an important part of a good security policy. If your OS supports them, it is wise to use them.

Default warning days for new users

The system can warn users when they log in through a terminal if an enforced password change is approaching within the number of days specified here.

Default inactive days for new users

If a user is inactive for the specified number of days after the maximum days specified above is reached, the account will be disabled. Only a system administrator will be able to re-enable the account.

Display Options

The following options configure how the user and group information will be displayed for the system user and group list page, as well as the edit user and group pages:

Maximum number of users to display

If there are more users than the number specified here, Webmin will display a search dialog allowing you to see only the users you need to see.

Sort users and groups by

Webmin will sort the users and groups according to the selection here. The default is not to sort the names, and simply list them in the order they appear in the passwd and group files.

Number of previous logins to display

When viewing the login history of a user using the **Display logins by** option, this option specifies how many previous logins will be displayed. Unlimited means Webmin will display all logins that exist in the log file. Because logs are rotated at some interval, you will never see logins older than the last log rotation.

Display users and groups by

Depending on the number of users you have, and how much information you need to see on the front page, you may wish to display them by name only, or display them categorized by primary group. Displaying by name only can allow a much larger number of names to appear on screen at once and may be more convenient than the default in environments with hundreds or thousands of users.

Conceal plain-text password?

If selected, the **Normal password** field in the **Edit User** and **Create User** pages will display * marks in place of the characters typed. If set to No, the typed characters will be displayed. It may be a security risk to leave this option disabled, if user passwords will be entered or changed in the presence of others.

Get user and group info from

Webmin can usually gather user and group information using standard system calls. In some operating systems this may not work, or may not work as expected. In such cases, you can configure Webmin to draw the information from the appropriate files on the system. This doesn't need to be changed from its defaults by the vast majority of users, as the Webmin default is usually right for your system.

Generate password for new users?

If selected, new users will be assigned a random password when created. This password will be visible in the password entry field on the **Create User** page if **Conceal plain-text password?** is set to No.

Show office and phone details?

Webmin can use the comment field in the /etc/passwd to store phone numbers and office information. If this option is selected, it displays the information when you view the user details. Modern implementations of the finger command can also display this information.

Display user email from

Webmin can be used to send and receive mail by users who have access to the mail module. This option should be set to your active mail server. If using postfix, choose the sendmail option, because it use the same mailbox format and locations.

Password Restrictions

The following options specify the restrictions that Webmin will place on passwords when creating a new user, or modifying an existing user password:

Minimum password length

When users change their passwords through the Webmin interface, it is possible for Webmin to enforce a minimum password length. It is recommended to enforce at least a minimum password length of six characters if security is at all a concern. Shorter passwords are easier to guess, and are weaker when assaulted with a brute force attack. Operating systems using the older crypt encryption mechanism are limited to passwords of eight characters or less, but MD5-based systems usually have no limit or a much larger limit.

Prevent dictionary word passwords?

Because a common method of attack against computer systems is to attempt logins using passwords pulled from a dictionary file, it is often wise to require passwords that do not match words in the system dictionary. This option will cause Webmin to display an error message if a user chooses a password found in the dictionary.

Perl regexp to check password against

Here you may enter any Perl regular expression against which you would like passwords to be compared. For example, if you fear your users will often choose the company name, or the name of a local sports mascot, for their password, you may create a regular expression to match those terms.

Prevent passwords containing username?

Users have a bad habit of choosing really bad passwords. Some even choose their own user name as a password. If enabled, this option will prevent a user from such a mistake. Unfortunately, in current versions of Webmin, it will not make jokes about the lack of intelligence of the user.

System Configuration

The following options specify the locations of the system user and group information files:

Password file

The password file is the location of the list of users, and it contains information about their home directory, their login shell, and their primary group. Usually, this is /etc/passwd. On modern systems this file does not contain user passwords. Passwords usually reside in the shadow file.

Group file

The group file is the location of the file that contains the names and membership information of groups on the system. Usually, this is /etc/group.

Shadow password file

The shadow password file is the file that contains the actual passwords. It is only readable by users with root permissions, and therefore is a more secure location than the /etc/passwd file, because the password file must be readable by everyone in order to allow groups and commands like finger to work. Usually, this is /etc/shadow.

BSD master password file

Much like the shadow password file on Linux and some other UNIX variants, the BSD master password file is only readable by root and is usually the location of passwords on a BSD system rather than the /etc/passwd file. This is usually /etc/master.passwd.

Shadow group file

If group passwords are in use on a system that supports shadow passwords, there will be a group shadow password file in addition to the shadow password file. This is usually named /etc/gshadow.

Creating a New User

Creating a user with Webmin is a simple task. The steps can be simplified further through careful configuration of the module to set up users to suit your environment. Webmin can create a user manually, or it can import a text file list of new users or users to modify in an automated batch mode. This can be used, for example, to migrate an existing user list from a legacy system. Batch mode can also be useful for large organizations with a constantly shifting user base, such as a university or military installation.

To create a user manually, click the **Create a new user** link. Fill in the appropriate details. If you've chosen your defaults in the module configuration file wisely, you should be able to get away with entering just a few details for each user. In Figure 5-12 below, I've added a few extras just to make the example more interesting.

A username is always necessary, and because our user's name is Seymour, I've given him the username seymour. I've let Webmin choose the UID for me, which is the next available UID on the system above the minimum that is set in the module configuration. I've also entered Seymour's real name and his work telephone number. The password that appears in the normal password text entry box was selected at random by Webmin. It appears secure enough to me, so we'll leave that one alone. In the password options section, I've specified some reasonable timeout information. Finally, I've selected for Seymour to be a member of the users group, because I think he will be involved in many group projects that require him to be able to share files with co-workers easily.

Create User and Edit User Options

When creating a new user or editing an existing user, the following options are available:

Username

This is simply the username under which the user will log in. UNIX has a long tradition of using all lowercase letters for usernames, but capitalized names will work if you feel a strong urge to go against 30 years of tradition. Usernames may contain all alphanumeric characters, but no spaces or other special characters. Names must be unique and begin with a letter.

User ID

The user ID is usually chosen automatically by Webmin, although you may enter a specific UID instead.

NOTE *Recycling a UID or GID, i.e., reusing a deleted users old ID, can be dangerous, because file ownership is maintained at the OS level by the UID and GID number of the file rather than the name of the user. Thus if you create a new user with an old users UID or GID, and any files remain on the system owned by the previous user, the new user will have access to the files at the same level as the old user. There are reasonably reliable methods of locating such file permission problems using the* find *command, although it is beyond the scope of this book. A better choice is to never delete old users. Instead, disable their account by turning off logins, and if the user will never need to be re-enabled you may delete their home directory and other files. By doing this you ensure that Webmin will never reuse an old ID, unless you force it to.*

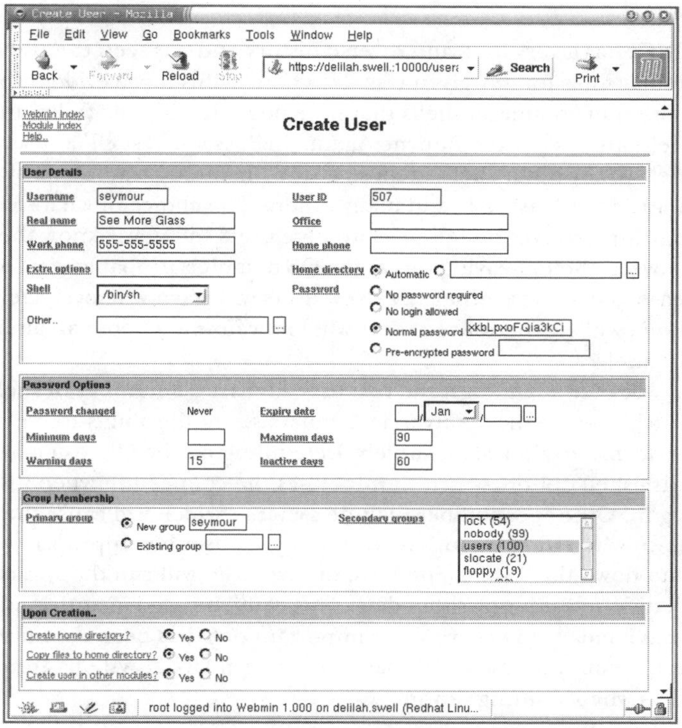

Figure 5-12: Creating a new user

Office, Work phone, Home Phone, Extra options

The UNIX passwd file has a comment field that may be used for mostly free-form text entry. Many programs, however, have standardized on a few comma-separated field values for the comment. For example, running the finger command on a username that has provided these extra fields will result in these numbers being displayed in addition to the usual information, such as recent logins. The **Extra options** field may be used on some systems to configure the initial umask, nice level, and ulimit values for the user.

Home directory

Users on a UNIX system generally have a directory that belongs to them called their home directory. Within their home directory, a user may read, write, delete, or execute files with no permissions restrictions. Quotas may limit the amount of space available to the user, but the user can otherwise work unrestricted in their home directory. The UNIX tradition places home directories in a partition labeled /home, with each user having their home directory named after their own username within it. For example, if our system has a user named slim it would not be unreasonable to expect his home directory to be /home/slim. As discussed previously, if you let it, Webmin will select the home directory for you based on the policy selected in the module configuration.

Shell

UNIX has a very long and diverse history and has seen the rise of a number of similar tools for any given task. Nowhere is this more evident than in the proliferation of command shells that have been developed. Today, the most popular shells are bash or the Bourne Again Shell, csh or C shell, and kshell or the Korn shell. Many other shells are also in use, including traditional sh or the original Bourne shell, ash, zsh, and many others. The choice of what shell to use is highly personal, though most average users will never know the difference between them. Leaving this at the OS default is probably wise, barring any strong reasons to choose otherwise. New users will learn whatever shell is provided for them, while experienced users will know how to choose an alternate shell for themselves.

Scattered amongst the real user shells are a number of shell replacements, which provide the ability to lock out a user or the ability to create special users to perform certain tasks remotely. Depending on the OS, you may have a nologin or false shell option, which simply closes the connection when the user attempts to log in. Other possibilities include shutdown, which will cause the system to shutdown when the user logs in, assuming the user has appropriate permissions to shut down the system. Similarly, the sync user will run the sync command to cause all disks to flush unwritten data. This could be used in anticipation of a shutdown or as a means to ensure some important data has been committed to disk. sync is not in common use today, because modern UNIX systems automatically sync disks when shutting down.

No password required

This option means that the user need not provide a password to log in. You don't want this option for any user that has shell access, as it means anyone that can reach a login prompt or the su command can become the user.

No login allowed

If set to this option, the system will never allow a user to log in under this username. This is often used for system users, like the syslog or nobody users. It is also used to lock an account, temporarily or permanently, without deleting it. This helps prevent accidental reuse of a user and group ID, which can have security implications.

Normal password

Here you may enter a new password for the user in plain text. If creating a new user, and you have configured Webmin to generate a password automatically, it will be prefilled with the generated password. If the configuration is set to hide plain-text passwords, the letters of the password will be replaced with asterisks. Existing passwords will never appear in this field, as the encryption used by the system is a one-way hash. There is no way, short of a brute force attack, to convert the encrypted password to a plain-text password.

Pre-encrypted password

If a password exists for this user, either in crypt or MD5 hash format, it will appear in this field. If you are importing UNIX users from an existing UNIX system, you may simply copy the password verbatim into this field. In most cases, the old password will continue to work on the new system. If importing many users, it may be more efficient to use the batch user creation feature instead of adding each user manually.

NOTE *As the **Password options** and **Group Membership** options have already been covered in the module configuration section they will not be covered again here.*

Upon Save . . .

When saving user information, Webmin can be configured to perform additional actions, based on the following configuration options:

Move home directory if changed?

If selected, and you have modified the value of the **Home directory** field, the path of the user's home directory will be altered to the new location. If unselected, the contents of the old home directory will remain unaltered. The default is Yes.

NOTE *Webmin attempts to rename the home directory rather than copy its contents. Because of this, the change must occur on the same filesystem, otherwise the change will fail.*

Change user ID on files?, Change group ID on files?

If you have altered the users **User ID** field and/or **Group ID** field, and these options are enabled, Webmin will change the user or group ownership of the files selected to the new UID or GID. If you have selected Home directory, only files within the user's current home directory will have ownership altered, while the All files option will change ownership of all files on the system that are currently owned by the user. Changing all files may take a very long time, depending on the size of the filesystems to be searched.

Modify user in other modules?

Because a UNIX system may maintain more than one user and password database for various services, Webmin provides a means to synchronize passwords and user creation across multiple files. For example, Samba and Squid may have their own user files and if configured to synchronize, Webmin will make changes to those files automatically when changes are made to system users. If this option is selected, changes made here will be made to all other modules that are configured for user synchronization.

Creating or Editing a Group

Groups are used in UNIX to provide means of providing access to common resources to more than one user. For example, if a group of users is working on the same project, the directories and files for that project can be owned by a common group that has read and write access. Modern UNIX systems use a two-layered approach to groups, including a single Primary group and some number of Secondary groups, also called supplementary groups. When a user creates a new file, the ownership will probably default to the user and her primary group. The default group membership of newly created users varies quite a bit between OS vendors and versions. Most modern UNIX versions create a new group whenever a new user is created that shares a name with the user. This becomes the primary group of the user. Because modern systems support a large number of Secondary groups transparently, this provides a very flexible means of configuring permissions. Many UNIX variants that have been around longer than Linux, like Solaris and the BSD-derived systems, may set the Primary group of new users to a users group or something similar.

NOTE   *Linux, and most other recent UNIX systems, support at least 32 groups per user. However, because the NFS protocol only supports 16 groups, most of them have imposed a soft limit of 16 groups. There are very rarely circumstances that require more than 16 groups, but it is usually possible to use more if the system will not be exporting or using NFS mounted filesystems.*

Creating or editing a group (Figure 5-13) is performed by clicking the **Create a new group link** or clicking the name of an existing group in group list.

Group Details

When creating a new group of editing and existing groups, the following options are available:

Group name

Like the username, this is a unique alphanumeric identifier. The name must follow the same rules as usernames, so must start with a letter and contain no non-alphanumeric characters. If editing the group, the name will be shown but cannot be edited.

Group ID

This is the numeric identifier that the system uses to identify this group. It is not necessary for this ID to be unique, but there is very rarely a reason to have multiple groups with the same GID. When creating a new group, Webmin can select a new unused ID for you.

Password

A little known and even less used feature of groups under most UNIX variants is that they can have a password just like users. When using this option, a user who normally is not part of a group can log in to a group using the newgrp command and providing the password. Because of the flexibility now available with the supplemental groups system, this feature is rarely used, but is still widely available.

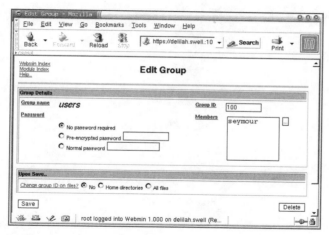

Figure 5-13: Editing a group

Members

This field lists all current members of the group and allows adding any number of new members. The **...** browse button allows you to choose from a selector popup containing all existing users.

Upon Save ...

When saving group information, Webmin can be configured to perform additional actions, based on the following configuration options:

Change group ID on files?

Much like the similarly named option for users, this provides the option to change the group ownership of files in either home directories or all files on the system. Selecting Home directories will cause Webmin to search all user home directories for files owned by this group, and change the group ownership to match the new group ID. Choosing All files will search the entire system, which may take a very long time, depending on the size and speed of the mounted disks. This change does not impact the user ownership of files. A file owned by seymour:users will still be owned by seymour after the change (and still owned by users for that matter, just under a different GID).

6

SERVER AND DAEMON CONFIGURATION

Clicking the Servers tab on the Webmin category bar brings you to what is probably the most interesting of the Webmin pages. It is here that all of the various complex servers and daemons can be configured. Webmin provides standard modules for a large number of the most popular servers and daemons in use on network systems in the world today, and more are being written all the time.

Introduction to Servers

The Servers Webmin category allows for administration of the server applications that run on a system, which provide some service to clients on the network. One example is the Apache web server daemon. Clicking on the Apache icon in this category allows you to edit the Apache configuration files, which are usually located in /etc/httpd/

conf. Most modules located in **Servers** will enable you to edit some configuration file found in /etc or some subdirectory therein. One of the most impressive features of Webmin is the ability to allow you to edit files without damaging existing hand-edited configuration details.

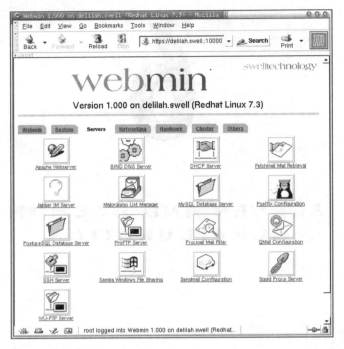

Figure 6-1: Servers category

The root of much of Webmin's popularity is the ability for an administrator to perform some tasks through the Webmin interface without being forced to do *all* tasks with Webmin. Unlike some graphical front ends for UNIX systems, Webmin leaves an edited file intact as much as is possible. Comments are untouched, and the ordering of directives is not changed. This results in a system that can be configured through Webmin and through hand-editing of configuration files, but with no conflict between the two methods.

A side effect of this feature is that Webmin generally must provide a one-to-one interface to configuration files in order to ensure that configuration options are not confused and to ensure that a savvy administrator gets what is expected from the Webmin output. This means that Webmin is not an "easier" way to administer a UNIX system. The administrator still must understand the tools he or she is administering with Webmin. For example, configuring DNS from Webmin requires an understanding of **named** and its required configuration files. The same applies to **squid**, **httpd**, **sendmail**, and so on. Webmin *can* make the learning process somewhat quicker, however, as all of the options are present on the display, which may or may not be the case with configuration files.

7

APACHE WEBSERVER

The **Apache** module is broken up into several sections to address different aspects of an Apache configuration. On the main page, these sections are grouped into **Global Configuration** and **Virtual Servers** groups. Using virtual servers it is possible to locate several websites with unique domain names on a single IP address, in order to conserve the rapidly diminishing IPv4 address space.

In the context of the **Apache** module, **Global Configuration** refers to configuration information that will apply to *all* virtual hosts that are run from the same httpd daemon. It is usually unnecessary to run more than one httpd daemon on a single machine but it is possible. It is also possible to manage more than one such daemon with Webmin via the module cloning feature.

NOTE *The official Apache documentation [http://httpd.apache.org/docs/] is a good source of additional information about Apache and its modules.*

Global Configuration

Global Configuration is found on the top half of the divided **Apache** module page, as shown in Figure 7-1. It provides access to the various options that will be shared across all virtual servers, such as which modules to load, network addresses, MIME types, etc. The options configured here will apply to every virtual server and the default server. To configure an option for one specific virtual server it must be configured in the Virtual Servers Configuration section.

Figure 7-1: Apache Global Configuration

Processes and Limits

This page provides the following options, which set many of the limits for Apache. Generally, the defaults are reasonable, but may need to be altered for high load or low memory situations. The options on this page cover two distinct but related limits that are configurable in Apache.

The first set of limits is related to the length or number of request headers that will be accepted by the server. A request header is a term that refers to all of the information that a client sends to the server to indicate the object it would like to receive. The most important portion of the request header is usually made up of the HTTP method (such as GET, POST, HEAD, and so on), the URI (the complete path and domain name of the object being referred to), and the HTTP protocol version number.

The second set of limits refers to connection and process specific limits of Apache. Apache usually operates in what is known as a process-per-connection mode, wherein each client connection to the server will be served by a single and independent httpd process. Thus to provide service to 30 simultaneous clients, the system will run 30 Apache processes.

Maximum headers in request

Sets the maximum number of request headers accepted per request. Each time a web client (usually a web browser) makes a connection to a web server, it includes request headers to indicate information about the encoding capabilities, HTTP version support, cache-control, content negotiation and other information about the client agent. As HTTP standards and non-standard extensions to the HTTP protocol have been developed, the number of request headers usually received has risen slowly, but is rarely more than 20. The LimitRequestFields [http://www.apache.org/docs/mod/core.html#limitrequestfields] directive in the Apache configuration file is modified by this option and usually defaults to 100.

It may be possible to prevent certain types of denial-of-service attacks by restricting the number of headers accepted, though it is unlikely the be a problem at the default value. It should rarely need to be altered from its default, unless clients receive error messages from the server indicating too many headers were in the request.

Maximum request header size

Defines the maximum header field size that will be permitted. Apache sets aside a buffer for processing of header entries received from the client. This buffer must be large enough to contain a single header entry in its entirety. The LimitRequestFieldsize [http://www.apache.org/docs/mod/core.html#limitrequestfieldsize] directive is modified by this option, and it usually defaults to 8190 and this value is also the normal maximum value possible. It is worth noting that the maximum value for this option is system dependent and is compiled into the Apache executable when it is built. Raising this value above the default of 8190 may not be supported on your Apache and should not be necessary under any normal circumstances.

Maximum request line size

Defines the maximum length of an HTTP request line. The request line contains the HTTP method, the complete URI, and the protocol version. The accepted line size needs to be long enough to contain any resource name on the system, and the default is generally recommended. This option edits the LimitRequestLine [http://www.apache. org/docs/mod/core.html#limitrequestline] directive in the Apache configuration and defaults to 8190 bytes, which is also usually the compiled-in upper bound for this value.

This option rarely needs to be altered from its default, but may be useful in preventing certain types of denial-of-service attacks by preventing client applications from overloading the server with many extremely large and complex request lines.

Maximum concurrent requests

The maximum number of allowed concurrent requests. Each request to Apache spawns a new daemon, and this defines the upper limit on how many such daemons will be spawned to answer requests. This option correlates to the

MaxClients [http://www.apache.org/docs/mod/core.html#maxclients] directive. To configure more than 256 you will probably have to edit HARD_SERVER_LIMIT entry in httpd.h and recompile your Apache, unless the package that is installed has already been configured for high loads or you did so when building Apache from the source tarball.

Except in extremely high load environments it is rarely beneficial to raise this to very high levels. Because every new process requires resources, in the form of memory and CPU time, it can be counterproductive and cause service to become less responsive rather than more. If all processes are busy, the request will usually be queued up to the limit imposed by the **listen queue length** discussed in the next section of this chapter.

Maximum requests per server process

The maximum number of requests that each child process will answer before being killed and respawned. This is useful for a couple of reasons. First, if there are any accidental memory leaks (anywhere in the process, including its modules), the damage can be minimized by restarting processes regularly. Also, without using this option the system will always keep alive the largest number of processes it has ever needed, even during low load periods when far fewer processes are needed to answer requests. This option correlates to the MaxRequestsPerChild [http://www.apache.org/docs/mod/core.html#maxrequestsperchild] directive.

NOTE   *On* Keepalive *requests, only one request is counted per* connection *from a client. Thus, a number of requests from the same client may be served before the counter is incremented if the client supports Keepalive requests. In this case, this directive acts to limit the number of connections per process rather than number of individual requests.*

Maximum spare server processes

This defines the maximum number of unused server processes that will be left running. This option configures the MaxSpareServers [http://www.apache.org/docs/mod/core.html#maxspareservers] directive and defaults to 10. There is usually no need to tune this option, except on extremely high load servers.

CAUTION   *Though Apache is historically a quite solidly written program, and has rarely exhibited major memory leaks, many of the shared modules in use by Apache may not be quite as commonly used or as well tested. These modules may lead to memory leakage even if the Apache* httpd *process does not exhibit such leakage.*

Minimum spare server processes

The minimum number of child processes that will be left running at all times. For high load servers, this may need to be raised, and for low memory and low load systems it might be best to reduce the number. This option correlates to the MinSpareServers [http://www.apache.org/docs/mod/core.html#minspareservers] directive and defaults to 5.

CAUTION *It is a very common mistake to raise the above two options to extreme levels when perfor-mance of an Apache installation seems sluggish. It is very rarely actually the source of the problem, but it seems a popular first reaction among new Apache administrators. Tuning Apache for performance is well documented in a number of locations, and much documen-tation about tuning for specific OS platforms is also available on the Internet. A good place to start is the Apache Performance Notes page [http://httpd.apache.org/docs/misc/ perf-tuning.html]. The documentation found there will address nearly all performance issues that most users will ever run into.*

Initial server processes

The number of child processes that are spawned when the httpd is started. Cor-relates to the StartServers [http://www.apache.org/docs/mod/core.html#start-servers] directive and defaults to 5. This usually does not need to be modified, except on high load servers.

Display extended status information

If the status module is enabled on the server, turning this on will keep track of extended status information for each request and present them in a web page or machine readable format. This option edits the s ExtendedStatus [http://httpd. apache.org/docs/mod/mod_status.html] directive. This option requires the mod_status module to be loaded.

NOTE *To access the extended status information from a running Apache server, you can browse to the address [http://www.yourdomain.com/server-status]. Note that access control should generally be configured to tightly restrict access to this URL, as it may contain sensitive data about your web server environment.*

The information provided by mod_status, with extended status enabled, includes statistics about the number of child processes and the number of con-nected clients, the average number of requests per second being served, the aver-age number of bytes per request, and the current CPU percentage being used by each Apache process. A machine readable form of this data may be collected from [http://www.yourdomain.com/server-status?auto]. The latter is ideal for use in scripts to gather statistics from your server automatically.

CAUTION *Because of the persistent nature of this type of data, this module is only functional when Apache is run in standalone mode, and not when run in inetd mode. Because of the large number of problems involved in running Apache under inetd, and problems inherent to inetd, it is simply best to avoid inetd altogether, anyway.*

Networking and Addresses

This section is for configuring the network addresses and ports where Apache will listen, and some other access limits, timeouts, and queue options (Figure 7-2).

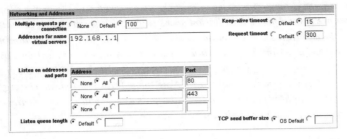

Figure 7-2: Networking and Addresses

Listen on addresses and ports

This option defines the addresses and ports where Apache will listen for requests. The default is to listen on port 80 on all addresses, and this is often all that is needed. Port 80 is the standard port for web traffic and should generally be used for all normal web traffic. It is also possible to configure multiple Apaches to run on the same machine with different global configurations on different ports or addresses. Also, because ports below 1024 are *privileged ports*, regular users running Apache without administrator access will have to run it on a non-standard port. 8080 is a common port for web servers run by unprivileged system users who cannot bind to port 80. A good overview of these options can be found at *Setting which addresses and ports Apache uses* [http://www.apache.org/docs/bind.html]. These options correlate to the Listen [http://www.apache.org/docs/mod/core.html#listen] and Port [http://www.apache.org/docs/mod/core.html#port] directives.

Multiple requests per connection

When KeepAlive [http://www.apache.org/docs/mod/core.html#keepalive] is enabled the server will support persistent connections, which can result in improved performance and a generally better experience for the end user. This option sets the maximum number of requests to be handled per client connection. If set to 0, the server will impose no limit on the number of requests during a single connection. This option correlates to the MaxKeepAliveRequests [http://www.apache.org/docs/mod/core.html#maxkeepaliverequests] directive. The default is usually 100.

CAUTION *If you develop websites, resist the temptation to rely on persistent connections to maintain state. An unfortunate effect of persistent connections becoming available on most browser clients, as well as most web servers, is that some web application and commerce site developers have attempted to use a long-lasting persistent connection to maintain the shopping cart or other state information of the user. This seemingly easy method of keeping up with users is fraught with problems in the real world, and the time spent doing it right using back-end storage and cookies or similar session ID information will be well rewarded in the decrease of support problems you run into. Problems caused by the abuse of persistence include older web proxies that do not support persistence breaking the connection and causing your application to not work for anyone behind such a proxy. Even some network address translation* *devices and load balancing systems can cause mysterious failures of the site. It is also an inefficient use of resources, potentially leading to many more server processes running than are necessary to service requests.*

Keep-alive timeout

The number of seconds Apache will wait for a subsequent request before closing a connection. This option edits the KeepAliveTimeout [http://www.apache.org/docs/mod/core.html#keepalivetimeout] directive. The default is 15 seconds. A too large value for this directive may lead to performance problems, as many clients may hold open idle connections to Apache processes that cannot exit or process requests for other users, thus they take up resources but remain idle.

Listen queue length

The maximum length of the queue of pending connections. Generally no tuning is needed or desired, however on some systems it is desirable to increase this when under a TCP SYN flood attack. As discussed in the **Processes and Limits** section, the listen queue is where requests that cannot be served immediately end up. If this number is exceeded, subsequent requests will be dropped. Correlates to the ListenBacklog [http://www.apache.org/docs/mod/core.html#listenbacklog] directive.

Addresses for name virtual servers

This option is used to configure the IP address on which Apache will listen for requests to virtual servers. Virtual servers are name-based servers, wherein several different domain names can answer on the same IP address. For example, I run two test servers on my local network. One is named *liberty* while the other is named *constitution*. Both run on the same server, but they answer on different named addresses and provide different root directories. So a visit to each will bring up different web pages. This, of course, works for real domain names as well (www.nostarch.com or www.swelltech.com, for example). Note that your DNS server, or the DNS server that is authoritative for the domain you wish to run virtual servers on, will also have to have entries for each virtual server you run that resolves to the IP of your server. It is also possible to specify a different port for a given name virtual server to listen on, by appending the port following a colon (i.e., 192.168.1.1:8080) would cause Apache to listen on port 8080 on the given IP. This option affects the NameVirtualHost [http://www.apache.org/docs/mod/core.html#namevirtualhost] directive. A tutorial on setting up Apache virtual hosts is provided later in this chapter. Another good source of information on virtual servers in Apache is the *Apache Virtual Host documentation* [http://www.apache.org/docs/vhosts/index.html].

TCP send buffer size

Sets the size of the send buffer for TCP packets. It is usually safe to leave this at the default, which is determined by the default of your operating system. This option edits the SendBufferSize [http://www.apache.org/docs/mod/core.html#sendbuffersize] directive.

Request timeout

Defines the maximum number of seconds that Apache will wait for a request after a connection has been established. Correlates to the TimeOut [http://www.apache.org/docs/mod/core.html#timeout] directive.

Apache Modules

Apache is designed in a modular fashion, so that the base server can be a small, easily debugged application, while nearly unlimited additional functionality can be added easily by loading additional modules. The base process can then be smaller, and only those additional features that are needed can be loaded. This Webmin module allows you to select the available Apache modules that you can load (Figure 7-3).

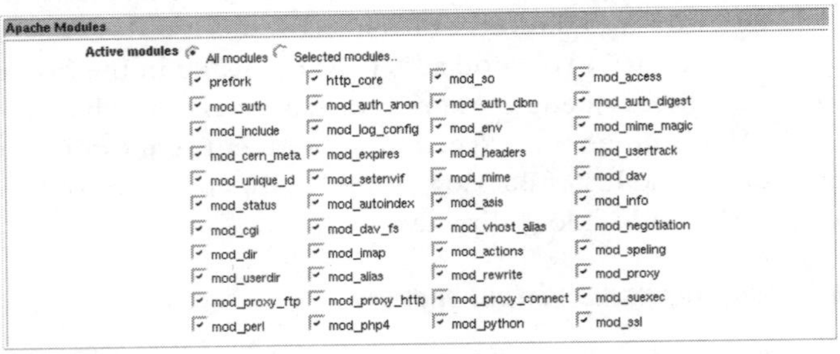

Figure 7-3: Apache Modules

The first module listed in the figure above is mod_so [http://www.apache.org/docs/mod/mod_so.html], which is the module that provides shared object loading at runtime. This module is required if you are using run-time module loading and is the only module other than core.c that cannot be a dynamically loaded module. It must be compiled into the Apache binary at build time if you will be using dynamically loaded modules. Dynamic Shared Objects are not supported by all operating systems, currently, but they are supported by the majority of modern systems including UNIX variants that support loadable .so libraries and Windows systems in the form of DLLs. There are several other modules in common use listed in the above figure, some of which will be discussed below. A good place to go to find out more about available standard modules and third-party modules is *Apache modules* [http://www.apache.org/docs/mod/index-bytype.html] and *Apache Module Registry* [http://modules.apache.org/].

Configured modules are loaded into the Apache process on startup, thus it is possible to add new modules without recompiling the server. The modular nature of Apache is one of its primary benefits over other web servers. Without modules, Apache would be just another web server. But because modules are relatively easy to program, the variety available has proliferated, providing functionality for Apache that is unavailable in any other web server product, commercial or Open Source.

About Apache Modules

Because of the importance modules play in the configuration and management of an Apache web server, it is worthwhile to step out of Webmin for a short time to discuss some of the lower-level details of Apache and its modules. While the usage of these modules via Webmin is discussed throughout this chapter, an overview of the modules will help put the modular structure of Apache into perspective, and hopefully make clearer the interaction between Webmin and the underlying configuration files.

NOTE *The official* Apache *modules [http://httpd.apache.org/docs/mod/] documentation page is an informative, and more comprehensive list of modules that are part of the Apache distribution. Only the most commonly used modules and their purposes will be discussed here. A similar page covers the* Apache 2.0 *modules [http://httpd.apache.org/docs-2.0/mod/].*

Apache Core

The Apache *Core module* [http://httpd.apache.org/docs/mod/core.html] provides the basic functionality that is required to provide web service as described by RFC 2616. The features in core are always available in any Apache installation, regardless of what other modules are available. Most of the basic network, system, and HTTP limits and functions are handled by the core module, and many of the configuration directives are available with no additional modules required.

Multi-Processing Modules

Beginning with Apache version 2.0, a new model (or more accurately, a number of new models) for handling connection concurrency has been added to the system. Concurrency in Apache versions prior to 2.0 used a model known as *connection-per-process*, with some enhancements to that model like *pre-forking*. New versions provide what are known as *Multi-Processing modules*, which allows Apache to use the concurrency model that makes the most sense for a give operating system. Most UNIX and UNIX-like systems use a module called *worker*, which implements a hybrid model utilizing a pool of multi-threaded processes.

When the worker module is enabled, Apache runs a single control process that is responsible for launching child processes. The child processes spawn a configurable fixed number of threads each, and these individual threads listen for connections and serve them. Threads are lighter weight, or less resource intensive, than real processes, and thus a machine of a given capacity can provide higher throughput from a worker-style Apache than from a traditional pre-forking Apache. This was a primary motivation in the development of the new Apache 2.0 service modules.

If your UNIX variant doesn't support threads, or supports them in an incompatible way, Apache will likely use the prefork model instead. Windows machines will likely use the mpm_winnt Multi-Processing module, which creates a single control process that spawns a child process, which in turn creates threads to handle requests. Because Webmin only runs on UNIX-like operating systems at this time, you will likely have no use for the Windows module.

mod_access

This module provides access control based on client host name, IP address and other information taken from the client request. This module also provides some of the functionality involved in supporting directory .htaccess files to control access to certain parts of the server.

mod_auth

User authentication of several types is supported by Apache. The oldest and most commonly used is supported by this module. It is known alternately as *HTTP Basic Authentication* or *NCSA authentication*. This method authenticates users from a plain-text file located somewhere on the system. The password file can be generated using the htpasswd program that is included with Apache.

NOTE *To generate a password file using* htpasswd, *simply run the program with the* -c *option, a new file name, and the first username to add to the file:*

```
[joe@delilah mydocs]$ htpasswd -c .htpasswd joe
```

This file can then be used by the mod_auth module to authenticate users based on this file. This must be explicitly configured in the Apache configuration file or in the local .htaccess file. Creating an .htaccess file is discussed in the tutorial section of this chapter.

mod_cgi

The *CGI module* must be used in order to run scripts or programs on the server to generate content dynamically for users. It is possible to configure at runtime the file types that will be handled by the CGI module. Configuration of the CGI module can be handled separately for virtual hosts, or it may be applied globally to all virtual hosts on the server, or a combination of global defaults with specific differences in some virtual hosts.

mod_expires

The HTTP specification defines a set of rules for clients and intermediary devices (specifically, web-caching proxies, like Squid) to follow when deciding whether to serve a cached document, re-validate the object, or fetch a new copy. A primary method for the website maintainer to dictate the result of these decisions for any given object is the Expires header. This module provides a flexible and simple method for configuring server-wide, as well as per-directory or by file type.

mod_rewrite

This module provides an extremely flexible (some would say too flexible) means of redirecting user requests to different URLs based on information contained in the request. The basis of this module is a regular expressions–based parser and rewriting engine. The URL alterations can depend on a large variety of additional data, including environment variables, client headers, time, external database lookups, and more.

NOTE *To fully understand URL rewriting, it may be worth your time to study the* URL Rewriting Guide *[http://httpd.apache.org/docs-2.0/misc/rewriteguide.html] written by Ralf Engelschall, the original author of the* mod_rewrite *module.*

mod_ssl

Normally, the HTTP protocol is not encrypted, and thus, not secure from prying eyes at any stage along the request path. Ordinarily, this is okay, and *man-in-the-middle* security problems of this sort are extremely rare (because the vast majority ISP and backbone administrators are honest folks who have no inclination to snoop on your web-browsing habits). However, for extremely private matters, such as online banking, investing, or making online purchases, it is important to have a more secure means of communication. The solution is *Secure Sockets Layer,* also known as simply SSL. The Open Source implementation is called OpenSSL, and it is the core of the mod_ssl Apache module.

To use SSL connections, you must generate or purchase an SSL certificate from one of several *Certificate Authorities.* A locally generated certificate can be used for authentication within a company, or for a small number of users whom you already have a trust relationship with. However, if your secure site will be used by a number of users who have no direct relationship with you, a certificate from a trusted certificate authority will be required so the user will know that the site is operated by who it claims to be.

NOTE *Certificate Authorities, or CAs as they are often called, supported by most modern browsers include VeriSign [http://www.verisign.com/], GeoTrust [http://www.geotrust.com/], and Thawte Consulting [http://www.thawte.com/] in the U.S. Options outside of the U.S. include Internet Publishing Services [http://www.ips.es/] and BelSign [http://www.belsign.be/].*

mod_suexec

In many web-hosting environments, a single server is shared by a number of users, and it would be inappropriate to allow the files of all users to be viewed by any other user. Because CGI scripts are run, by default, with the permissions of the web server itself, and the web server must have access to all content and scripts, it would be possible for a malicious user to use a CGI script to browse the contents of any other users private directories using Apache as an intermediary. In order to combat this problem in virtual hosting environments, the server may be configured to run CGI scripts as a specified user rather than as the more privileged Apache user (usually nobody). This module makes this feature possible by performing a suexec function on the created process when CGI scripts are run. There is some complexity in this solution, and there are many security pitfalls to beware of, but it is a required step to providing a secured virtual hosting environment with CGI script capabilities.

MIME Types

MIME Types is the method by which the server and its clients know what type of data a given object is. This information is generally more important to the client, as they must know how to interpret the data where the server only needs to send it to the client along with MIME identification information. MIME, or *Multipurpose Internet Mail Extensions,* was originally defined to easily allow sending of data other than text via email. It has now become the standard method for many types of network connection to declare data type. The **MIME Types** module merely provides a list of the currently accepted MIME types and their optional extensions. At the bottom of the page, the **Add a MIME type** link allows you to add new MIME types easily (Figure 7-4).

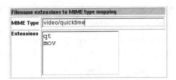

Figure 7-4: Apache MIME types

A great resource for more information on MIME types can be found at the *MIME Page* [http://www.oac.uci.edu/indiv/ehood/MIME/MIME.html] maintained by Earl Hood. Links to relevant RFCs as well as a *MIME FAQ* [http://www.faqs.org/faqs/mail/mime-faq/mime0/] can be found there.

Miscellaneous

The **Miscellaneous** options page is just what it sounds like (Figure 7-5). It's the global options that didn't seem to fit anywhere else. As such, there aren't very many fields on this page, but nonetheless there are a few items of interest.

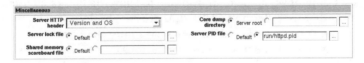

Figure 7-5: Apache Miscellaneous page

Core dump directory

This is the directory where Apache will send its core dump file, in the event of a crash. By default this will be the same directory as the Apache server's root directory. However, the server process will not normally have write access to this directory, so in order to get a core dump on crashes, it is necessary to change it to a directory that is writable by the Apache process. Core dumps are often used for debugging purposes. This option affects the CoreDumpDirectory [http://www.apache.org/docs/mod/core.html#coredumpdirectory] directive.

Server lock file

This sets the location for Apache's *lock file* to the file named. A lock file is the file that is used to notify a new instance of a process that one is already running. This prevents Apache from trying to start again, *using the same configuration,* if it is already running. Note that if you use a different configuration and a different lock file, it is possible to start multiple instances of Apache. This option corresponds to the LockFile [http://www.apache.org/docs/mod/core.html#lockfile] directive.

Server PID file

The PID file for Apache. Edits the PidFile [http://www.apache.org/docs/mod/core.html#pidfile] directive.

Shared memory scoreboard file

Some architectures require a file for the children and parent processes can communicate. For performance this can be placed on a RAM disk. This corresponds to the ScoreBoardFile [http://www.apache.org/docs/mod/core.html#scoreboardfile] directive.

Server HTTP header

This option allows you to set the data that will be contained within the HTTP header. This corresponds to the ServerTokens [http://www.apache.org/docs/mod/core.html#servertokens] directive.

Server execution

Defines how the server will be started. **Standalone** indicates that it will run as a standalone daemon, while **Run from inetd** will cause it to run periodically, as called by the **inetd** daemon. It is strongly recommended to avoid the **inetd** option, as it does not always work as expected. This option edits the ServerType [http://www.apache.org/docs/mod/core.html#servertype] directive.

CGI Programs

CGI, or *Common Gateway Interface,* provides a means for a website to have dynamic, program-generated content on a web page. CGI programs can interact with the user through the use of input fields and can provide different data based on the information returned. CGI programs can be written in nearly any language, though it is most common for them to be written in Perl, PHP, Python, Java, C, and bash or other shell scripting languages. The **CGI Programs** module provides an interface to the global CGI options of Apache (Figure 7-6).

Figure 7-6: Apache CGI Programs

CGI Script log

Is the log directory for the CGI script error log file. If none is given, no log is created. Edits the ScriptLog directive found at [http://www.apache.org/docs/mod/mod_cgi.html#scriptlog].

Maximum logged post data size

Data from a PUT or POST request to a CGI script that is written to the error log file can be limited in size, because PUT and POST requests can be extremely large. The default is 1024 bytes. This option correlates to the ScriptLogBuffer [http://www.apache.org/docs/mod/mod_cgi.html#scriptlogbuffer] directive.

Maximum CGI log post size

Limits the size of the CGI script log file. When the log file exceeds this size, no more errors will be written to the log file. Corresponds to the ScriptLogLength [http://www.apache.org/docs/mod/mod_cgi.html#scriptloglength] directive.

Variables set based on browser type

If the server should set some environment variables differently depending on the client browser type, it is possible to enter that data here. This option edits the BrowserMatch [http://www.apache.org/docs/mod/mod_setenvif.html#BrowserMatch] directive. Note that the mod_setenvif and mod_browser modules should be loaded when using these features.

Variable set based on request headers

Allows you to set environment variables based on attributes of the request. This corresponds to the SetEnvIf [http://www.apache.org/docs/mod/mod_setenvif.html#SetEnvIf] directive.

Per-Directory Options Files

Apache offers the ability to modify many global settings on a per-directory basis (Figure 7-7). This module provides access to that feature. To create an options file for a directory, simply enter the path and file name in the field and click **Create Options File**. By convention these files are called .htaccess, but that is a configurable option in Apache. This file also allows configuration of per-directory authentication among other access control features.

More information on options files can be found in the Apache docs under the Options [http://www.apache.org/docs/mod/core.html#options] directive.

Virtual Servers

The lower half of the **Apache** page contains a list of configured virtual servers (Figure 7-8). Each virtual server entry on this page shows the address and port the virtual server listens on, the server name, and the document root. Clicking the icon for the virtual server will bring you to a page filled with many new options and many of the same options found in the **Global** section discussed earlier. The options that are repeated from that section generally behave the same, and so are not covered again.

Figure 7-7: Per-Directory Options File

It's important to remember that each virtual server has its own configuration. While it is possible to set *default* behaviors by editing the **Default** server (the first in the list of Virtual Servers), each virtual server may have configuration directives that override the default behavior. Each may have its own directory structure, server settings, MIME types, logging configuration, and more. Apache provides near-infinite options, and most of those can be applied to any individual virtual server, as well as to the server as a whole.

Log Files

Logs provide a window into the operation of your web server, and Apache provides a great set of logging options so you can keep up with what your server is up to. In short, Apache allows you to configure each virtual host as though it were an independent server. This includes the ability to independently log information to a separate file and in a custom format.

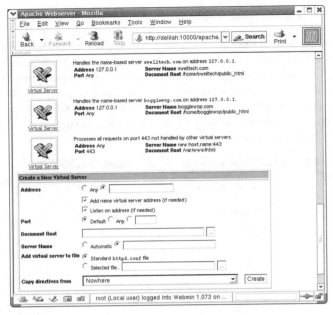

Figure 7-8: Virtual servers

CAUTION *Beware that there are particular security issues associated with logging in Apache. Because any logging helper programs will be started as the user that started Apache (usually root), the program* must *be secure. A good resource for further security information is the* Security Tips *[http://httpd.apache.org/docs/misc/security_tips.html] section of the official* Apache documentation.

Error log to

This sets where Apache sends error information for this virtual server. Usually this goes to the syslog daemon, which writes it to the primary web server error log. However, Apache can send this to an alternate logging program or to a file. This option configures the ErrorLog [http://httpd.apache.org/docs/mod/ core.html#errorlog] directive and usually defaults to logging to the syslog daemon, if available.

Browser log file

Here you can define whether Apache will keep logs of the user agents (browsers, most often, though robots and autodownloaders will show up also) that access the web server. This information is usually only of passing interest, except perhaps when you're thinking of implementing some technology that is incompatible with some browsers (like Flash, Shockwave, and a host of lesser-known and even less widely accessible data formats). Reviewing these logs will often remind you of what percentage of your clients such technologies may alienate. Agent information is not logged by default. This option configures the AgentLog [http://httpd.apache.org/docs/mod/mod_log_agent.html#agentlog] directive.

Default log format

This option allows you to configure Apache to write logs in an arbitrarily chosen format. If you want Apache to log in the *Common Log Format* you simply leave this on the default. However, to log in a different manner, you would select the Format choice and fill in the field either with a nickname of a named log format (discussed next) or with a log format string. This option configures the CustomLog [http://httpd.apache.org/docs/mod/mod_log_config.html#customlog] directive.

Named log formats

A named log format is a custom log format, as discussed above, that has been defined and given a nickname for use by other log directives. A custom log format is created by entering a series of variables to indicate the data fields that should be present and the order in which they will appear. For example, a custom log type that mimics the *Common Log Format* looks like this:

```
%h %l %u %t \"%r\" %>s %b
```

This option configures the LogFormat [http://httpd.apache.org/docs/mod/mod_log_config.html#logformat] directive.

Access log files

Here, you can define additional locations, formats, or programs for Apache to send logs to. Configuration is much like the **Default** log above, except that you may have any number of access log files. This allows you, for example, to log accesses of images to a separate file or to log visits to another format for processing and analyses. This option correlates to the TransferLog [http://httpd.apache.org/docs/mod/mod_log_config.html#transferlog] directive. Beware that the same security implications that affect all of the other logging directives affect this option as well.

Don't log references from

This option adds the host names provided to a list of hosts from whence referral information will not be logged. For example, if I wanted my web server at penguinfeet.org to ignore referrals from my other web page, swelltech.com, I would enter swelltech.com here. Then, my statistics wouldn't be skewed by the large number of referrals from my own pages. This option correlates to the RefererIgnore [http://httpd.apache.org/docs/mod/mod_log_referer.html#refererignore] directive.

Referer log file

Here you define where referer information is logged to. This can be a file or a program. This option configures the RefererLog [http://httpd.apache.org/docs/mod/mod_log_referer.html#refererlog] directive.

Document Options

Here you have access to many of the virtual server specific options that will affect permissions, locations, and behaviors.

The first field of this page has no label. It is the document root. This is usually set when the virtual server is created, and it is created automatically by Webmin. This option correlates to the DocumentRoot [http://httpd.apache.org/docs/mod/core.html#documentroot] directive.

User WWW directory

Here, you configure the location where users can publish HTML documents via Apache. The syntax has several forms that perform different types of expansion to create the actual path. First, a relative link of the form htmldocs translates for user joe to ~joe/htmldocs. An absolute link, such as /usr/htmldocs, will translate to /usr/htmldocs/joe. Finally, it is possible to use an * to represent the username in the translation. For example, /home/*/htmldocs, will translate to /home/joe/htmldocs. This option configures the UserDir [http://httpd.apache.org/docs/mod/mod_userdir.html#userdir] directive.

The following fields are continued options connected to the above **User WWW directory** option. They control which users' directories will have the translation performed. Selecting **All users accessible** means that for any username entered in the URL, the translation will occur and the users' web directories will be browsable. **All users except** allows you to disallow some users, while the rest are translated. This could be used, for example, to disable the website of a user who violated the terms of service. Finally, **Only users** means that only those users explicitly named will have directory translation performed.

Per-directory options file

Here you can specify a file name to be checked for directory access options. Unless prohibited elsewhere in Apache's configuration, options found in a file by this name in any directory will override the default permissions for that directory. For example, if I chose the file name .acl, and in one of my directories I created such a file that included instructions to Generate directory indexes, then for that directory such indexes would be generated. This would apply even if the default is to not generate indexes. If you are operating a virtual hosting server, this can allow your users to have some freedom in the behavior of the web server for their individual site, without interfering with or altering the behavior of other sites on the same server. This can be thought of as one more layer of the onion of configurability that is Apache. This option configures the AccessFileName directive and defaults to .htaccess.

Directory options

Here, you can choose to use the default options for this directory. This effects the root directory for your virtual server and all subdirectories, except those the contain and AccessFileName file as discussed in the **Per-directory options file** section above. This option correlates to the Options [http://httpd.apache.org/docs/mod/core.html#options] directive and defaults to all, except for Generate Multiviews.

The available directory options are as follows:

Execute CGI programs Allows execution of CGI scripts located in this directory.

Follow symbolic links The server will follow symbolic links in this directory. This correlates to the ExecCGI directive.

Server-side includes and execs Server-side includes are permitted. This correlates to the FollowSymLinks directive.

Server-side includes Permits server side includes, but disallows #exec command and the use of #include for CGI scripts. This correlates to the IncludesNOEXEC directive.

Generate directory indexes When a URL maps to a directory in which there is no index HTML file (usually index.html, but this is a configurable option), then Apache can generate a formatted file list for the directory. This option correlates to the Indexes directive.

Generate Multiviews Content-negotiated multiviews are permitted. This allows for multiple languages, character sets, and presentations to be referenced by the same URL. The client browser then negotiates with the server to select the appropriate one for the user. For more, see Content Negotiation [http://httpd.apache.org/docs/content-negotiation.html]. This option correlates to the MultiViews directive.

Follow symbolic links if owners match Apache will only follow symbolic links for which the target file or directory ownership matches that of the link. This option correlates to the SymLinksIfOwnerMatch directive.

Note that if multiple items apply (inherited from a parent directory), then the ones specific to the selected directory apply, unless **Merge with parent** is selected. For example, if /home/httpd/penguinfeet has All permissions, but the subdirectory /home/httpd/penguinfeet/users has only ExecCGI, then that directory would only have the execute CGI option available. Merging with the parent, however, gives the subdirectory the same options, except where explicitly turned off.

Generate MD5 digests

This option turns on generation of Content-MD5 digest headers. When enabled, Apache will generate a message digest, or fingerprint, for each static page served. When using MD5 digests, the client can be assured with a very high degree of confidence that if the content has been altered during transit from the origin server those alterations will be reflected in alterations in the message digest. The Content-MD5 standard is described in RFC 1864 [http://www.ietf.org/rfc/rfc1864.txt?number=1864] and RFC 2616 [http://www.ietf.org/rfc/rfc2616.txt?number=2616]. This option configures the ContentDigest [http://httpd.apache.org/docs/mod/core.html#contentdigest] directive. Be aware that this option can have performance implications, because the digest is generated for each request, and digests will not be created for any requests that are served by modules.

Generate ETag header from

ETag is an HTTP response header to provide a means of differentiating two or more objects with the same URL. The header is useful for intermediary devices that perform caching, as well as client browsers that cache results. Using the ETag, an object can be uniquely identified to the client. Usually, Apache generates the ETag based on the i-node number of the file, the last modified time of the file, and the size of the file. If **Select attributes** is chosen, you may select any or all of these criteria. This option correlates to the FileETag [http://httpd. apache.org/docs/mod/core.html#fileetag] directive.

Virtual server path

Very old browsers and proxies cannot address name-based virtual servers and know only how to request a site by its IP. This leads to the unfortunate effect that those browsers will only be able to reach the default website on a given IP. A workaround for this problem is to provide a path from the default server to each virtual server. Using this directive, you can define where in the path of the default server this particular virtual server will reside. So, if my virtual server www.penguinfeet.org resides on a server at IP 123.45.67.89, and an older browser visits that name, it will end up browsing to the default server on the host — which can provide the user with a list of links to virtual servers hosted on this server. If this were set to /penguinfeet, the link would then take the user to http://www. penguinfeet.org/penguinfeet/, which is the correct page! Not exactly pretty, but the web wasn't always as well thought out as it is today. And who can blame the original designers of the web for not realizing the one day everyone would have their own domain name! The good news is that those old web clients are simply no longer in use in any statistically significant quantity (they don't show up on any of my web server logs, anyway; your mileage may vary). This option configures the ServerPath [http://httpd.apache.org/docs/mod/core. html#serverpath] directive. For more on virtual hosts and the potential issues, see also the *Apache Virtual Host* documentation [http://httpd.apache.org/docs/ vhosts/].

Error message footer

This option allows you to add a footer to all server-generated documents (such as error pages, mod_proxy ftp directory listings, mod_info output, and so on). This is usually only needed when your Apache is acting as a proxy, as it is most useful in discovering where an error message originates from in a chain of multiple proxies. This option configures the / ServerSignature [http://httpd.apache.org/ docs/mod/core.html#serversignature] directive and defaults to Off.

Automatically correct misspelled URLs?

This option configures whether Apache will attempt to correct user spelling errors in the URL. If enabled, and a URL does not match a document on the server, a check will be performed of all of the objects available that could possibly match the user's request. If one object is found that closely matches what the user requested — for example, if there was incorrect capitalizations but the object is spelled correctly or only one letter is missing — Apache will silently redirect the user to the corrected URL. If multiple possible matches are found, the user will be redirected to a page containing a list of possible pages so they may select the correct page. If no possible matches are found, the request traverses the normal error path and will result in a 404 not found error. This option correlates to the CheckSpelling [http://httpd.apache.org/docs/mod/mod_speling.html#checkspelling] directive and defaults to Off.

Error Handling

In the event of a server error, Apache can be configured to provide custom error messages, or redirect to a local or external URL, or by default output a simple har-coded error message. Here, you may configure any error types for which you'd like to provide a custom message. So, for example, if you wanted a custom 404 message that directed users to a local site search page (a convenient and polite thing to do), you could do that on this page. To configure the custom error responses feature of Apache, simply enter to error code, and then enter the URL or message to be displayed. See the Custom error responses documentation [http://httpd.apache.org/docs/custom-error.html] for more on this feature.

User and Group

This page configures the user and group under which the Apache server will run. This sets the privileges the Apache and child processes will have while operating. It is strongly suggested that you set this to a user and group with as little privilege as possible (while still allowing the server to do its job). This is often configured to nobody and nogroup on many UNIX operating systems, and this is a good choice in most cases. Do *not* set this to root unless you know exactly what you're doing and the security implications of doing so. Note that the Apache parent process, if started as root, will remain as root, while the child processes that actually service requests will run as the user and group set here. If the parent process is started by a non-root user, Apache will not be able to su to another user, and so will run as the user that started the process. This option configures the User [http://httpd.apache.org/docs/mod/core.html#user] and Group [http://httpd.apache.org/docs/mod/core.html#group] directives.

Aliases and Redirects

Apache provides several forms of alias and redirection. This allows you to present more unified or simpler paths to your users in the URL, as well as serve objects from outside of your server's root directory. It also allows you to redirect users to a new website during a transition period or direct their browser to the correct link if directory structure has changed.

Document directory aliases

This allows objects to be stored in directories other than the root directory. Be aware the aliases that end in a / will require the slash in the requested URL to be translated. This option correlates to the Alias [http://httpd.apache.org/docs/mod/mod_alias.html#alias] directive.

Regexp document directory aliases

This option is very similar to the above, except that it allows the use of regular expressions to match paths to be translated. This option correlates to the AliasMatch [http://httpd.apache.org/docs/mod/mod_alias.html#aliasmatch] directive. For more on regular expressions, consult the regex man page.

URL redirects

This option redirects an old URL into a new one. The new URL is returned to the client, which will attempt to fetch again with the new address. You can also specify a status message for the redirect, which can be one of several HTTP status codes, as described below. This option configures the Redirect [http://httpd.apache.org/docs/mod/mod_alias.html#redirect] directive.

Redirect status codes

301 Moved permanently.

302 Moved temporarily.

303 See other, meaning the resources has been replaced.

410 The object is no longer available. When this status is used, the redirect **To** URL should be omitted.

Regexp URL redirects

This option behaves exactly like the above, except the **From** field can contain a regular expression to match. This option correlates to the RedirectMatch [http://httpd.apache.org/docs/mod/mod_alias.html#redirectmatch] directive.

Permanent URL redirects

This option behaves as the above **URL redirect** with a status of 301 (moved permanently). Correlates to the RedirectPermanent [http://httpd.apache.org/docs/mod/mod_alias.html#redirectperm] directive.

Temporary URL redirects

This option behaves as the above **URL redirect** with a status of 302 (moved temporarily). Correlates to the RedirectTemp [http://httpd.apache.org/docs/mod/mod_alias.html#redirecttemp] directive.

Map local to remote URLs

This option allows a remote server to be mapped onto the space of the local server; the local server does not act as a conventional proxy, but appears to be a mirror of the remote server. For example, if the **local URL** is /mirror/otherdomain and the **remote URL** is http://www.otherdomain.com then users will be able to access http://www.otherdomain.com via http://www.thisdomain.com/mirror/otherdomain. This option corresponds to the ProxyPass [http://httpd.apache.org/docs/mod/mod_proxy.html#proxypass] directive.

Map remote Location: headers to local

This option provides roughly the reverse functionality of the previous option. It adjusts the location header on HTTP redirect responses, which is necessary when Apache is being used as a reverse proxy in order to avoid having the reverse proxy bypassed by a redirect request. This option configures the ProxyPassReverse [http://httpd.apache.org/docs/mod/mod_proxy.html#proxypassreverse] directive.

Directory Indexing

An *index* in Apache is simply a page that is displayed when a client browses to a directory on the server rather than an object or document. For example, if someone browses to my Squid patches directory on my server, which is located at http://www.swelltech.com/pengies/joe/patches/, Apache will serve an index page. If there is no file in the directory that matches Apache's definition of an index page, it will instead generate an index page containing a file list, or it will serve an error page, if index generation is prohibited. This page allows you to configure the behavior of Apache when displaying index pages.

Directory index options

This option sets the appearance and information contained in Apache-generated indexes. This option configures the IndexOptions [http://httpd.apache.org/docs/mod/mod_autoindex.html#indexoptions] directive. The following options are available:

Display fancy directory indexes This turns on fancy indexing of directories, which means that icons will be provided for files and directories. This configures the FancyIndexing sub-directive.

Display HTML title as description If files within the directory contain HTML title information, those titles will be displayed as the file names for their respective files. This option configures the ScanHTMLTitles sub-directive.

Icon height This sets the height of the icons in fancy directory listings. This correlates to the IconHeight sub-directive.

Icon width This sets the width of the icons in fancy directory listings. This correlates to the IconWidth sub-directive.

Allow user sorting of columns By default, Apache will generate listings that can be sorted by the user by clicking the column headings. If you do not wish for users to be able to sort by last-modified date or size, then you may disable this, and no sorting links will be provided. This option configures the SuppressColumnSorting sub-directive.

Show file descriptions Enable this to display descriptions of the files in the fancy index listings. This option correlates to the SuppressDescription sub-directive.

Output HTML header tags If using a header file (also configured on this page) for directory indexes, you may choose to allow Apache to output a standard HTML preamble containing enough to *start* a legal HTML page. If this is disabled, your header will have to contain its own preamble to make it into a legal HTML page. This option configures the SuppressHTMLPreamble sub-directive.

Show last modified times By default, Apache will display the last modified time of each file in a generated index. Unselecting this option will cause Apache not to do so. This option configures the SuppressLastModified subdirectory.

Show file sizes This option is much like the previous option, except that it allows you to disable display of the size information about the files listed in a generated index. This option correlates to the SuppressSize sub-directive.

Include icon in link This will cause Apache to display icons as part of the link. This option configures the IconsAreLinks sub-directive.

Filename width Here you may configure the number of characters Apache will display in the filename of indexes. This option correlates to the NameWidth= sub-directive. If this is set to * Apache will set the length to the length of the longest file name in the directory.

Description width The number of characters that will be displayed in the description field of generated indexes. This option correlates to the DescriptionWidth= sub-directive. As above, if this value is set to * the description length will be set to that of the longest description in the directory.

Display directories first You may choose to have Apache sort the listing such that directories are listed first in the index. This option corresponds to the FoldersFirst sub-directive.

Directory index files

Here you configure the file names that Apache will look for when entering a directory, and if one of them exists it will be displayed as the index of the directory rather than an auto-generated file index. This file will be displayed to clients who request any directory on the server by specifying a / at the end of the URL. This may be any file name or list of file names, though those used by convention include index.html or index.htm on operating systems with file name limitations. It is now not uncommon to use script suffixes on index pages, such as index.pl, index.cgi, or index.php. This option correlates to the DirectoryIndex [http://httpd.apache.org/docs/mod/mod_dir.html#directoryindex] directive.

Files to ignore in directory index

If an auto-generated index is being displayed, you may specify files that are not to be listed in the index. This option configures the IndexIgnore [http://httpd. apache.org/docs/mod/mod_autoindex.html#indexignore] directive.

Directory index default icon

Apache will automatically add icons to index listings when the file types of files are recognized. When no icon is known for a file type, you may configure an icon to be displayed here. This option correlates to the DefaultIcon [http://httpd. apache.org/docs/mod/mod_autoindex.html#defaulticon] directive.

Directory index header file

Indexes may have a custom header file attached to them using this option. The file may be either a plain-text file or an HTML file. This option correlates to the HeaderName directive [http://httpd.apache.org/docs/mod/ mod_autoindex.html#headername].

Directory index footer file

Sets the path to the file to append to the end of an index. This option corresponds to the ReadmeName directive [http://httpd.apache.org/docs/mod/ mod_autoindex.html#readmename].

Sort directory index by

This option allows you to select how Apache will sort the entries on the index page. The order may be Ascending or Descending, and it may sort based on the Name of the file, Date of last modification, Size of the file, or the Description of the file. This option correlates to the IndexOrderDefault [http://httpd.apache.org/docs/ mod/mod_autoindex.html#indexorderdefault] directive and defaults to sorting by file name in ascending order.

Directory index icons

Here you may select the graphic icons that will be displayed beside file name links in the fancy directory listing index pages. The Icon is the relative path to the image file. The Alt text is the text to be displayed if the clients browser does not support images. Match by is the attribute to match against when deciding which icon will be displayed, and it can be one of Filename, MIME type, or Encoding. The Filenames, Types, or Encodings are simply the terms to be matched for this icon type to be displayed. This option configures the AddIcon [http://httpd.apache. org/docs/mod/mod_autoindex.html#addicon], AddIconByEncoding [http:// httpd.apache.org/docs/mod/mod_autoindex.html#addiconbyencoding], and AddIconByType directives [http://httpd.apache.org/docs/mod/mod_autoindex. html#addiconbytype]. When matching against the file name of the MIME type, you can use wildcards to match any of several variations. For example, to match all backup files (as generated by ispell and other software), you could use the file match *~. Or, for a MIME type wildcard example, to match all images types, you could use image/*. It is generally recommended to match based on the MIME type rather than file extensions, when possible, as it tends to be less prone to missing files of certain types or misidentifying a file type.

NOTE   *When adding a file name matched icon, there are a couple of special names that allow you to match directories and blank lines (Apache uses blank lines to format the list). These are* ^^DIRECTORY^^ *and* ^^BLANKICON^^, *respectively.*

Directory index ALT tags

Much like the previous option, this option allows you to configure the text to be displayed for files instead of icons. The possible values and wildcard usage are the same as for the previous option. This configures the AddAlt [http://httpd. apache.org/docs/mod/mod_autoindex.html#addalt], AddAltByEncoding

[http://httpd.apache.org/docs/mod/mod_autoindex.
html#addaltbyencoding], and AddAltByType [http://httpd.apache.org/ docs/
mod/mod_autoindex.html#addaltbytype] directives.

Directory index descriptions

Here you may define what descriptions will be displayed for a given file name
extension. The length of this will be limited by the Description width option discussed above. This option configures the AddDescription [http://httpd.apache.
org/docs/mod/mod_autoindex.html#adddescription] directive.

Imagemaps

Imagemaps provide a method to make images clickable in regions, where each
region results in a different URL. Options on this page dictate default paths for
imagemap URLs, actions to take on clicks within imagemaps, and the handling
of error conditions.

Default base for imagemaps

This option sets the base directory for imagemaps. If this is not set, the default is
http://servername/. This correlates to the ImapBase [http://httpd.apache.org/
docs/mod/mod_imap.html#imapbase] directive.

Default action for imagemaps

Sets the default used in imagemap files. This will be overridden by a default
directive within the imagemap file. The default is nocontent or Do nothing which
sends a 204 No content message to the browser. The browser should continue to
display the original page. This option correlates to the ImapDefault [http://
httpd.apache.org/docs/mod/mod_imap.html#imapdefault] directive.

Action on incorrect use of imagemaps

This option determines what action Apache should take if an imagemap file is
called without valid coordinates. This correlates to the ImapMenu [http://httpd.
apache.org/docs/mod/mod_imap.html#imapmenu] directive. The options are
as follows:

Imap Menu Options

none If ImapMenu is none, no menu is generated, and the default action is
performed.

Show formatted menu A formatted menu is the simplest menu. Comments
in the imagemap file are ignored. A level one header is printed, then an
hrule, then the links each on a separate line. The menu has a consistent,
plain look close to that of a directory listing.

Show semi-formatted menu In the semi-formatted menu, comments are
printed where they occur in the imagemap file. Blank lines are turned into
HTML breaks. No header or hrule is printed, but otherwise the menu is the
same as a formatted menu.

Show unformatted menu Comments are printed, blank lines are ignored. Nothing is printed that does not appear in the image map file. All breaks and headers must be included as comments in the imagemap file. This gives you the most flexibility over the appearance of your menus, but requires you to treat your map files as HTML instead of plain text.

For more on image map files in Apache visit the mod_imap Module documentation [http://httpd.apache.org/docs/mod/mod_imap.html#imapmenu].

Proxying

This page configures the mod_proxy module, which allows Apache to act as a full-featured HTTP proxy. While Squid is a higher performance and more featureful option in most cases, Apache can also provide some interesting functions and features for proxying and reverse proxying in very simple environments. For additional information on proxying with mod_proxy see the mod_proxy module documentation [http://httpd.apache.org/docs/mod/mod_proxy.html]. Generally, however, if you need HTTP proxying or web caching, Squid [http://www.squid-cache.org] is a far better choice and is usually no more complicated to configure.

Act as proxy server?

This option simply turns proxying on or off in Apache. This is not required for passing requests on to another server using the ProxyPass directive, which was documented briefly in the **Directory Options** section, and also is configurable on this page. This option correlates to the ProxyRequests [http://httpd.apache.org/docs/mod/mod_proxy.html#proxyrequests] directive, and defaults to Off .

Cache directory

This option sets the directory where cached files will be stored. This directory must be writable by the server. If this option is not set, proxying will still function, but not caching will occur. This option correlates to the CacheRoot [http://httpd.apache.org/docs/mod/mod_proxy.html#cacheroot] directive and defaults to none.

Block requests to domains

Provides a simple means of access control, wherein any domain or domain containing a word listed will be inaccessible through the proxy. The sites listed will be blocked even if the site is accessed via IP address, as Apache will resolve the names on startup and cache the IP information. This option correlates to the ProxyBlock [http://httpd.apache.org/docs/mod/mod_proxy.html#proxyblock] directive and defaults to none.

Requests to pass to another proxy

This option configures remote proxies that requests will be sent to if the request contains the words or domains in the match field. This option correlates to the ProxyRemote [http://httpd.apache.org/docs/mod/mod_proxy.html#proxyremote] directive and defaults to none.

Don't pass requests to another proxy for

Here you can configure any number of domains, IP addresses, IP subnets, or host names that will not be forwarded to another proxy via the above option. This option correlates to the NoProxy [http://httpd.apache.org/docs/mod/mod_proxy.html#noproxy] directive, and defaults to none.

Domain for requests with no domain

This option is useful for proxy servers on intranets. It allows you to configure a domain name to be redirected to if a request is encountered without one. This option correlates to the ProxyDomain [http://httpd.apache.org/docs/mod/mod_proxy.html#proxydomain] directive and defaults to none.

Domains not to cache

If caching is enabled above, here you can select some number of domains that will not be stored on the local proxy. This is useful for local domains, for which no benefit would be gained by locally caching the content thereof. This option configures the NoCache [http://httpd.apache.org/docs/mod/mod_proxy.html#nocache] directive and defaults to none.

Ports to which CONNECT is allowed

This option dictates which ports Apache will allow the proxy CONNECT method on. This method is used to set up a tunnel for https connections. This option correlates to the AllowCONNECT [http://httpd.apache.org/docs/mod/mod_proxy.html#allowconnect] directive and defaults to ports 443 (https) and 563 (snews). Enabling this option overrides the default, so if you add ports here, you must include at least the https port for secure connections to work correctly through your proxy.

Cache default expiry time

If an object is fetched via a protocol that does not support expiry times (such as ftp), or no expiry time is present, the cached data will be stored the specified number of hours. This option configures the CacheDefaultExpire [http://httpd.apache.org/docs/mod/mod_proxy.html#cachedefaultexpire] and defaults to 1 hour.

Cache directory name length

Sets the number of characters in proxy cache subdirectory names. This option correlates to the CacheDirLength [http://httpd.apache.org/docs/mod/mod_proxy.html#cachedirlength] directive and defaults to 1.

Cache directory levels

Sets the number of levels in the proxy cache subdirectory hierarchy. This option correlates to the CacheDirLevels [http://httpd.apache.org/docs/mod/mod_proxy.html#cachedirlevels] directive and defaults to 3.

Finish and cache transfer after

If a transfer is canceled before completion, but after this percentage of the object has been received, Apache will continue to fetch the object in order to cache the complete object. Entering 0 here will cause the default to be used, and 100 will not store an object unless the whole transfer was completed. A number between 60 and 90 is suggested. This option configures the CacheForceCompletion [http://httpd.apache.org/docs/mod/mod_proxy.html#cacheforcecompletion] and defaults to 90.

Cache garbage collection interval

If this is configured, Apache will perform periodic garbage collection, wherein it deletes files if the space used for cached objects is greater than the configured **Cache size**. This option accepts floating point values, so can be configured to perform garbage collection every 30 minutes, for example, by entering 0.5 here. If this is unset, the cache will grow indefinitely. This option configures the CacheGcInterval [http://httpd.apache.org/docs/mod/mod_proxy.html#cachegcinterval] and defaults to none.

Cached file expiry time factor

If the origin HTTP server does not provide an expiry time for the object, Apache can estimate one by multiplying the time since the last modification by this factor. This option configures the CacheLastModifiedFactor [http://httpd.apache.org/docs/mod/mod_proxy.html#cachelastmodifiedfactor] directive and defaults to 0.1.

Cached file maximum expiry time

After an object has been stored for this many hours, Apache will check for new content with the origin server, even if the expiry time supplied by the origin server has not yet been reached. This option configures the CacheMaxExpire [http://httpd.apache.org/docs/mod/mod_proxy.html#cachemaxexpire] directive and defaults to 24 hours.

Cache size

Assuming garbage collection has been configured, Apache will restrict the size of the cached object storage directories to this number of kilobytes. This option correlates to the CacheSize [http://httpd.apache.org/docs/mod/mod_proxy.html#cachesize] directive and defaults to 5 KB.

Server Configuration

This page allows you to reconfigure the basic configuration details of your virtual server. For example, if when you created your virtual server you placed it on port 8080 for testing, but now want to move it over to port 80 for production, you can perform that update here.

Address and Port

If your system has multiple interfaces, Apache will answer on any of them by default on port 80. However, you can configure your virtual server to only answer on one address using this option. You can also configure a different port here.

Document Root

This is the root directory, from whence the paths to access objects on your server will begin. This option configures the DocumentRoot [http://httpd.apache.org/docs/mod/core.html#documentroot] directive.

Server Name

When using name based virtual servers, this name should match the name under which this server should answer. This is also used when creating redirection URLs. If not specified Apache will try to deduce it from the IP address, which isn't always reliable. This option correlates to the ServerName [http://httpd.apache.org/docs/mod/core.html#servername] directive.

Tutorial: A Basic Apache Configuration

Apache is an extremely large and feature-rich piece of software. Approaching it for the first time can be daunting. Luckily, it is extremely easy to install, configure, and maintain as long as you proceed with care and pay attention to the documentation relevant to your installation and environment. Installation of Apache is not covered here, as it is well documented on the Apache website, and it is also very likely that your OS vendor provides a suitable package to make installation automatic. What will be covered is the initial hurdle of setting up Apache to serve HTML web pages. The next section will take the configuration one step further to configuring a virtual hosting service. Later, a section in the BIND module chapter will cover adding name service for your web server.

Configuring Apache Paths

NOTE *If you've installed Apache from a package from your OS vendor or if your vendor does not provide a package and it has been installed in the default location selected by the program, you can probably skip this section and proceed to the next section covering initial module selection. For any supported OS, Webmin has a configuration file that includes sensible default paths for the programs that it administers. These configurations assume an installation in the default location for your operating system. So, for example, on a Red Hat Linux system, Webmin will expect to find the* httpd.conf *file in the* /etc/httpd/conf *directory, while on Solaris it is expected to be in* /usr/local/apache/conf.*

Webmin works directly with the Apache configuration files, and so must know where to find them. When you browse to the Apache module of Webmin for the first time you may be greeted with an error stating that the configuration file could not be found. You'll need to locate the configuration files, as well as the Apache binary, and possibly startup and shutdown scripts for your system, and configure Webmin to search the appropriate locations. The most important paths are probably **Apache server root directory** and the **Path to httpd executable**.

Module Selection

Apache is extremely modular, and the vast majority of its available functionality is broken out into small modules that can be loaded at runtime depending on the needs of the specific environment in which it runs. Webmin needs to know about the modules that are available to your Apache so that it can provide configuration options for options that are available and hide options that are not. So, the first time you visit the Webmin Apache module, you'll be presented a list of Apache modules with check boxes beside them. If you've used a package or a default Apache source installation, you can simply click **Configure**. If you've built your Apache from scratch with customizations, you'll need to choose the modules that you have made available in your installation, and then click **Configure**.

Adding Content

Believe it or not, we're now very nearly ready to serve up content with Apache. Once you've reached the primary Apache module page in Webmin, you'll see a set of icons for the global server options as well as a single virtual server configuration section labeled **Default server**. The default server is the server that will answer a request when no other virtual servers do. Because we have no virtual servers configured on our system yet, the default server will answer all HTTP requests that reach our machine. Take note of the path in the **Document root** field, as this is where we'll be placing our first web page.

On my system the **Document root** for the default server is /var/www/html, which was automatically created during the installation process. So I will create a web page called index.html and drop it into that directory, making sure the page has permissions that will allow the Apache process to read it. The name index.html is significant, and you must use the correct file name for your default page, or else Apache won't serve it without having the file specified after the address in the URL. Other common names for the index page are index.htm and default.htm.

Starting Apache

Now all that is left is to start up your Apache server. Assuming Webmin has been configured correctly for your installation it can even be started from within Webmin with the click of a button. Simply browse to the Apache module main page, and click the **Start Apache** link in the upper right corner of the page.

To test your new website browse to the IP on which your server resides with your favorite browser. For example, my testing server is located on IP 192.168.1.1, so I would enter http://192.168.1.1 into my browser URL field. Assuming everything went right, you'll see your new web page.

Tutorial: Name-Based Virtual Hosting with Apache

In the real world, it is rare to only operate one website on a machine. For all but the most demanding websites, it would be a waste of resources to do so, because a single modest computer can serve hundreds or thousands of web requests every minute without much effort. It would also be a waste of the finite IP space on the Internet, as there is a fixed number of IP addresses available, and the majority of them are already in use. To solve both problems Apache provides a feature known as name-based virtual hosts. With name-based virtual hosts, you may serve hundreds or thousands of websites, each with their own domain name, from a single machine running on a single IP!

NOTE *The terms* virtual host *and* virtual server *are generally interchangeable for our purposes. The terminology is constantly shifting, however, and you may hear the terms used differently in different contexts. In our case, the terms have the same meaning, but the term* virtual host *may be used to indicate a concept, while the term* virtual server *will generally be used to indicate a specific configuration detail.*

In this short tutorial we will convert our existing default server into a virtual server, and create a new server that can be hosted alongside our first website on a different domain name. With the mention of domain names, you may have realized we won't be able to test our new virtual servers until domain name service has been configured. Luckily, there is a short tutorial for that as well in the BIND chapter to which you can refer when you are ready to try out your new virtual hosts.

Converting a Default Server to a Virtual Server

The first step to using virtual servers in a generic, and thus easily scalable and flexible manner, is to convert our already configured default server to a virtual server. Though this isn't strictly necessary to make this change, it is common practice to instead provide an appropriate error page or a page of links to all of the virtual hosts on the machine using a traditional URL syntax for web clients that are incompatible with name-based hosts (however extremely rare such clients may be). Because the default server will be used in the event no virtual servers match, it could also be left as-is, with all other hosts being configured using the virtual hosts mechanism.

To create a new virtual server, fill in the form at the bottom of the primary Apache module page. You may leave the address and port empty and select the **Any** option for the address, unless your server has many IP addresses and you only want this virtual host to respond on one of them or you want this virtual host to respond on one or more nonstandard ports. For our example setup, we'll just leave them empty.

The **Document Root** can be any directory on your system to which the Apache process has read access; however, there are some conventions that you can follow in order to make your server more immediately comprehensible to subsequent administrators. If all of the virtual servers on your system are to be under the control of your company and you will be administering all of them yourself, it is wise to place all of the document roots into subdirectories of whatever the default server document roots parent directory is. For example, on my system the default document root is /var/www/html, so it makes good sense for my virtual server document roots to reside in subdirectories of /var/www. The more common convention, however, is used in environments where many users will be maintaining many websites, and none of the users should have access to the other users' website directories directly. In this case, the normal practice is to place the document root into the user's home directory, in a sub-directory called htdocs or www.

Finally, fill in the server name, which is the domain name on which you'd like this server to answer (Figure 7-9). If you don't happen to own a domain that can be used for experimenting, you can simply make one up. We'll be configuring our own local domain name server later on, so there are no rules about how you have to name it. You could call it google.com, or whitehouse.gov, or just george, if you wanted to. However, because it is likely you intend to put the server online for production use at some point in the future, you'll likely just name it whatever domain name it will be at that point. In my case, I'd call it swelltech.com.

Figure 7-9: Creating a new virtual host

Click **Create**. Now move your content from your default server document root directory into your new document root. In my case it is /var/www/swelltech.com. After applying the changes to your server, your Apache configuration should be finished, though we'll tackle a few more small issues before calling it done.

NOTE *To test your new virtual server, you can't simply browse to your IP as you did in the previous tutorial. The browser request must contain the domain name for the virtual host in the URL. There are a couple of ways to achieve this. The first is to configure a local name server to temporarily provide name service for your new domain; the second is to set up your system hosts file to point to the appropriate IP for the domain name. The easiest is obviously to add it to your hosts file. You can do this in Webmin, if your client machine is a UNIX machine running Webmin, using the **Networking:Network Configuration:Host addresses** module. On a Windows client machine, you'll need to edit the hosts file manually. It is located in c:\windows\hosts on Win 98 and Me; c:\winnt\system32\drivers\etc\hosts on Win NT, 2000, and XP Pro; and c:\windows\system32\drivers\etc\hosts on XP Home. The more interesting and educational method is to configure BIND to serve your new address, and then configure your client to get name service from the newly configured BIND. This is documented later in the BIND chapter; feel free to skip ahead and work through that tutorial now. I'll wait for you here. . . .*

Adding Other Virtual Server Names

Perhaps you noticed when we configured the above virtual server, it was named simply swelltech.com. Did you wonder why I didn't call it www.swelltech.com instead? The reason is simple: I'd like for users to be able to browse to either address and get the same website. So I named the virtual server swelltech.com, and now a new server alias can be added to cause it to answer on both names. To add a new virtual server name to an existing virtual server, click the icon for the virtual server on the main Apache module page. Then click the **Networking and Addresses** icon. Now fill in all of the other domain names on which you'd like your website to appear. Note that these names must each have their own DNS record for users to be able to use them, just like the original swelltech.com name. Every additional host name in the domain is a new address, so www.swelltech.com and mail.swelltech.com have to have their own name record in the name server even if they are on the same machine.

8

BIND

DNS, or the Domain Name System, is absolutely vital to the functioning of the Internet. In fact, though you rarely interact directly with the DNS the Internet as we know it could not exist without its constant presence. DNS associates, or *binds*, host names and domain names to IP addresses and thus allows you to type `http://www.swelltech.com` instead of the much less memorable IP 216.40.244.74.

Further, it makes it possible for mail servers to easily locate the correct host to send mail to for a given domain, the correct administrative contact when strange things are originating from the domain, and more. But for our purposes, as ordinary system administrators, all we need to really keep in mind is that BIND is our method of providing DNS information for our network. It will provide information to our local users when their client applications need to access various sites by name. And it will provide information to clients (primarily other DNS servers acting as DNS clients in order to fetch the correct information for their clients) on the Internet at large in order to advertise to the world how host names on our network can be reached. Think of it as a fancy telephone book, or even better, a telephone operator, for networked computers. The client computer has a name, but needs the number in order to reach it across the vast Internet. So it contacts the DNS server and asks for the number, and BIND is happy to do its best to return the correct number.

Every host on a TCP/IP network has an *IP address*. This address must be unique for the network on which the address is routable. So, every host that is accessible via the Internet has a unique IP address that may, theoretically, be reached from anywhere else on the Internet. Because these addresses are doled out, roughly, according to physical location on the network, and because routers keep up with which other routers have access to which subnets, this simple number is all that is needed for your computer to establish a connection with any other computer on the Internet in seconds. Unfortunately the topic of routing on the Internet falls quite outside of the scope of this document, as Webmin is not designed to manage routers or the more complex routing features of Linux, FreeBSD, and the other operating systems that are supported.

A Brief History of BIND

We have established already that BIND can provide name service for your network, allowing you to enter a host name rather than an IP when connecting to another computer on the network. However, we did not address how BIND, and DNS in general, works on the Internet at large. DNS on the Internet is really a multi-tiered system, wherein clients make queries of local name servers that serve a tiny fraction of the clients found on the Internet, usually on a single subnet. These local name servers then act as clients of somewhat larger name servers, which in turn act as clients for name servers above even them. At some point in this hierarchy the server will be one of the ROOT, or top-level domain, name servers, which will know what other lower-name server to query regarding the requested name. Each name server in the chain will likely save the results of the query, or cache the result, so will have no need to go all the way up the chain the next time the same query is made. Shockingly, perhaps, this system works quite well and has scaled as the Internet has grown from a few thousand hosts to hundreds of millions.

Walking Through an Example Query

When you open your favorite browser and enter a request for a web page — for example, http://www.swelltech.com — quite a lot goes on behind the scenes before the browser can even begin to load data from the server. First, the URL you entered must be parsed and interpreted by the browser. But we don't care about that step. Next, the domain and host name where the data is located must be found on the Internet. The name, www.swelltech.com, tells the browser very little about the physical or network location of the data, so it queries a tool that can make some sense out of that information: the DNS server.

The DNS server receives the request and checks its internal cache for the host named www, in the second level domain swelltech, in the top-level domain (aka TLD) com. If the DNS server does not have this information cached, it becomes a client and asks its parent name server the same question: "What is the IP for the host www.swelltech.com?" Eventually, assuming no lower-level name servers have information about this host, a top-level domain name server (in this case, the one for the com TLD) will receive the query. The difference here is that the top-level domain name server knows the address of the name server that is responsible for that domain name, or at least the next level down, swelltech. Finally, the name server for the swelltech.com domain is queried, and the IP for the host www is returned. As mentioned earlier this data will then be cached by each name server in the query path so that next time, they won't have to work so hard to answer the request.

The BIND Module

The BIND module opens to a screen with two sections (Figure 8-1). The upper portion of the page is devoted to global BIND options, such as other DNS servers, logging, access control, and more. The lower portion of the display provides a number of icons, one for each of the *zones* your BIND is responsible for. This will include all Master, Slave, Forward, and Stub zones.

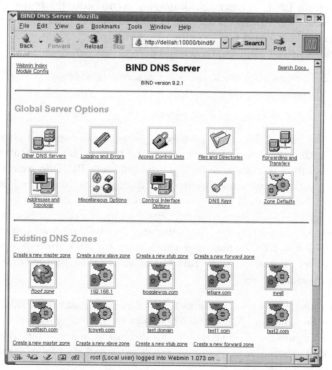

Figure 8-1: The BIND start page

Configuring your BIND server is an area where Webmin can really make things simpler. Even though DNS is a very simple service on the surface, the BIND configuration files are notoriously confusing, and it is very easy to make a mistake that will render your name server useless. That's not to say you can't misconfigure your name server with Webmin, but it does make it a lot easier to generate a syntactically correct BIND configuration.

NOTE *There are three BIND versions in common usage today, specifically versions 4, 8, and 9. BIND 8 and 9 are functionally identical in many ways and share a configuration file syntax, so that a working BIND 8 configuration will very likely also be a working BIND 9 configuration. BIND 9 adds a few new features, but is primarily a rewrite of BIND 8 (the reasons for the rewrite are irrelevant for general users). Webmin has two BIND modules, one for 4 and one for 8 and 9. Because version 4 is extremely old and pretty rarely used outside of OpenBSD and older UNIX environments, it will not be covered here. BIND 8 and 9, because they share the same module and configuration syntax, can be covered together. Features available only in BIND 9 will be noted as such.*

Global Server Options

Other DNS Servers

The Other DNS Servers page allows you to configure the behavior of DNS servers that BIND will communicate with in one way or another in a zone transfer relationship. This allows you to explicitly configure several aspects of the transfer relationship for each server (Figure 8-2).

Figure 8-2: Configuring other servers

The first field is the **IP address** of the server to configure. If you are receiving zone transfers for several servers and one of them is to be treated differently, here is where to configure it. The next field tells BIND to treat replies from this server as bogus, meaning incorrect. Future results that come from this domain will not be trusted. Next, in the **Zone transfer** format field, you can configure whether BIND will receive zone transfers one at a time or in a batch of many. Finally, though it is not yet implemented in BIND (at least not the latest version of BIND 8 — BIND 9 may have this feature by now), there is a placeholder for a per-server limitation on the number of transfers to initiate concurrently called **Maximum transfers**.

NOTE *If you have configured any security keys as documented later in the **DNS Keys** section, there will be an additional field containing a check box for each of the keys configured. Selecting one will require the server to authenticate itself using the key selected. A copy of the key must exist on both the local server and the remote server and must be configured in the BIND configuration for each.*

This page configures the server directive and related options in your named.conf file. By default, no other servers are defined.

Logging and Errors

This page provides a list of existing *logging channels* that are active for bind. It also allows you to add new logging channels. Generally speaking, the logs provided by BIND by default are enough for most purposes, providing a general overview of operations (starting, stopping, and so on) as well as any errors that occur during operation. However, if you need additional logging or logging of specific information to a separate file, you can configure it here.

Logging in BIND 8 is very flexible but also a little confusing at first glance. To add a new log, you first create a new channel that can be set to log to a file or to a syslog level. You then configure the level of information to log there, as discussed next. Finally, you assign logging categories to that channel. The categories dictate what types of information are logged to this particular channel (Figure 8-3).

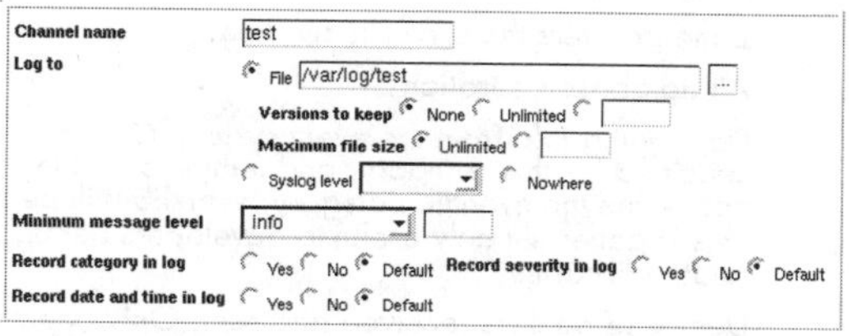

Figure 8-3: Creating a new logging channel

In the example, I've created a logging channel called test. I've chosen to send it to a log file located at /var/log/test (I know what you're thinking: "Where does he come up with these great names?"). So far it's all pretty self-explanatory, but then we come to **Minimum message level**. Here we can set the logging level for the information we'd like logged. There are five presets, and you can also choose a numeric debug level. The five presets are, from order of least important, info, notice, warning, error, and critical, which are pretty much what they sound like. The info level is almost everything the server has to say about the subject, making for quite a chatty little log. On the other hand, the critical level is reserved for things that usually mean your name server is experiencing one or more serious problems, possibly leading to improper functioning of the server. These first five levels are the same as those used by syslog. The Debug level option allows you to set a debug level for debugging messages to be sent to your log. Note that debug messages cannot be sent to syslog, and must be logged to a file. Finally, the Global level sets this log to the same level as the global server logging.

Next, I assigned a logging category to the logging channel *test*. In this case I decided to send security information to this channel. There are currently 22 supported categories of information that can be logged. They are as follows.

default	If no categories are specified, then default is used. Default contains most messages from the other categories, but a few are left out.
config	Configuration file processing information. BIND writes these messages as it loads the configuration file.
parser	Configuration file parsing information. BIND writes these messages as it parses the configuration file.
queries	Logging of queries.
lame-servers	Notifies you of the detection of a bad delegation.
statistics	Provides periodic reports of general system runtime information.
panic	Logging of problems that will cause the shutdown of the server.
update	Dynamic updates.
ncache	Negative caching.
xfer-in	Zone transfers the server is receiving.
xfer-out	Zone transfers the server is sending.
db	All database operations.
eventlib	Debugging info from the event system. Only one channel may be specified for this category, and it must be a file channel. If you do not define the eventlib category, eventlib will be directed to default. This is generally only useful to developers debugging BIND or its related libraries.
packet	Dumps of packets received and sent. Only one channel may be specified for this category, and it must be a file channel. If you do not define the packet category, it will be directed to the default category at the debug level.
notify	The NOTIFY protocol, which provides asynchronous change notifications.
cname	CNAME errors.
security	Approved and unapproved requests.
os	Problems with the underlying operating system.
insist	Internal consistency check failures.
maintenance	Periodic maintenance events.
load	Zone loading messages.
response-checks	Messages arising from response checking, such as "Malformed response...", "wrong ans. name...", "unrelated additional info...", "invalid RR type...", and "bad referral...".

Access Control Lists

This page is for entering any number of named address match lists. The lists defined here are used later in the configuration for a number of purposes, though having an ACL by itself does nothing. To create an ACL, simply enter a name in the ACL Name field, and the addresses, networks, and other ACLs that this ACL will match in the second field. There are a few ACLs that are built in and do not need to be defined manually. These are any, which matches all hosts; none, which matches no hosts; localhost, which matches the IP address of all interfaces on the system where BIND is running; and localnets, which matches all hosts on the local networks for which the system has an interface configured.

Files and Directories

Here you configure a few of the file locations for files that your BIND process may need to read from or write to. These usually do not need to be changed, but it may be useful to know what each of them refers to.

Statistics output file

This option allows you to choose a different file name and path for the statistics that BIND generates when signaled. To cause BIND to dump statistics to this file, you can use the ndc program with the stats option, which will send the correct signal to BIND. This corresponds to the statistics-file directive in the options section of named.conf and defaults to named.stats.

Database dump file

Configures the location of the file where BIND dumps its database when it receives the correct signal. The signal can be generated by using **ndc dumpdb**. This option correlates to the dump-file directive in the options section of named.conf and defaults to named_dump.db.

Process ID file

This is the location of BIND's process ID file. This location and file must be writable by the BIND process.

Path to zone transfer program

This sets the path to the named-xfer program that BIND uses for inbound zone transfers. This option configures the named-xfer directive of the options section in named.conf.

Forwarding and Transfers

This page allows you to configure parent DNS servers (Figure 8-4). Here, you declare what servers your BIND can query and how to behave towards them.

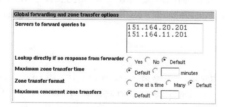

Figure 8-4: Forwarding and Transfers

Servers to forward queries to

With this field, you enter any name servers that you wish your BIND process to query in the event it does not have a cached result to serve to the client. Usually this will be the name servers that your ISP or hosting service provides for you, but it may also be other servers on your local network. It's a good idea to have at least two, which will be called the *primary* and *secondary* name servers, respectively. This option configures the forwarders directive in the options section of named.conf.

Lookup directly if no response from forwarder

This option allows you to choose whether BIND should query the TLD servers directly if the forwarders do not reply. You may need to turn this off if you have a non-Internet-connected DNS server, or a server isolated by a firewall on your local network that can only communicate with the forwarders. This option configures the forward directive.

Maximum zone transfer time

This allows you to put an upper limit on the time allowed for inbound zone transfers. This option correlates to the max-transfer-time-in directive, and defaults to 120 minutes. After this time, a transfer will be terminated.

Zone transfer format

Sets the global transfer format (which can be overridden on a per server basis, in the Other Servers section). Here you can choose whether BIND should receive a message for each resource record transferred. The many choice tells BIND to accept several per message, which is more efficient. This option correlates to the transfer-format directive.

Maximum concurrent zone transfers

Places a limit on the number of concurrent transfers. This corresponds to the transfers-in option and defaults to 10. Increasing this may improve performance but at the cost of more system resources being consumed.

Addresses and Topology

The following options specify network-specific details:

Ports and addresses to listen on

BIND can answer on any number of ports and addresses on your server. By default, BIND will answer on port 53 on every active IP address. If you choose to listen on one or more specific addresses and/or ports, then BIND will answer on only those allowed by the match list. It is also possible to negate a port or IP by prepending an !.

Source IP address for queries

If your BIND does not know the answer to a query, it will query other name servers. Here you can define the local addresses and ports on which to query those name servers. By default it can use any IP or port that is available on the system.

Nameserver choice topology

When querying other servers, BIND can be configured to choose name servers that are closer in the topology address list. The order the servers appear in the list indicates their distance from the local name server, where the first is closest and the last is furthest. It is also possible to force one or more name servers to be last resorts, by prepending them with !. Those servers prepended by an exclamation point will be placed at the end of the queue, regardless of placement in the topology address list.

Miscellaneous Options

The BIND options with no other obvious locations ended up in this section, so it has a relatively large number of options. Luckily for you, most administrators don't have to worry about these options very often. Unluckily for me, to achieve my goal of fully documenting the BIND module, I have to document these features just as completely as those that are more often used. So, on this page you'll find several configurable memory usage settings, some timing options, and some general behavior choices.

Maximum core dump size

This is the maximum file size of a dump file that BIND will generate in the event of a crash. This option configures the coresize option in the named.conf file. Your operating system may also impose a limit on core size, which may or may not be smaller than the value configured here.

Maximum data memory usage

This defines the maximum amount of memory that BIND will use for storage of data. This is not the complete memory usage of BIND, as the process itself must have memory, but it can be used to limit BIND somewhat. This option correlates to the datasize in named.conf.

Maximum open files

Defines the number of files that BIND can have open at any given time. The default is the limit of the OS; however, BIND is not always able to determine this at runtime if the operating system does not accurately report it. In this case, it may be necessary to use the correct value here. This is not a problem under the most popular operating systems where Webmin and BIND are used, such as FreeBSD and Linux. This option configures the files directive.

Maximum stack memory usage

Defines the maximum amount of stack space that the BIND process may use. This correlates to the stacksize directive.

Interval between cleaning expired records

BIND will periodically remove expired records from the cache. This option configures how often this cleaning occurs. This corresponds to the cleaning-interval and defaults to 60 minutes.

Interval between check for new interfaces

BIND will scan the network interface list periodically, and this option configures the interval, in minutes, between scans. The default is 60 minutes. This option configures the interface-interval directive.

Interval between logging stats

This setting controls how often BIND writes general server statistics to the logs. By default this occurs every 60 minutes, and if set to 0 statistics logging will be turned off. This option correlates to the statistics-interval directive.

Do full recursive lookups for clients?

BIND can respond in one of two ways if it does not have an answer for a client. If this option is set to Yes, the default, then BIND will perform the lookup itself on a parent or root server. If this is turned off, BIND will simply refer the client to another name server that can answer the query. This option configures the recursion directive.

Allow multiple CNAME aliases for one name?

Older versions of BIND allowed multiple CNAME resource records for a single domain, and many sites used this for load balancing. However, this usage is against standards and is not recommended. Turning this on allows you to use multiple CNAMES, as in older versions of BIND. The default is off, and it correlates to the multiple-cnames directive.

Fetch glue records?

If this option is set to Yes, the default, the server will fetch "glue" resource records it does not have when constructing the additional data section of a response. Setting this to No can be used in conjunction with recursion no to prevent the server's cache from growing or becoming corrupted. However, doing this increases the work for the client. This option configures the fetch-glue directive.

Set authoritative AA bit on responses?

BIND normally caches negative responses (i.e., NXDOMAIN, or "this does not exist"), however, some very old servers and clients may have problems with this and generate errors. It's probably wise to upgrade those old clients and servers rather than turning this off. This option configures the auth-nxdomain directive and defaults to Yes.

Control Interface Options

BIND provides a command-line utility called rndc (or ndc in older versions) that allows an administrator to perform some administrative tasks. The newer rndc version allows these tasks to be performed on remote BIND servers as well as a server running locally, as it operates via a network socket. Common uses for this utility include stopping the named process, forcing a reload of configuration files, refreshing zone information, and triggering a dump of server stats. Because the rndc tool can be used to shut down the server, as well as other potentially dangerous actions, its use should be limited to a few trusted client addresses.

This page of the BIND module provides access to the controls section of the BIND configuration file and configures the hosts that are allowed to connect to the running BIND server.

Internet port access

If enabled, the first field must contain the local address on which the named server will listen for control requests. The port field can be the port on which you'd like the process to listen, or you can simply fill in an asterisk, "*", to specify a randomly selected unprivileged port (unprivileged ports on a UNIX system are usually those above 1024). Finally, the allow field should contain the addresses of the hosts you would like to be able to administer your server from. Generally, unless you have a reason to do otherwise, security is most easily maintained by preventing access to all outside addresses. In such a case you would choose an address of 127.0.0.1 in the first field, a port of *, and an allow list containing only 127.0.0.1. Assuming your local machine is trusted, your server will be relatively secure.

Unix filing system access

As in the previous set of options, this directive specifies which clients will have access to the administrative channel of the running named process, but in this case, it is for the older style of communication using a UNIX FIFO pipe. A pipe in UNIX, is a mechanism by which a stream of data can be treated as a file, and vice versa. Or, in other words, it allows a running process to accept data being written into it as though it were a file and it can output data likewise in a form that can be read like a file.

If using this mechanism for communicating with your named process, you can choose a file name for the pipe, the permissions for the pipe, and the owner and group of the pipe. Care should be taken to make the file inaccessible to all but the administrative users of the system.

NOTE *The UNIX pipe mechanism is not available in BIND 9. It has been deprecated in favor of using the network socket interface along with security keys. It is supported in BIND version 8.*

DNS Keys

Newer BIND version support secure keys for the purpose of authentication and authorizing access to certain functions. This page allows you to generate keys for use in other sections. Specifically, after generation, a key can be used to secure your **Other Servers** connections.

Installing a Key

To create a new key, simply fill in a new **Key ID**, which must be an alphanumeric string with no whitespace, for example, mynewkey or supersecret or HenryThe8th. The **Algorithm** can usually safely remain at the default of hmac-md5. Finally, the **Secret string** must be a base64-encoded string.

Creating a Key with dnssec-keygen

To generate a base64-encoded string for use in the **Secret string** field, you can use the dnssec-keygen or dnskeygen utility that is included in most installations of BIND. You can even use a plain string encoded with the mmencode utility, though this will be significantly less secure than using an MD5 key. To create a key using dnssec-keygen, the following command line can be used with minor modifications to suit your server:

```
[root@delilah]# dnssec-keygen -a HMAC-MD5 -b 128 -n HOST delilah.swelltech.com
Kdelilah.swelltech.com.+157+06448
```

In the above example, the second line is the output from the command, which gives you a hint about the filenames under which your new key is stored. In this case, two files were generated, named Kdelilah.swelltech.com.+157+06448.key and Kdelilah.swelltech.com.+157+06448.private. Both contain the newly generated key, and so you can view either to copy the key for pasting into the Webmin **Secret string** field. This key will also need to be made available to any servers that will be communicating with this server using security features.

Zone Defaults

Here you can define several default options for new zones on your server and zones for which you provide backup service (Figure 8-5). These options can often be overridden in the definition of the individual zone; however, most such items are best configured here, and any differences from the norm can be configured in the individual zone. These options are only documented here, though they apply to individual zones as well. Note also that these do not affect the named.conf file at all. These are merely default values used by Webmin when creating new master zones, similar to the /etc/skel file used when creating new users. You'll also find on this page settings for some default zone permissions options.

Refresh time

This is interval for which your zones will be cached before being refreshed by slaves. Lowering this will increase the load on your master server but will help ensure fresh data reaches clients from your slave DNS servers. This option configures the refresh field in the SOA record in each new zone you create, and defaults to 10800 seconds, or 3 hours. Note that the introduction of the DNS NOTIFY protocol into BIND 8 removes the reliance of slaves on refresh times for prompt updates. To find out more take a look at *RFC 1996* [http://www.ietf.org/rfc/rfc1966.txt?number=1966]. BIND 4 and some other name servers may not have NOTIFY, so if your slaves are not all known to be NOTIFY capable, you should still be aware that your slaves will take the full refresh time to be guaranteed to be fresh.

Transfer retry time

This defines the amount of time between retries if a refresh attempt fails. If you have reduced the refresh time, this value should be reduced accordingly. This option correlates to the retry field in an SOA record and defaults to 3600 seconds, or 1 hour.

Defaults for new master zones

When creating a new master zone, Webmin can be configured to fill in some of the values with defaults for your network. The following options allow these defaults to be configured (Figure 8-5):

Default time-to-live

This sets the minimum time to live for a zone. Downstream name servers will no longer consider the information they have cached accurate if it is older than this. They will continue to serve the old data if new data cannot be retrieved, until the expiry time has been reached. This option can be used very effectively to ensure that server or address changes can be performed without interruption of client services. For example, if you are aware that your website will be moving to a new server on a new address in a week, you can alter this to something very short, perhaps 30 seconds. By the end of the week, when your change happens, all name servers that have cached your information will know to check with a name server that is authoritative for your domain often. No one will even notice you changed! This option configures the TTL field in the SOA record and defaults to 38400 seconds, or 10 hours.

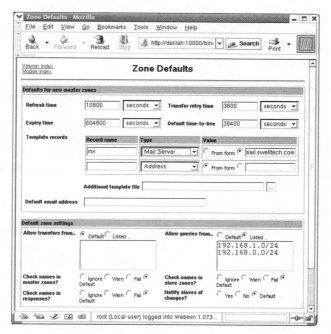

Figure 8-5: Zone Defaults

Template records

This section can be a nice time-saver if you create a large number of domains with Webmin (for example, if you run an ISP or a web-hosting company). Here you can define several template records that can be automatically inserted into some or all of your new zones. For example, if you have a single mail server and two name servers that are the same for all of the domains you create you can create templates for each of those. When you create a zone file later, you can choose to have the templates included. It is also possible to add a single host, whose IP can be defined at zone creation time. The mail server, name alias, and name server templates must have addresses assigned to them from the beginning, however. There is no default template, and this section does not directly affect any BIND configuration files.

Default Zone Settings

This section configures zone settings that will be applied by BIND for zones that do not override them. Unlike with the **Defaults for new master zones** section, these options do impact the BIND configuration file.

Allow transfers from

Here you can define other servers that will, by default, be allowed to receive transfers from this server. This option correlates to the allow-transfer directive and defaults to allowing zone transfers to all hosts.

Allow queries from

This one allows you to define what hosts or networks will be allowed to query your server. Any host that will use your name server should be listed here. However, by default, the server will allow requests from all hosts. This option configures the allow-query directive.

Check names in master zones? and Check names in slave zones?

These two allow you to choose how strict your name server will be with regard to checking names within their expected client context. This means that, for example, a domain name used as a host name can be checked for compliance with relevant standards regarding domain names and host names. These options configure check-names master and check-names slave and default to fail and warn, respectively.

Check names in responses?

Similar to the previous two options, but checks the names in responses to queries sent by the name server. If this is set to fail, your name server will REFUSE a query it receives and invalid name. This option configures the check-names response directive and defaults to ignore.

Notify slaves of changes?

This option allows you to configure whether BIND will use the NOTIFY protocol to inform its slaves of updates. In this way, its slaves can query the master to see if a zone transfer is needed. If so, the transfer takes places immediately, and all servers are brought up to date much more quickly than if the slaves awaited their usual refresh age to be reached. This option configures the notify directive.

Existing DNS Zones

This section of the BIND main page displays a list of all existing DNS zones. There are four types of zones (actually there are five, but the hint needs little configuration and is usually set up only once), master, slave, stub, and forward. And each of these types may then be either a forward zone (meaning it maps names to addresses) or a reverse zone (maps addresses to names). Each of the four types has a specific purpose, depending on your name server's relationship to the data it presents to clients:

Zone Types

The following are the types of DNS zone:

master

The server has the master copy of the zone data, and will provide authoritative answers for it.

slave

A slave zone is a copy of a master zone. Each slave zone will have a list of masters that it may query to receive updates to its copy of the zone. A slave may, optionally, keep a copy of the zone saved on disk to speed startups. A single master server can have any number of slaves in order to distribute load.

stub

A stub zone is much like a slave zone, and behaves similarly, however, it only replicates the NS records of a master zone rather than the whole zone.

forward

A forward zone directs all queries in the zone to other servers. In this way it can act as a caching DNS server for a network, or provide Internet DNS services to a network behind a firewall that limits outside DNS queries (obviously the forwarding DNS server must have DNS access to the Internet!). Note that this is similar to the global forwarding facility, but allows per-zone selection of forwarders.

Creating a New Zone

To create a new zone, click on one of the zone creation links in the **Existing DNS Zones** section of the screen. Each zone type will present you with the various fields necessary for Webmin to generate the new zone file for a zone of the selected type. The fields present differ for each zone type, except slave and stub, so we'll document each in turn.

Creating a Forward Master Zone

A master zone is one that contains the authoritative and complete data for a DNS zone, and therefore has the most configurable options (Figure 8-6). When creating any type of zone, it is necessary to create at least two zone database files, one for forward mappings and one for reverse mappings. This is to provide both name to address translation, as well as address to name translation. Luckily, once you've created a forward and reverse master zone, Webmin can automatically add the correct reverse records for each host you add to your master zone.

The options when creating zones are pretty straightforward, but I'll discuss them briefly, as well as give an example of creating a new master forward and master reverse zone database.

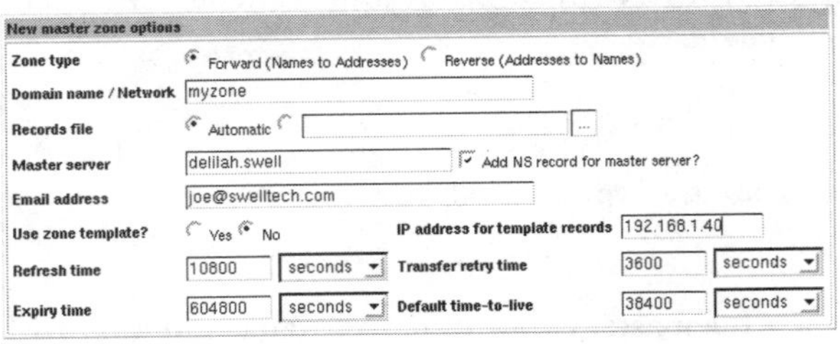

Figure 8-6: Creating a new master zone

Zone type

The zone type is either Forward or Reverse, as discussed earlier. In the example shown, I'm creating a new forward zone.

Domain name/Network

This option will be either the domain name of the zone in the case of a forward zone or the network in the case of a reverse zone. Here, I'm creating a zone named myzone. Note that in my case, my domain is for a local network and will not be able to be resolved from the Internet at large (which requires registration in one of the top-level domains, such as .com, .org, or .net). Registration of a domain zone and obtaining addresses and other related tasks are well beyond the scope of this book, but the steps for creating Internet domains are precisely the same.

Records file

This option allows you to choose the name and location of the db file while you would like your zone information stored. Webmin will automatically create a correctly named file in the system default location for you if you leave this option set to Automatic. Unless you have good reason for breaking convention it is recommended that you leave this as it is.

Master server

Here you select the name of the master server for this domain. Because we are creating a master zone, this should be the host name of the server that will be the master for this file; in my example, I've selected the host name delilah.swell, a host on my local (non-Internet) domain swell. The sub-option **Add NS record for master server?** when checked, will add a name server record in this zone for this name server. It's usually good to leave this checked and let Webmin handle one more of the many minor details it will handle if you let it.

Email address

This should be the email address for the maintainer of this domain. In the case of Internet resolvable domains, this will be the person contacted in the event of problems with your DNS server(s).

Use zone template?

If you created a zone template in your **Global Server Options:Zone Defaults** you can include that template information here. This can include any number of automatically generated records of several types (host address, mail server, name server, name alias, and host information). If you chose From form as a source for one of your host addresses, then you can enter that information in the **IP address for template records** field. Using the template facility in Webmin can prove a very powerful tool for administrators who manage a large number of zones that have the same name servers and mail servers. Creating a new domain can be done almost automatically in this way.

Refresh time

This is the same as the option of the same name in **Global Server Options:Zone Defaults**, though it will only apply to this zone. This option will override the global zone default. The same applies to **Transfer retry time**, **Expiry time**, and **Default time-to-live**.

Clicking Create takes you to the primary page for this new zone. We'll come back to these options after discussing the creation of a reverse master zone, as it makes good sense to create your reverse zone for this domain before adding any records to the zone. In this way, Webmin can keep the two files in sync for you automatically.

Creating a Reverse Master Zone

After creating a forward master zone, you may then want to return to the main BIND module page and create another master zone (Figure 8-7). This time, you will choose to create a reverse zone, in order to provide mapping from IP addresses to names.

NOTE *Reverse address resolution is somewhat different than forward resolution. With forward zones, there can be any number of addresses associated with a single IP, whereas there should only be one reverse record for a given IP. Thus if you are hosting many virtual services on a single IP, they can have their own domain name, but the IP can only map back to one of them in the event of a reverse lookup. Also, unless you own your own network IP block, or are using a private netblock, your name server will not necessarily be authoritative for your range of IP addresses. Reverse lookups are not frequently used, and when they are, it is usually only to confirm that an IP does resolve to some legitimate network.*

Here, you'll see that creating a reverse master zone is exactly like creating a forward master zone. In this case, I've chosen a zone type of Reverse, as this zone will map addresses to names. The only other difference between this and the previous example, is that I've entered the network address, 172.16.1, instead of the domain name. After creating this, I'm taken to the primary page for the new zone. We will rarely edit the reverse master zone records directly, as it is easier and safer to allow Webmin to do it for us. So let's return to the primary BIND module page and then edit our new myzone master zone.

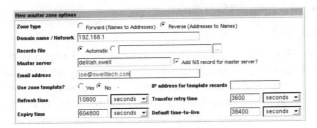

Figure 8-7: Creating a reverse master zone

Adding Records to a Master Zone

Assuming you successfully created a Forward Master Zone, it will now appear in the **Existing DNS Zones** section of your main BIND page. Clicking it takes you to a page that allows adding records of all types, as well as a few general zone options at the bottom of the page (Figure 8-8). The options at the bottom of the page are the same as those documented in the **Global Zone Options** sections earlier, except they only affect the one zone you are editing, so these options will not be covered here.

Figure 8-8: Edit Master Zone

Address

An address record allows you to enter the host name, the time to live, and the address for a host. Every host on your network should have an Address Record (Figure 8-9). In the example, note that I've entered the fully qualified host name, and ended with a period. I've also chosen to have Webmin update the reverse master zone with this address, as well. This option creates an A record.

Name Server

If you have another name server that is responsible for another subdomain (such as joeszone.myzone.), you can add it here. You can also add other name servers for this domain, including slaves and redundant masters. This option creates an NS record.

Name Alias

Name aliases provide a means to name a host more than one name. For example, if you wanted your mail server (real name mail.myzone.) to also be addressable by the name smtp.myzone., you could create an alias for it here, and both names would resolve to the same machine. Also, it allows you to create shortcuts for your users. If for example, you wanted users to be able to simply enter *news* to reach a news server, even though your news server is actually in another domain. This option creates a CNAME record.

Mail Server

Every mail server in your domain should have an entry here. On this page, the **Name** field should contain the name of the domain, and the **Mail Server** field should contain the name of the mail server. When creating a mail server record, you are given an extra option that is not present in any of the other records, called **Priority**. The Priority of a mail server is a relative value to indicate which mail server has precedence. The lower the value, the higher its precedence. Every mail record must have a Priority. In the event that the server with the highest precedence is down, mail servers can then deliver mail to the next server on the list. This option creates an MX record.

Figure 8-9: Adding an address record

Host Information

This record type allows you to identify the type of host that is referenced by an address record. Here, you enter the name of the host and the **Hardware** type and **Operating System** type. These types are entirely optional, but if you do enter them, you should be aware of the security implications (identifying your hardware and OS is the first step a cracker takes in identifying ways to crack your system). Also, there are several rules documented in *RFC 1700* [http://www. ietf.org/rfc/rfc1700.txt?number=1700] regarding how one *should* identify hardware and OS. However, these rules are not at all strictly enforced and it is usually quite safe to use this record for internal record keeping purposes (i.e., instead of keeping a notebook or separate database of all of your hosts and what OS and version they run). This option creates a HINFO record.

Text Record

Here you can enter any arbitrary text string up to about 2K. You can use this for notes regarding the host, perhaps the location or primary user of the host, as well as for other notes that can be referenced by other records, for example, in a Responsible Person record. This option creates a TXT record.

Well Known Service

The Well Known Service record type allows you to configure what types of services a particular host provides. So, for example, you could advertise that the host myhost.myzone. can provide telnet, ftp, and smtp services. The services are identified by the same name as is found in the services file. This option creates a WKS record. More on Well Known Services can be found in section 3.4.2 of *RFC 1035* [http://www.ietf.org/rfc/rfc1035.txt?number=1035]. WKS records are optional, and are not in very common usage, nor is it supported by all domain name servers.

Responsible Person

Here you define the person who is responsible for a given host or domain. The **Name** field is for the host name or the domain name, ending in a period if an absolute name. You can also enter the email address for the responsible person. The **Text Record** field can contain the name of a previously configured Text record. For example, if I were maintaining a domain and wanted people to be able to locate me in the event of a problem, I could create a text record named joe containing my cell phone number. Then for each host and subzone I manage, I could create a Responsible Person record that contains not only my email address, but also refers to the joe Text record. This option creates an RP record.

TIP   *When entering an email address in the **Responsible Person** section, Webmin will automatically convert it to the dot-separated format required by BIND. You should enter email addresses in their real world form, i.e.,* joe@swelltech.com.

Location

The Location record is a rather new and experimental record type that allows one to include precise (on a global scale, anyway) information about each host and network in your zone. The location is defined in latitude, longitude, and altitude. The current Webmin version does not distinguish the separate parts of this information, so you must enter it yourself in the correct format. *RFC 1876* [http://www.ietf.org/rfc/rfc1876.txt?number=1876] provides a more complete description of the Location record. One good resource to help you understand and use the LOC record, provided by one of the co-creators of the LOC specification, is *DNS LOC: Geo-enabling the Domain Name System* [http://www.ckdhr.com/dns-loc/]. There you can find links to sites that will provide the coordinates for your location for free. There is also a link to AirNav, which will provide altitude information for public landing sites (airports) in your area. This isn't as precise as a GPS system, but it's better than nothing and a lot more information than most DNS servers are configured to provide.

Edit Records File

This option merely provides a simple text editor window that contains the complete db file for your zone. This allows you to edit it manually; however, this is not recommended unless you are familiar with the BIND configuration file grammar as it is not checked by Webmin for correctness.

Creating a Slave or Stub Zone

Slave and Stub zones are created in exactly the same way, and are quite similar in some ways though their purposes are very different (Figure 8-10). Slave zones keep a complete copy in memory, and sometimes also on disk, of a zone that it receives via a zone transfer from a master zone. A slave zone can answer any queries for a zone, and as long as network connectivity remains intact between the master and slave and the servers are configured correctly, it will stay in sync with the master server. A stub zone also syncs to a master server; however it only keeps NS and SOA record information from the master server. This allows BIND to keep up with delegation information automatically.

Figure 8-10: Creating a Slave Zone

Creating a slave is extremely simple. The only information required is the domain name or the network (as was used in the master zone earlier), and the addresses of one or more master name servers. As with master zones, you configure both a forward and reverse zone type for each zone. This server can then be used by clients just as the master zone is used. In fact, whether it is a slave or master is entirely transparent to the user.

Creating a Forward Zone

A forward zone is simpler still. It's only possible configuration options are whether it is a forward (name to address) or reverse (address to name) zone type, the name or network of the domain, and the master servers to forward requests to. A forward zone is just specific instructions for BIND that it should forward requests for a specific zone to one or more specific name servers. BIND does not perform zone transfers with a forward zone, as it does in the case of slave and stub zones.

Tutorial: Setting Up a Caching Name Server with BIND

A caching name server can be beneficial in a number of situations. First, because it brings name service closer to the user, performance of all name-based services will likely be improved. Also, in secured environments with a strict firewall implementation, it can be used to allow local clients to obtain name service without having to pierce the firewall for all users. Only the local caching DNS server must have access to outside name servers. Finally, it provides a simple mechanism for providing a private name space to local users, by allowing users to obtain all name service from the local caching name server, which also acts as a master name server for the local network name space.

A caching name server is perhaps the simplest type of name server to configure, and Webmin makes the configuration even easier. Because caching is a core part of how DNS scales, it is an automatic part of any BIND configuration. All that is left for us to do is allow Webmin to create our initial configuration files and alter a couple of options in the configuration.

Initializing the named.conf

When first opening the Webmin BIND module, you'll be given a few choices about how to generate the initial configuration files. The ideal choice is to allow Webmin to initialize your configuration and download the root name server list. If you are not currently connected to the network you can choose to use the root name server list file that is included in the Webmin distribution.

Adding Forwarders

After Webmin has completed the download, and initialized your files, click the **Forwarding and Transfers** icon. Add the primary and secondary name server addresses provided by your ISP to the field labeled **Servers to forward queries to**. Then select Yes for the option **Lookup directly if no response from forwarder**. Click **Save**.

Believe it or not, your configuration is finished. Simply click the **Start BIND** button, point your client workstations to the IP of your server for their primary name server, and test it out. Check the later section on troubleshooting BIND if problems arise.

Tutorial: Name Resolution for Virtual Hosts

As discussed earlier in the Apache chapter, a name-based virtual host has to have a name mapped to an IP address before you can even access its contents with a browser. BIND, of course, will be our means of providing lookup of those names. Because we're only concerned with web service for this tutorial, we only need to concern ourselves with the creation of a forward zone (a forward zone maps names to addresses).

Create a New Master Forward Zone

Assuming you've already allowed Webmin to initialize your named configuration files you're ready to add a master forward zone for your domain (Figure 8-11). Click the **Create a new master zone** link on the front page of the BIND module.

The **Zone type** should remain at its default of Forward. The **Domain name/Network** field should contain the second level domain name under which your virtual hosts will reside. For example, if I had one or more virtual hosts under the swelltech.com domain, that would be the domain name I would enter here. If you have other second level domains, you will create a zone for each. It is easiest to allow Webmin to automatically name the **Records file**, and the **Master server** will probably be correct if your host name is configured correctly. Enter your email address, or the address you would like to be the administrative contact for this zone, into the **Email address** field. Finally, click **Create**. You will immediately be directed to the new zone for further configuration.

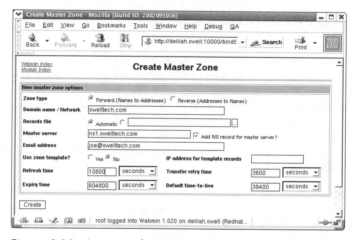

Figure 8-11: An example master zone

Adding Address Records

Now we can begin adding records to our new zone. The first record I would add to my swelltech.com domain would be swelltech.com itself, and it will be an address record, also known as an A record. Clicking the **Addresses** icon provides a simple form for adding the new record. Because this first record is for a host named simply swelltech.com, we enter nothing in the **Name** field. Then we enter the IP address of the server we'd like this name to point to, in my case it is the same address on which my Webmin server is running. All other fields can remain at their defaults. Clicking **Create** adds the record.

Follow the same steps to add another address record for www.swelltech.com, presumably on the same IP. All that changes from the above steps is to enter www in the **Name** field instead of leaving it blank. If you've worked through the examples in the Apache tutorial on virtual hosting, you'll now have all of the pieces for web service on both domain names.

Adding an Mail Server Record for Mail

Because no domain would be complete without mail service, and mail service for a domain does not have to reside on the same server as web service, we need to have some way to tell mail servers where to direct our mail. Luckily, the designers of DNS have thought of that already and provide the MX, or mail server, record as a means of notifying other mail servers where to send email destined for the domain.

Adding a mail server is usually a two part process. First, a new record is created pointing to the address of the mail server. In the case of small networks, this will likely be a machine that is providing other services. For example, the Swell Technology mail server resides on the same machine as our web server and our NTP time server. So, in most cases we can use a Name Alias record, also known as a CNAME record, for our mail server name. If you have a dedicated mail server you will use an address record instead.

Adding a Name Alias

Because my mail server is hosted on the same address as my web server, I've chosen to use a CNAME record, or name alias, for mail.swelltech.com. Creating a name alias record is a lot like creating an address record. Click the **Name Alias** icon, and fill in the appropriate fields. In this case, I will fill in mail for the **Name** and swelltech.com. for the **Real Name**. Notice there is a period at the end of my real name. This period is significant, and required to indicate a fully qualified domain name, otherwise the real name pointed to would be swelltech.com.swelltech.com, which is probably not what we want. Click **Create** to add the new record.

NOTE   *This step is not strictly necessary if your mail server is hosted on the same machine as other named services. However, traditionally mail servers have had a name record of their own, usually* mail.domain.com *or* smtp.domain.com. *It also makes it easier to plan for later network expansions if you begin your network design with appropriate names for all of the services available on your network. If you wish to avoid adding a CNAME for mail service, you can skip this step and point your MX record to an existing name.*

Creating an MX Record

Now that we have a name for our server, we can add an MX, or mail server, record. This is simply a record that indicates to other mail servers where mail for our domain should be delivered. In my case, I would like mail directed to swelltech.com and all names within the domain to be delivered to mail.swelltech.com. So when a mail server receives a mail from one of its users directed to joe@swelltech.com, it will first find out where that mail ought to be delivered by querying the name server that is authoritative for swelltech.com for its MX record.

To create a new mail server record, click the **Mail Server** icon. Because we are currently concerned with our primary domain, in my case swelltech.com, the **Name** field can be left empty. The **Mail Server** field can be filled in with the name of the mail server we created in the previous step, mail.swelltech.com in my case. There is an additional field required, called **Priority**, which is simply a number that dictates the preference of this mail server relative to others that may be configured, where lower numbers have higher priority with zero being the lowest. Traditionally, a priority of 10 is used for the primary mail server, and other servers will be given priorities higher in steps of ten. So a backup mail server could have a priority of 20. There is no enforcement of this de facto standard, so you could use priorities of 0 and 43 to represent your primary and backup mail servers, but following traditions is probably more polite to any administrator who might have to follow in your footsteps. Click Create to add the mail server record.

Applying Changes and Testing the Results

Now we have the bare minimum configuration required to make good use of our name server in the real world, so let's reload our BIND configuration and make sure it is working. First, return to the BIND module front page by clicking the **Module Index** link in the upper right corner of the page. Then click the **Apply Changes** button at the bottom of the page to signal BIND to reload its configuration files.

To test our work, we can use the host program. First, we'll test to be sure our domain is resolvable from our name server:

```
[joe@delilah joe]$ host swelltech.com 192.168.1.1
Using domain server:
Name: 192.168.1.1
Address: 192.168.1.1#53
Aliases:

swelltech.com has address 192.168.1.1
```

The host command is discussed further in the troubleshooting section of this chapter, but I will point out arguments I've used. Obviously, the first argument to the command is swelltech.com, which is the domain I'd like to look up. While the second argument is 192.168.1.1, which is the name server I'd like to query for the information. This allows us to easily set up a name server in isolation, without relying on it for real-world name service, so that it can be thoroughly tested and confirmed working. Because the above result is exactly what we expected to see, we can move on to testing the MX and NS records, to be sure they also match our expectations:

```
[joe@delilah joe]$ host -t mx swelltech.com 192.168.1.1
Using domain server:
Name: 192.168.1.1
Address: 192.168.1.1#53
Aliases:

swelltech.com mail is handled by 10 mail.swelltech.com.
```

This time, we've added an additional argument, "-t mx", to specify the type of record we'd like to retrieve. With this we can retrieve any record type we would like to test. Our only other currently configured record type is an NS record to indicate the authoritative name server for this domain, so we'll also check it:

```
[joe@delilah joe]$ host -t ns swelltech.com 192.168.1.1
Using domain server:
Name: 192.168.1.1
Address: 192.168.1.1#53
Aliases:

swelltech.com name server ns1.swelltech.com.
```

So far, so good! Just for completeness, let's run one last lookup, to see how a name alias differs from a normal address record:

```
[joe@delilah joe]$ host mail.swelltech.com 192.168.1.1
Using domain server:
Name: 192.168.1.1
Address: 192.168.1.1#53
Aliases:

mail.swelltech.com is an alias for swelltech.com.
swelltech.com has address 192.168.1.1
```

Assuming all went well with your results, you're ready to put your name server into service. The rest of this chapter is devoted to troubleshooting methods, and more advanced uses for the host and dig utilities, and working through the examples might provide some insight into the workings of DNS in a variety of applications and environments.

Troubleshooting BIND

There are a number of tools that are available to assist with testing and troubleshooting problems with your BIND configuration. The simplest tool on most systems is the host command, which simply performs an address lookup or a reverse address lookup. More complete information can be gathered using dig. On extremely old systems, nslookup might still be the only available option for this type of testing, but it is rather confusing and inconsistent in a number of ways and is not recommended.

Using Host

The host utility provides a very easy-to-use command-line interface for looking up a name or an address. In its simplest usage form it will return the IP address or addresses when given a host name as its argument. The mail host address or addresses will also be returned if available. If the command-line argument is an IP address, a reverse lookup will be performed and the host name will be returned. host also has a few additional options that may be helpful in tracing DNS problems or testing your configuration for correctness. You may query your system default name server, or you can query any name server you need to test by appending a server address to the end of the command line.

The simplest usage of host is to lookup an address, or a name:

```
[joe@delilah joe]$ host swelltech.com
swelltech.com has address 216.40.244.74
[joe@delilah joe]$ host 216.40.244.74
74.244.40.216.in-addr.arpa domain name pointer swelltech.com.
```

Above, I've requested the address for the domain swelltech.com, and then the name for the address 216.40.244.74. I could also ask for the name servers that are authoritative for a domain by using the -t ns command-line option.

```
[joe@delilah joe]$ host -t ns google.com
google.com name server ns2.google.com.
google.com name server ns3.google.com.
google.com name server ns4.google.com.
google.com name server ns1.google.com.
```

Finally, the MX record can be retrieved by using the -t mx option:

```
[joe@delilah joe]$ host -t mx yahoo.com
yahoo.com mail is handled by 1 mx2.mail.yahoo.com.
yahoo.com mail is handled by 5 mx4.mail.yahoo.com.
yahoo.com mail is handled by 1 mx1.mail.yahoo.com.
```

In the above MX record example, yahoo.com has three mail servers defined. The MX record has an additional field to indicate the priority of the server relative to other servers, in this case mx1.mail.yahoo.com and mx2.mail.yahoo.com have a priority of 1 so they will be preferred over mx4.mail.yahoo.com, which will only be used in the event the other two servers are unavailable.

NOTE *Not all options of the* host *utility are discussed here. For more detailed coverage of all of the command-line options consult the* host *man page, either via the Webmin man pages interface or from the command line.*

The -v option enables *verbose* output, which is in a format compatible with BINDs own master file format, so it can be directly imported into a BIND configuration without additional parsing or modification. The -t option allows you to specify the query type to make of the name server. There are many query types, but common types that may be useful include cname, which lists the *canonical name* entries for the host if available, and the ns type which lists the authoritative name servers for the host.

One of the more verbose options of host is the -a option, which will list all available fields for the host, including all A records, CNAME records, NS records, and so on. Using host with this option against your own name server is a good way to ensure it is providing all of the information you expect.

Using dig

The dig, or *domain information groper*, provides the ability to query any domain server for information about the domains it serves. It operates in both an interactive mode and a batch query mode. Using dig is much like using host, in that in its simplest mode you enter just the command and the name to lookup. However, dig is more verbose by default and presents a much wider array or information, though in a somewhat less readable form.

Just like host, it is possible to query your default system resolver, or you can query a name server specified on the command line. For example, I could query my local name server about the nostarch.com domain.

```
[joe@delilah joe]$ dig @192.168.1.1 nostarch.com

; <<>> DiG 9.2.1 <<>> @192.168.1.1 nostarch.com
;; global options:  printcmd
;; Got answer:
;; ->>HEADER<<- opcode: QUERY, status: NOERROR, id: 21448
;; flags: qr rd ra; QUERY: 1, ANSWER: 1, AUTHORITY: 2, ADDITIONAL: 2

;; QUESTION SECTION:
;nostarch.com.                  IN      A

;; ANSWER SECTION:
nostarch.com.           8585    IN      A       66.80.60.21

;; AUTHORITY SECTION:
nostarch.com.           8585    IN      NS      ns1.megapath.net.
nostarch.com.           8585    IN      NS      ns2.megapath.net.

;; ADDITIONAL SECTION:
ns1.megapath.net.       123591  IN      A       66.80.130.23
ns2.megapath.net.       123591  IN      A       66.80.131.5

;; Query time: 281 msec
;; SERVER: 192.168.1.1#53(192.168.1.1)
;; WHEN: Sat Oct 26 19:42:45 2002
;; MSG SIZE  rcvd: 126
```

Above, we have a large amount of information, though not all of it is generally useful to us. First is the version of dig and the command-line options we specified. The comes some status information, including the NOERROR designator that indicates the name was retrieve without error. If the domain did not exist, or could not be queried, there would be an NXDOMAIN error or some other error. Next are the flags of the query. In this case, we have one query and one answer which are contained in the QUESTION and ANSWER sections below it. The next two items inform us of the number of AUTHORITY and ADDITIONAL sections that follow. In this case, the authority section gives us the primary and secondary name servers for this domain, ns1.megapath.com and ns2.megapath.com, and the additional section provides the IP addresses of those name servers.

The last few lines give the time the query required, the server that was queried and the port on which it was queried, the time and date on which the query was made, and the size of the message received from the name server.

Like host, dig has a mode in which you can query all of the information available about the domain. This can be done by appending the ANY argument to the end of the command line. Furthermore, the options NS, MX, CNAME, and so on are also available and do just what you would expect.

9

FTP SERVER

The File Transfer Protocol is a lightweight protocol for transferring files over a network. It is a client-server protocol requiring an FTP server, such as WU-FTPD [http://www.wu-ftpd.org/] and a client such as ncftp [http://www.ncftp.com/]. WU-FTPD is the most popular FTP server on the Internet, and though it has had its problems (primarily security-related), it is a very feature-rich FTP daemon.

WU-FTPD has been in constant development for over ten years and has attracted a lot of users and developers during that time. This chapter covers all of the configuration files involved in running a WU-FTPD installation (Figure 9-1). It is highly recommended that you make sure your FTP server is running the latest version (2.6.2 is the version as of this writing), as all earlier versions have widely known security exploits.

Figure 9-1: WU-FTPD Server

Users and Classes

Here you configure the various user and group features of the ftpaccess file (Figure 9-2). For more on this file and its structure, see the ftpaccess man page [http://www.wu-ftpd.org/man/ftpaccess.html].

User classes

Here you define a class of users, and the networks from which they are allowed to log in. Note that the default includes a class all for users of all types (real, guest, and anonymous) which matches all networks with the *. This option configures the class directive.

Unix users and UIDs to treat as guests and Unix groups and GIDs to treat as guests

Here, you can define users and groups who would ordinarily qualify as real users who will be treated as guests, or anonymous users. In other words, a chroot will be done, and the user will not be permitted to use the USER or PASS commands. The users home directory must be properly set up, as an anonymous FTP directory would be. These two options correspond to the guestuser and guestgroup directives.

Unix users and UIDs not to treat as guests and Unix groups and GIDs not to treat as guests

If your server is configured to treat all users as guests, then you can selectively allow a few users to be treated as real users (i.e., with access to the system directories, and without performing a chroot). These options configure the realuser and realgroup directives.

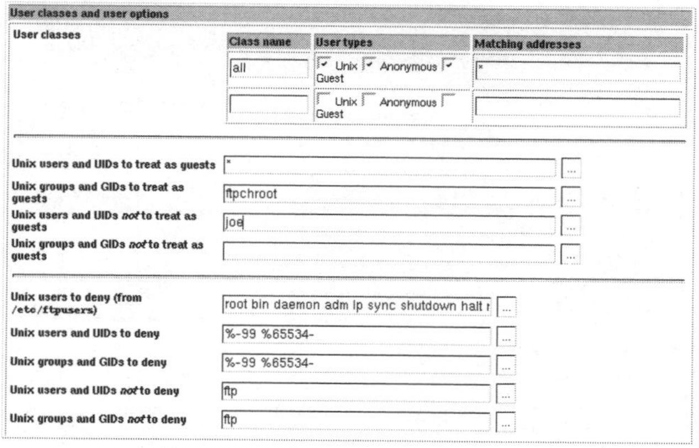

Figure 9-2: Users and Classes

Unix users to deny (from /etc/ftpusers)

This is simply a list of users to deny access to the server to. This information is drawn from the /etc/ftpusers file. Adding to this list will add to the file. Note that if the next two sets of options are used to precisely control access to the FTP server (i.e., by blocking all access except for explicitly permitted users), then the ftpusers file becomes unnecessary.

Unix users and UIDs to deny and Unix groups and GIDs to deny

Here you can enter any users or groups you would like to deny access to. These options configure the deny-uid and deny-gid directives.

Unix users and UIDs not to deny and Unix groups and GIDs not to deny

These options can be used to negate the above options, if you chose to disallow all access from all users and groups. In this way, you could allow only explicitly configured users to access the server.

Messages and Banners

WU-FTPD provides a simple mechanism for informing users of important information regarding the server, or files on the server. As in the previous section, this page configures certain aspects of the ftpaccess (Figure 9-3).

Message files

This option configures the messages that will be displayed on login to the server. The default on many systems is to display a message contained in the file welcome.msg in the root FTP directory, if it exists, as soon as someone logs in. Also, when entering a directory the server will check for the existence of a file called .message in the new directory. If it exists, it will be displayed. Both of these are optional, and the names and actions can be changed at will. This option configures the message directive.

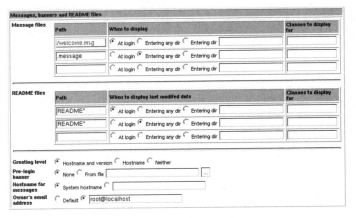

Figure 9-3: Messages and Banners

README files

Here, you can configure the behavior of the server with regard to README files. This, too, is set up by default on most systems. In this case, any file beginning README will be displayed to the user, both on logging into the server, and upon entering a new directory. This option configures the readme directive.

Greeting level

Here you can select how much information about your server will be presented to the user. This can include the host name, the server version, and nothing. This can be a mild security risk, as the first step to cracking a box is to figure out what software and version is running. However, if the system is kept up to date (religiously), and the system is otherwise secured, this should not be an issue. Many paranoid types (and there's no harm in being paranoid in a world where script kiddies are a dime a dozen) will disable all specific software and version information on all of their publicly accessible services. This option configures the greeting directive.

Pre-login banner

Here you configure a banner that will be displayed before the user is prompted for a user name and password. This option can cause problems with non-compliant FTP client software. This option configures the banner directive.

Hostname for messages

This will be the host name that is printed in the greeting message, and anytime the host name is inserted into a message for the user. This option configures the hostname directive.

Owner's email address

Here you can set the email address of the servers maintainer. This will be presented as the contact email for this server. This option configures the email directive.

Limits and Access Control

This page provides access to various resource limits, as well as provides system level access controls. If you wish to limit the system or network resources your server uses, this is the page to start with.

Deny access from

Here you may deny access to the server from any number of IP addresses, and you can provide a filename of a text error message file to send the client in the event they have been denied access based on this rule. This option configures the deny directive.

Concurrent user limits

Here you may limit the number of concurrent users from a given user class. To configure this option, you must provide a class for which the rule will apply, and the maximum number of users to allow to log in simultaneously. Next, you can choose times in UUCP L.sys format. This format is pretty simple, you choose the days by entering the first two letters with the first capitalized (i.e., Su for Sunday, or Mo for Monday), or Any for all days. Then the time is set in military format (1000 for 10AM, 2300 for 11PM, etc.). So to limit users during business hours, for example, we could enter MoTuWeThFr0800-1800. This option configures the limit directive.

File and data transfer limits

This option provides access to the transfer limits features of WU-FTPD. It is possible to limit user's downloads based on files or data or both. You may also configure limits for outgoing and incoming transfers, and to which classes the limits should apply. This option configures the file-limit and data-limit directives.

Deny access to files and Allow access to files even if denied

If there are files in your directory tree that you do not wish to be retrievable by one or more classes of users, you may enter it here. The path may be relative to the FTP chroot, or it may be an absolute path (select which using the **Relative to chroot** option). This option correlates to the noretrieve directive. The **Allow access to files even if denied** option allows you to unselect files that would ordinarily be made inaccessible by the previous option. This option correlates to the allow-retrieve directive.

Anonymous session limit Guest session limit

Anonymous users and guest users can be limited to the specified time. This option correlates to the limit-time directive.

Maximum login failures

This option allows you to define the number of failed login attempts to allow before a "too many login failures" message is presented to the user and the FTP connection is closed. This option configures the loginfails directive and defaults to 5.

Can switch groups?

If this option is turned on, a user may switch to a new group after login. The user will then have the privileges of the new group. This configures the private directive and defaults to off.

Networking

Here you configure a few of the networking-related options for WU-FTPD.

TCP window sizes

This option configures the window size of TCP packets for the data connection. This may be useful if clients are PPP dial-up users, as a smaller TCP window can provide faster transfers. Usually this does not need to be modified. This option correlates to the tcpwindow directive.

Addresses for PASV connections

Allows control of the address reported in response to a PASV command. This does not alter the address that the daemon listens on, only the address it reports to clients on a passive connection. This option configures the passive address directive.

Ports for PASV connections

Configures the port numbers which may be used for passive data connections. You may select port ranges for specific networks. When a control connection matches the network specified, a randomly selected port from the range provided will be used for the daemon to listen on. This feature allows firewalls that limit open ports to be used, while still provided FTP services. This option corresponds to the passive ports directive.

Logging

Here you configure the logging behavior of WU-FTPD (figure 9-4). Logging for this daemon is quite simple, and doesn't present nearly the options of servers like Apache or BIND. Nonetheless, it is possible to gather a large amount of useful information from your FTP daemon.

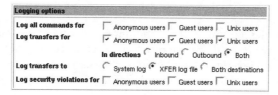

Figure 9-4: Logging

Log all commands for

Selecting one or more types of users here will provide a log of every single command executed by a user of the given type. This option configures the log commands directive.

Log transfers for

As above, you may select one of more types of users to log for. This option when enabled will log every file transfer made by any users of a given type. This option configures the log transfers directive.

Log transfers to

This option sets where transfer logs will be stored. If System log, transfers will be logged via the syslog daemon to the standard system log (configured by your syslog configuration). If XFER log, transfers will be logged to a separate transfer log file. This option configures the log syslog directive.

Log security violations for

It is possible to configure your server to log attempts by users of a given type to perform actions which are denied by the server. This option configures the log security directive.

Aliases and Paths

This page allows you to configure aliases that the FTP daemon will use when a client issues a cd command. If an alias is defined, in the **CD directory aliases** section, the **Alias name** is the directory name that the client can enter, while the **Alias to directory** field defines to what directory the client will switch to. So, for example, if the **Alias name** is bin and the **Alias to directory** is /home/ftp/pub/usr/local/bin, then when the client enters cd bin he will be directed to /home/ftp/pub/usr/local/bin.

Next comes the **CD directory search path**. With this option, you can configure any number of directories that can be in the search path. For example, if a client enters cd bin, and there is no bin directory in the current directory, then the server will check the directories in the search path. If the directory requested exists in one of those directories, the client will be directed there.

Anonymous FTP

WU-FTPD provides a number of capabilities for serving anonymous (i.e., non-authenticated) users. And anonymous user generally has very limited capabilities on the server, and is often unable to upload files, or modify any content on the server. This page provides access to many of the features related to anonymous users on your FTP server.

Anonymous FTP root directories

This option allows you to configure the root directory for anonymous users of a given class. So setting this to /home/ftp for the all class, will cause the server to chroot to the directory specified for any anonymous user. The initial directory (somewhere above the chrooted directory) will then be the home directory indicated in /etc/passwd for the user ftp. The server will then Using this option, is becomes possible for local network users to be chrooted to a different directory than users from the Internet, for example. This option configures the anonymous-root directive.

Guest root directories

This option, much like the previous option, configures the chroot behavior of the server. In this case, however, it configures for guest users who have logged in with a valid user name and password. So, it is possible to set the chroot environment to /home, causing users to be unable to traverse the directory tree below that point. The initial working directory, unless otherwise specified, will be the users home directory specified in the /etc/passwd. This option configures the guest-root directive.

Unix groups for anonymous users

Here you may configure the default UNIX group whose permissions will apply to anonymous users of a given class. This option configures the autogroup directive.

Anonymous FTP password check

The server always performs a user name and password authentication check, before permitting access. The convention is to accept a blank user name, and the valid email address of the user. Here you can configure how strict the checking of the given email address is, and whether to issue a warning, but still allow the login, or deny access, if the email address is invalid for some reason. This option configures the passwd-check directive.

Anonymous FTP passwords to deny

If you wish to be more stringent about disallowing generated passwords, such as those presented by some web browsers, you may enter those addresses here. This will not prevent browser client users from accessing your server, it will merely force them to configure their browser to provide a legitimate email address. This option configures the deny-email directive.

Permissions

This page allows you to configure the permissions that users of each type will have for given classes. You may create any number of permissions rules.

Command restrictions

This section creates a number of different types of rules to regulate the various commands that a user may be able to perform on your server. The **Command** options are chmod, delete, overwrite, rename, and umask, which match the directive names. You may choose a user type, and a class for each rule.

Disallowed upload filenames

Here you may specify regular expressions to match filenames that may not be uploaded by a specified type or list of types and classes. The option also allows you to specify the path to a message file to be displayed if an upload is disallowed by the rule. By default, the message is located in /etc/pathmsg, and the server will revert to this if the path you provide is invalid. This option corresponds to the path-filter directive.

Miscellaneous Options

This page provides access to a few of the configuration options that don't quite fit anywhere else. You are unlikely to need to alter any of these settings from their defaults.

Long listing command, Short listing command, Plain listing

Defines the command to be used for each of the types of file listing that a user may specify. The defaults are usually sane, and should only be modified if necessary. These options correlate to the lslong, lsshort, and lsplain directives.

Shutdown notification file

Here you configure the path to the message that the server will display prior to shutting down. This option correlates to the shutdown directive and usually defaults to /etc/shutmsg.

Service process nice level

This sets the niceness level for the FTP daemon process. This may be set per class of user, or for all classes. This option correlates to the nice directive.

Default umask for uploaded files

This option defines the umask that is applied to uploaded files by users of the given class. This option correlates to the defumask directive.

10

POSTFIX

Postfix is an efficient and feature-rich mail server that was designed by Wietse Venema at the IBM T.J. Watson Research Center (Figure 10-1). It was intended to be a replacement for the popular Sendmail. While it still represents only a small percentage of mail server installations worldwide, its popularity is growing rapidly, due to its simple configuration, secure implementation, and high performance architecture.

Also, because Postfix is designed to behave outwardly like Sendmail, it is a mostly drop-in replacement for the older, larger, and slower mail server. It does lack some of the obscure features of Sendmail, but the features it lacks are rarely used by the vast majority of users, so they are not often missed.

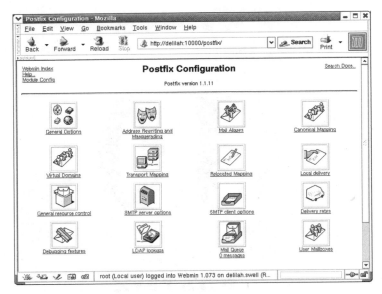

Figure 10-1: Postfix

The Postfix project, originally named VMailer (fortunately for everyone, the name was changed before release due to legal entanglements of the VMailer name), is designed as a group of related but separate executable components, providing security through segmentation. Smaller parts are easier to debug, as well. The Internet home of Postfix is www.postfix.org [http://www.postfix.org]. Postfix is an ideal mail server choice for new mail administrators, and even experienced Sendmail administrators might find its simplicity appealing. Because it provides a quite compatible Sendmail-ish exterior, and provides programs of the same names (such as `sendmail` for sending mail, `mailq` for managing the queue, etc.), and can utilize the same type of aliases and forwarding files that Sendmail uses, it is possible to replace Sendmail without reconfiguring existing mail-related tools, or rewriting local scripts. After such a switch, local users may not even notice the difference.

NOTE   *The previous statements should not be viewed as an endorsement of Postfix as being a better mail transport agent than Sendmail. The two projects have different emphasis, and have had very different development models. Sendmail has been in use all over the world for over 20 years in one form or another, and thus has an extremely large head start on Postfix with regard to maturity, available documentation, number of experienced administrators, and support tools. Postfix is only a few years old and has much more limited supporting documentation and tools to enhance it. The decision for which mail transfer agent is appropriate for your network will be dictated by the requirements and the availability of local expertise.*

General Options

The **General Options** page configures a number of options regarding the general behavior of Postfix. Specifically, most of the configuration options that impact all users and all messages are configured here. Postfix, keeping with its philosophy of simplicity, usually requires only a few configuration file changes to get a mail server running efficiently and securely.

The **General Options** page is divided into two parts. The upper section is labeled **Most Useful General Options** and the lower section **Other General Options**. In many standard installations, it may be possible to start up a Postfix installation with just configuration of one or more of the three directives in the upper section. Unless otherwise stated, all of the options on this page correspond to directives in the main.cf file in the Postfix configuration directory.

Most Useful General Options

The three options in this section are, in some installations, the only options that need to be altered to get Postfix running for both sending and receiving email (Figure 10-2).

Figure 10-2: Most Useful General Options

What domain to use in outbound mail

Here you may specify the domain or host name to use to identify the source on outgoing mail. Postfix defaults to using the host name of the server, but you most likely will want it to identify mail as coming from your domain name instead. If your mail server will be accepting mail for a large number of users under a single domain name, you will most likely configure domain name here, and create a domain-wide alias database to map user names to their respective local mail servers. This option correlates to the myorigin Postfix directive.

What domain to receive mail for

This option accepts a list of domains and addresses to receive mail as its final destination. In other words, when mail reaches the server destined for addresses in this field, it will deliver the mail to a local user, rather than forward it to another mail server. By default, this is all configured addresses on the machine as well as localhost within the local domain. You may specify any number of domains or host names separated by commas, or you may provide a full path to a file containing similar entries. The variables $myhostname and $mydomain may be used to represent those concepts to Postfix automatically. The ability of Postfix to use such variables throughout its configuration files makes it easier to maintain a number of Postfix servers with very similar configurations. This option correlates to the mydestination directive.

What trouble to report to the postmaster

Postfix provides the ability to select what types of error messages will be mailed to the designated *postmaster* of the mail server. Assuming you have setup a postmaster alias that directs mail to a real person, Postfix will send reports of all of the types of trouble designated here. The available classes are:

bounce When this option is selected, whenever a message is undeliverable, a bounce message (called a *single bounce message* will be sent to the sender of the message and the local postmaster. For the sake of privacy only the headers will be sent in the message to the postmaster. If the first bounce to the sender is returned as undeliverable, a *double bounce message* will be sent to the postmaster with the entire contents of the first single bounce message.

2bounce Causes double bounce messages to be sent to the postmaster.

delay If the delivery of a message is delayed, the postmaster will receive a notice, along with the headers of the delayed message.

policy Notifies the postmaster of messages that were rejected due to a unsolicited commercial email policy restriction. The complete transcript of the SMTP session is sent.

protocol Notifies the postmaster of protocol errors, or client requests that contained unimplemented commands. The complete transcript of the SMTP session is included in the message.

resource Informs the postmaster of undelivered mail due to resource problems, such as a queue file write error.

software Notifies the postmaster of mail not delivered due to software failures.

This option correlates to the notify_classes directive, and defaults to reporting only problems that usually indicate a misconfiguration or serious problem (specifically resource and software). In some high load environments, altering this to include bounce notifications could lead to a large number of notices.

Other General Options

The lower section of this page is devoted to global options which are less likely to need to be altered (Figure 10-3). In many installations these options will remain at their defaults.

Send outgoing mail via

This option configures whether outgoing mail should be delivered directly to the recipients mail server, or if a parent mail gateway should be used as an intermediary. If the server is behind a firewall, behind a network address translating router/gateway, or similar, it may be necessary to use an intermediary server to achieve reliable service. Many mail servers on the Internet will not accept mail from a server that does not have a working DNS entry and a routable IP address, in order to help prevent spam from forged addresses. Also, local network use policy may require the use of an intermediary for logging, virus scanning, or other purposes that require aggregation of outgoing mail traffic onto a central server. This option corresponds to the relayhost directive and defaults to sending mail directly.

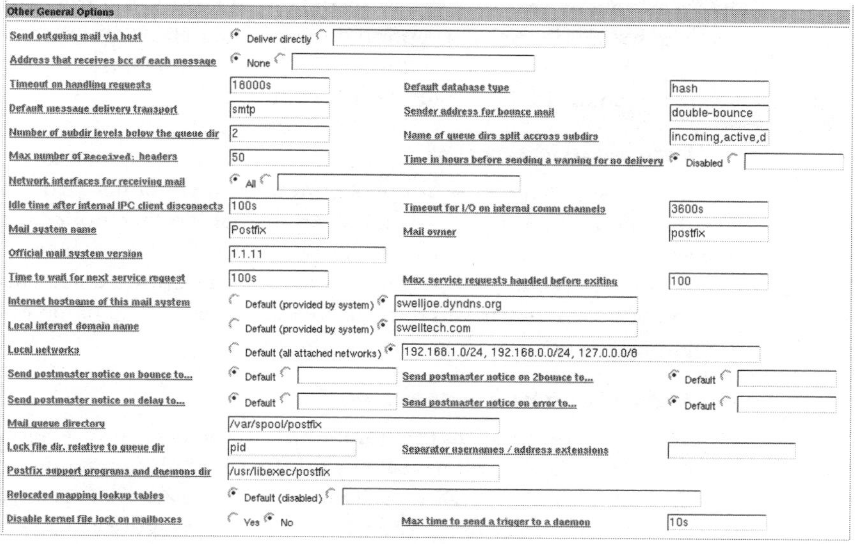

Figure 10-3: Other General Options

Address that receives bcc of each message

With this option, an optional email address may be specified that will receive a copy of every message that enters the Postfix system, excluding locally generated bounce messages. This can represent a breach of privacy in many circumstances, and may be illegal in some countries. It is advisable to be especially cautious about utilizing this option. It can be useful in some environments, however, where central archival of email is valuable for legal or technical reasons. This option correlates to the always_bcc directive and defaults to none.

Timeout on handling requests

This option determines how long a Postfix daemon will wait on a request to complete before it assumes the daemon has locked up, at which time the daemon will be killed. This option corresponds to the daemon_timeout and defaults to 18000 seconds.

Default database type

This option determines the type of database to use in the postalias and postmap commands. This option corresponds to the default_database_type directive and the default depends on the OS and installed system libraries at the time of building Postfix. Ordinarily on UNIX systems this will be hash or dbm.

Default message delivery transport

The term *delivery transport* refers to the protocol, or language, used to deliver the message from one mail server to another. The transport on modern systems is nearly always snmp, and this is the default in Postfix, but there are still a few legacy uucp systems in use. This option is merely the default choice, when no transport is explicitly selected for the destination in the optional transport table. This option corresponds to the default_transport directive.

Sender address for bounce mail

In the event a message double-bounces, or first bounces from the recipient and then bounces from the sender when the first bounce notice is sent, the message will be sent to this address. All messages to this address will be silently discarded. In this way bounce-loops can be avoided. This option correlates to the double_bounce_sender and defaults to double-bounce. The name may be any arbitrary name, but must be unique.

Number of subdir levels below the queue dir

This option configures the number of subdirectory levels below the configured queue directories will be used by Postfix for mail storage. Because of the design of the traditional UNIX filesystem, which includes UFS used by all modern BSD systems and the Linux ext2 and ext3 filesystems, performance becomes measurably slower when an extremely large number of files are stored in a single directory. Thus, programs that generate a large number of files often provide the ability to split files out to a number of subdirectories to keep lookups fast. This option correlates to the hash_queue_depth directive and defaults to 2, which is suitable for most moderate and even relatively large installations. Because the number of directories in use increases the search time for object seeks, using a too high value here can be harmful to performance.

Name of queue dirs split across subdirs

Postfix uses a number of queues to organize messages with varying states and destinations. Each of these queues can be configured to use hashed subdirectories or not. If a queue is selected here, it will be stored in a hashed subdirectory. In some cases, a queue mus not be listed here as performance will be severely impacted, specifically the world-writable mail drop directory. The defer log file directory, on the other hand must be stored in hashed directories or performance will suffer. This option corresponds to the hash_queue_names directive and defaults to incoming,active,deferred,bounce,defer,flush and it is rarely necessary or beneficial to alter this configuration.

Max number of Received: headers

A message that contains more Received: headers than this will bounce. An extremely large number of this header may indicate a mail loop or a misconfigured mail server somewhere in the path of this message. This option correlates to the hopcount_limit directive and defaults to 50. This value rarely needs to be altered from its default.

Time in hours before sending a warning for no delivery

If a message cannot be delivered immediately, it will be queued for later delivery. If after this number of hours, the message still cannot be delivered, a warning will be sent to the sender notifying them that the server has been unable to send the message for a specified time. This correlates to the delay_warning_time directive and defaults to not sending a warning.

Network interfaces for receiving mail

This option configures the network addresses on which Postfic will accept mail deliveries. By default Postfix will accept mail on every active interface. Here, Postfix will accept the variables discussed earlier. This option configures the inet_interfaces directive.

Idle time after internal IPC client disconnects

This option sets the time in seconds after which an internal IPC client disconnects. This allows servers to terminate voluntarily. This feature is used by the address resolution and rewriting clients. This option correlates to the idle_time directive and defaults to 100s. This option should probably never need to be altered under normal circumstances.

Timeout for I/O on internal comm channels

This option determines the amount of time in seconds the server will wait for I/O on internal communication channels before breaking. If the timeout is exceeded, the server aborts with a fatal error. This directive corresponds to the ipc_timeout directive and defaults to 3600 seconds, or 60 minutes.

Mail system name

This option identifies the mail server system in use to connecting users. It will be used in the smtpd_banner which is sent in Received: headers, the SMTP greeting banner, and in bounced mail. Some security experts, who promote security through obscurity, suggest anonymizing all server software to prevent potential crackers from being able to identify the software in use on the server. It is probably not the best use of an administrators time or effort in most environments, however, and many other security tactics are more effective, without negatively impacting the ability to track software problems. This option correlates to the mail_name directive and defaults to Postfix.

Mail owner

This option specifies the owner of the Postfix mail queue, and most of the Postfix daemon processes. This user should be unique on the system, and share no groups with other accounts or own any other files or processes on the system. After binding to the SMTP port (25), postfix can then drop root privileges and become the user specified here for all new daemon processes. Because of this, if the Postfix daemon is ever compromised the exploiter will only have access to mail and a few other files. Obviously it is good to avoid this as well, but it is certainly better than a root exploit which would allow the exploiter to access and alter anything on the system. This option correlates to the mail_owner directive and defaults to postfix.

Official mail system version

This parameter configures the version number that will be reported by Postfix in the SMTP greeting banner, among other things. This correlates to the mail_version directive and defaults to the version of Postfix that is installed. Once again, security by obscurity promoters may encourage obfuscation of this value.

Time to wait for next service request

A Postfix daemon process will exit after the time specified here, if it does not receive a new request for service during that time. This option corresponds to the max_idle directive and defaults to 100s. This directive does not impact the queue manager daemon process.

Max service requests handled before exiting

This option configures the maximum number of requests that a single Postfix daemon process will answer before exiting. This option configures the max_use directive and defaults to 100.

Internet hostname of this mail system

This option specifies the Internet host name of the mail server. By default this value will be set to the fully qualified host name of the server, as determined by a call to gethostname(). This option sets the $myhostname variable which is used in the defaults to many other options. This option correlates to the myhostname directive.

Local Internet domain name

This option corresponds to the mydomain directive and defaults to the contents of the $myhostname variable minus the first component. This option defines the $mydomain variable and is used in a number of other configuration option defaults.

Local networks

Postfix provides a flexible set of options to help prevent UCE, or other unauthorized uses of the mail server. This option defines what networks will be considered to be local by Postfix. The value is used to determine whether a client is a local client or a remote client. Policies can be more relaxed for local clients. This option configures the mynetworks directive and defaults to a list of all networks attached to the server. For example, if the server has an IP of 192.168.1.48, and a netmask of 255.255.255.0, all of the 192.168.1.0 network will be considered local. If you would like stricter control, or the ability to treat other network blocks as local clients, you can specify them here in the form of network/mask pairs (i.e., 172.16.0.0/16. Network/mask pairs may be inserted from a separate file, if preferred, by specifying the absolute path to the file here.

Send postmaster notice on bounce to...

This option configures the user name or email address to whom bounce notices will be sent. This option correlates to the bounce_notice_recipient and is set to postmaster by default.

Send postmaster notice on 2bounce to...

This option configures the user name or email address to whom second bounce messages will be sent. This allows an administrator to watch for second bounces warnings more closely than first bounce messages, because first bounces are far more common and less likely to indicate serious problems. The option configures the 2bounce_notice_recipient directive and defaults to postmaster.

Send postmaster notice on delay to...

This option configures where delay warnings will be sent. This option correlates to the delay_notice_recipient directive and defaults to postmaster.

Send postmaster notice on error to...

Specifies where error warnings will be sent. This option correlates to the error_notice_recipient directive and defaults to postmaster.

Mail queue directory

This specifies the directory where Postfix will store queued mail. This will also be the root directory for Postfix daemons that run in a chroot environment. The queue is where messages that are awaiting delivery are stored, thus enough space to accommodate your user mail load should be provided in this directory. This option correlates to the queue_directory directive and usually defaults to a sensible location for your OS. Many Linux systems will have the mail queue in /var/spool/mail or /var/spool/postfix.

Lock file dir, relative to queue dir

This option configures the location of the Postfix lock directory. It should be specified relative to the queue directory, and generally will simply be a subdirectory of the queue directory. This option configures the process_id_directory directive and defaults to pid.

Separator between user names and address extensions

This option specifies the separator character between user names and address extensions. This option correlates to the recipient_delimiter directive and defaults to using no delimiter. This option impacts **Canonical Mapping**, **Relocated Mapping**, and **Virtual Domains**.

Postfix support programs and daemons dir

This option specifies the directory where Postfix will look for its various support programs and daemons. The directory should be owned by root. This option correlates to the program_directory directive and defaults vary depending on installation method and OS variant. On many Linux systems this will be /usr/libexec/postfix.

Relocated mapping lookup tables

Postfix can provide a relocation notice in response to messages sent to users who no longer receive mail from this server. If enabled, this option specifies the location of the file containing a table of contact information for users who no longer exist on this system. By default this feature is disabled. This option correlates to the relocated_maps directive. If enabled a reasonable choice for this option might be /etc/postfix/relocated.

Disable kernel file lock on mailboxes

On Sun workstations, kernel file locks can cause problems, because the mailtool program holds an exclusive lock whenever its window is open. Users of other OS variants, or Sun systems where no Sun mail software is in use, may ignore this option. This option correlates to the sun_mailtool_compatibility directive and defaults to No.

Max time to send a trigger to a daemon

This option specifies the maximum amount of time allowed to send a trigger to a Postfix daemon. This limit helps prevent programs from getting hung when the mail system is under extremely heavy load. This option correlates to the opts_trigger_timeout directive and defaults to 10s.

Address Rewriting and Masquerading

Postfix offers a relatively easy to use, and flexible, address rewriting system, allowing it to act as a mail gateway for a large network, or as a gateway between legacy mail systems and the Internet at large (Figure 10-4).

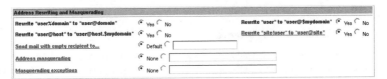

Figure 10-4: Address Rewriting and Masquerading

NOTE   *The options on this page are also discussed on the Postfix Configuration - Address Manipulation [http://www.postfix.org/rewrite.html] page at the Postfix homepage. It is worth reading if advanced address rewriting is required in your mail system.*

Rewrite "user%domain" to "user@domain"

This option is useful for some legacy systems that used strange address trickery such as, *user%domain@otherdomain*. It is not generally useful in modern environments, but it is not harmful so usually defaults to Yes. This option correlates to the allow_percent_hack directive.

Rewrite "user" to "user@$mydomain"

This option configures how Postfix will handle an address that has no domain name in the destination. If enabled, it will append the value of $mydomain to the address. This option correlates to the append_at_myorigin directive and defaults to Yes. Because most Postfix components expect addresses to be of the form user@domain it is probably never appropriate to disable this feature.

Rewrite "user@host" to "user@host.$mydomain"

This option configures whether simple host addresses will have the value of $mydomain appended to them. This option correlates to the append_dot_mydomain directive and defaults to Yes. Some administrators may find that this explicit rewrite has unexpected consequences, but it is very rarely a problem.

Rewrite "site!user" to "user@site"

Legacy UUCP networks use a different addressing format than modern SMTP systems. This option enables Postfix to convert the old-style address to a modern address for delivery via the standard SMTP protocol. This option configures the swap_bangpath directive and defaults to Yes.

Send mail with empty recipient to...

The specifies the destination of mail that is undeliverable. Typically, this will be bounce notifications and other error messages. This option correlates to the empty_address_recipient directive and defaults to MAILER-DAEMON, which by default is simply an alias to postmaster.

Address masquerading

Address masquerading is a method whereby hosts behind the gateway mail server may be hidden, and all mail will appear to have originated from the gateway server. If enabled, the host and/or subdomain portion of an address will be stripped off and only the domain specified here will be included in the address. For example, if $mydomain is specified here, an outgoing mail from joe@joesmachine.swelltech.com would become simply joe@swelltech.com, assuming the $mydomain variable contains swelltech.com. This option correlates to the masquerade_domains directive and it is disabled by default.

Masquerade exceptions

It is possible to skip over the masquerade rules define above for some user names. The names to be excepted from those rules can be entered here. This option corresponds to the masquerade_exceptions directive and by default no exceptions are made.

Mail Aliases

Mail aliases provide a means to redirect mail to local recipients. Specifically, it allows mail destined for a number of different addresses to be delivered to a single mailbox. A common use for this is to direct mail for users like postmaster to a real person. This page is divided into two sections. The upper section labeled **Aliases Options** contains the location and format of the alias files that Postfix should use to construct its alias databases and specifies the type of database to use. The lower section provides a list of all configured aliases on the system, and what the alias maps to.

Aliases Options

The following options specify the location and types of alias databases that Postfix will use:

Alias databases used by the local delivery agent

This option sets the filenames that Postfix will use for local delivery alias translation. The filename will have a suffix appended to it based on the file type. This option correlates to the alias_maps directive and the default is system dependent. Some common defaults include hash:/etc/aliases or hash:/etc/postfix/aliases. The first part of the entry, preceding the colon, is the type of database to use, which will be one of hash for systems with a modern Berkeley DB implementation, dbm for older style systems that only have dbm available, or nis for systems that run NIS. The after-colon portion of the entry is the path to the filename from which the database name is derived. The databases will be built from the contents of the flat files by Postfix on startup, or when running the newaliases command.

Alias databases built by Postfix

This option, closely related to the above, specifies the alias database file(s) that are built when the newaliases or sendmail -bi commands are run. These commands generate the alias database from the flat file in the above option, in order to speed alias lookups performed by Postfix. Because there may be thousands of aliases on a large mail server, importing them into a database is necessary to maintain efficiency. This option correlates to the alias_database directive. Defaults are system dependent, but will commonly be the same as the above option, with the appropriate database file suffix appended.

Aliases

This section of the page provides a list of all configured aliases. To edit an alias, click on the name of the alias. To create an alias, click on the **Create a new alias** button and fill in the alias Name, and Alias to... fields. Whenever the aliases files have been modified, it is necessary to recreate the aliases database files as well in order for the changes to take effect. When using Webmin this step is performed automatically, and no additional steps are required.

Canonical Mapping

Canonical mapping in Postfix is used for modifying mail in the incoming queue, and it alters both the message headers and the message envelope information for local or remote mail. This mapping can be useful to replace login names with *Firstname.Lastname* style addresses, or to clean up odd addresses produced by legacy mail systems.

Canonical Mapping Tables

If you use any canonical mapping tables, they must be specified in the first section of the **Canonical Mapping** module. After defining them, you can edit them from the second section of the module.

Address mapping lookup tables

This option specifies the location of the optional canonical address mapping table file. This mapping is applied to both sender and recipient addresses, in both envelopes and headers. This option configures the canonical_maps directive and is disabled by default. Much like the aliases files discussed in the last section, canonical mapping files are specified by a database type and a filename. The accepted database types depend on your operating system, and installed components. Usually hash and dbm are used as the database type. A common choice for this value, then, might be hash:/etc/postfix/canonical.

Tables for RECIPIENT addresses

This parameter configures address mapping only on recipient addresses, and not sender addresses. Mapping is performed on both envelopes and headers. These lookups are performed before the above configured **Address mapping lookup tables**. This option correlates to the recipient_canonical_maps directive and is disabled by default.

Tables for SENDER addresses

Similar to the previous option, this configures mapping for sender addresses only, and not recipient addresses. Both envelope and header information is modified. This option correlates to the sender_canonical_maps directive and by default is disabled.

Editing Canonical Mappings

Once a filename is selected for any of the canonical mapping tables, it may be edited by clicking the appropriate **Edit** buttons. A new page will open, listing any existing mappings and allowing creation of new mappings. The format of mappings in all files is the same.

Canonical mappings may seem, on the surface, to be similar to aliases or virtual domains. However, they are quite distinct and are useful for other purposes. While aliases merely make a decision about which user will receive an email, and virtual domains only impact the envelope address, the canonical mapping alters both the envelope address and the SMTP header address. This change can be used to make mail appear to come from a different user or domain, or direct mail to a different user or domain by changing the address on the message.

For example, if I have a number of local subdomains, but would like all mail to appear to originate from a single domain, it is possible to create a canonical mapping to make the translations. In the **Edit a Map** page, the Name will be a subdomain that is to be mapped to the domain, such as @lab.swelltech.com. The Mapts to... value will simply be the domain I'd like this subdomain converted to, @swelltech.com. After saving the mapping and applying changes, all outgoing mail from lab.swelltech.com will appear to originate from swelltech.com.

Virtual Domains

Virtual domains functionality in Postfix provides a means to redirect messages to different locations by altering the message envelope address. The header address is not altered by a virtual domain mapping. While some functionality of virtual domains overlaps with features available in aliases, virtual domains can be used for local or non-local addresses, while aliases can only be used for local address.

Domain mapping lookup tables

Much like aliases tables and canonical mapping tables discussed in the previous sections, this is simply the path to a file containing the mapping tables for virtual domains. This is usually something along the lines of hash:/etc/postfix/virtual, and must be converted to a database format for use in Postfix. Webmin will perform the database generation step for you.

Transport Mapping

The term transport refers to the mechanism used to deliver a piece of email. Specifically, SMTP and UUCP are mail transports that are supported by Postfix. Transport mapping can be used for a number of purposes, including SMTP to UUCP gatewaying, operating Postfix on a firewall with forwarding to an internal mail server, and so on.

Transport mapping lookup tables

This option configures the path to a file containing one or more transport mappings. These tables are much like the mapping tables discussed already, and are converted to a database and used by Postfix in the same way. This option correlates to the transport_maps directive. This feature is disabled by default. A common value for this option is /etc/postfix/transport.

To create a new mapping, first define the mapping file. Then click **Add a mapping**. If your goal is to redirect mail to an protected internal host from Postfix running on a firewall, for example, you could enter the outside domain name into the **Name** field, swelltech.com and then enter into the **Maps to** field the address of the internal machine, smtp:privatehost.swelltech.com. To further improve upon this, local delivery on this machine could be disabled, and increased controls over where and to whom mail should be accepted. There are more examples of such a configuration in the tutorial section of this chapter.

Relocated Mapping

Using this option it is possible to notify senders if a local user has moved to another address. For example, if a user leaves an organization but still receives occasional mail at her local address, it may be convenient to notify anyone sending mail to the user of the move and new contact information for that user. Usage is just like the previous types of mappings and so won't be documented specifically here, though an example of a relocated mapping will be given to display the types of information that can be provided by this feature.

As an example, let's say I move from my current company to the far more relaxed atmosphere of the Oval Office. To make sure all of my friends and clients can keep in touch with me, I could provide a relocated mapping with a **Name** of joe@swelltech.com with a **Maps to** of president@whitehouse.gov. While this won't redirect mail to me at my new home, it will notify the people trying to contact me that I've changed email addresses. Hopefully they will all update their address books and resend their mail to my new address.

Local delivery

Local delivery is what Postfix does when it reaches the end of all of its list of mappings and access controls, and still finds that the message is allowed and destined for a user on the local machine (i.e., a mapping could potentially send the message elsewhere for final delivery, so all mappings as well as various access checks are performed before reaching this stage). This page configures a number of options relating to how Postfix handles the delivery of mail for local users (Figure 10-5).

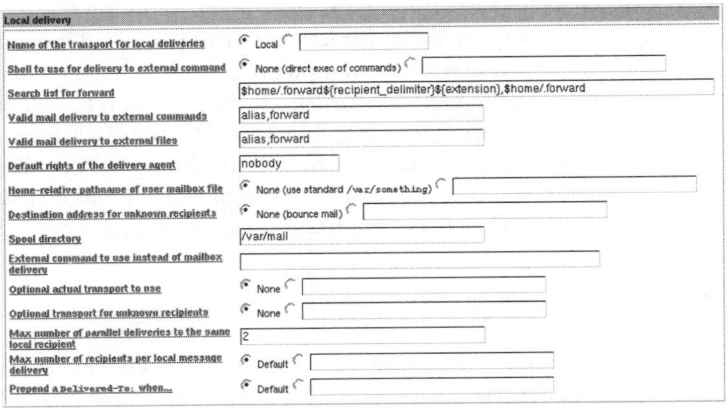

Figure 10-5: Local Delivery

Name of the transport for local deliveries

This configures the name of the transport that will be used for delivery to destination that match the $mydestination or $inet_interfaces variables. This can be a simple mailbox drop handled by the Postfix local delivery agent, or any appropriate delivery command. This option correlates to the local_transport directive and defaults to the defined transport type named local.

Shell to use for delivery to external command

If a command shell is required to communicate properly with your chosen local delivery transport, this option selects the shell that will be used. By default no shell is used, and the transport command will be executed directly. However, if the command contains shell meta-characters or shell built-in commands they will be passed to /bin/sh or whatever shell you configure here. A popular choice for this is smrsh, or *Sendmail's Restricted Shell*, which is included in recent Sendmail distributions. smrsh allows for more precise control over what commands users can execute from their .forward files. This option corresponds to the local_command_shell and defaults to /bin/sh.

Search list for forward

This is a comma-separated list of possible locations for user forward files. Postfix will try each entry in the list until a forward file is found or until all have been checked and no match is found. The forward file allows users to configure delivery options for themselves, including delivery-time processing by a program like procmail, as well as forwarding of messages to a different server. A number of variable expansions are performed on the entries. The expansions are currently:

Forward Search Path Variable Expansions

Entries in forward files can make use of the following variables:

$user	The username of the recipient.
$shell	The shell of the recipient.
$home	Recipient's home directory.
$recipient	The full recipient address.
$extensions	Recipient address extensions. This is a separate part of the email address, separated by the **Separator between user names and address extensions** defined on the **General Options** page.
$domain	The recipient's domain name.
$local	The entire local part of the recipient address.
$recipient_delimiter	The separation delimiter for the recipient.

Valid mail delivery to external commands

This parameter restricts mail delivery to only those commands specified here. The default is to disallow delivery to commands specified in :include: files and allow execution of commands in alias and forward files. This option correlates to the allow_mail_to_command directive.

Valid mail delivery to external files

This option restricts mail delivery to external files. The default is to disallow delivery to files specified in :include: but to allow delivery to files specified in aliases and forward files. This option correlates to the allow_mail_to_files directive.

Default rights of the local delivery agent

This option configures the privileges that the delivery agent will have for delivery to a file or a command. This option should never be a privileged user or the Postfix owner. This option corresponds to the default_privs directive and defaults to nobody.

Pathname of user mailbox file

When delivering mail locally, Postfix will drop mail in the directory configured here or in its default mail spool directory. If you wish to use the *maildir* format for mail storage, this value can be appended with a trailing slash. For example, to store mail in the user's home directory in the Maildir subdirectory, the value would be Maildir/. This option correlates to the home_mailbox directive and usually defaults to some location under /var/spool/mail or /var/spool/postfix.

Destination address for unknown recipients

If a message is received for a recipient that does not exist, the message is normally bounced. However, it is possible to instead have the message delivered to an alternate address. This option corresponds to the luser_relay directive. Variable expansions matching those discussed for the **Search list for forward** are also valid for this directive.

Spool directory

This option specifies the directory where UNIX-style mailboxes are stored. Defaults vary depending on OS variant and version, but a common choice is /var/spool/mail. This option correlates to the mail_spool_directory option.

External command to use instead of mailbox delivery

This option defines a command to use for delivery instead of delivering straight to the user's mailbox. The command will be run as the recipient of the message with appropriate HOME, SHELL, and LOGNAME environment variables set. This option is commonly used to set up system-wide usage of procmail. Beware that if you use a command to deliver mail to all users, you *must* configure an alias for root, as the command will be executed with the permissions of the $default_user. This option correlates to the mailbox_command directive and is disabled by default.

Optional actual transport to use

This option configures the message transport to use for all local users, whether they are in the UNIX passwd database or not. If provided, the value will override all other forms of local delivery, including **Destination address for unknown recipients**. This option corresponds to the mailbox_transport directive and is disabled by default. This option may be useful in some environments, for example, to delegate all delivery to an agent like the cyrus IMAPD.

Optional transport for unknown recipients

If a user cannot be found in the UNIX passwd database, and no alias matches the name, the message will ordinarily be bounced or handled via the **Destination address for unknown recipients** option. However, if you would like unknown users to be handled by a separate transport method, this option overrides the **Destination address for unknown recipients** option above. This option correlates to the fallback_transport directive and is disabled by default.

Max number of parallel deliveries to the same local recipient

This option limits the number of simultaneous deliveries to a single local recipient. If .forward files are allowed for users, a user may run a time-consuming command or shell script, leading to overload caused by several such processes being started up at once. This option correlates to the local_destination_concurrency_limit directive, and the default is 2. A low value is recommended for this option, unless it is certain that no complex .forward files will be in use.

Max number of recipients per local message delivery

This option configures the maximum number of recipients per local message delivery. This option correlates to the local_destination_recipient_limit and is set to the value of Max number of recipients per message delivery by default.

Prepend a Delivered-To: when . . .

This parameter determines when Postfix should insert a Delivered-to: message header. By default Postfix inserts this header when forwarding mail and when delivering to a file. The defaults are recommended, and it is generally preferable not to disable insertion into forwarded mail. This option corresponds to the prepend_delivered_header directive.

General Resource Control

This page provides access to the various memory and process limits for the Postfix processes (Figure 10-6). It is rarely necessary to alter the values on this page, except for highly loaded servers or very low resource machines.

Max size of bounced message

This option limits the amount of the original message content in bytes that will be sent in a bounce notification. This option correlates to bounce_size_limit and defaults to 50000.

General resource control

Max size of bounced message	50000	Max time for delivery to external commands	1000s
Max number of Postfix child processes	50	Max number of addresses remembered by the duplicate filter	1000
Max attempts to acquire file lock	20	Time in seconds between file lock attempts	1s
Max attempts to fork a process	5	Time in seconds between fork attempts	1s
Max memory used for processing headers	102400	Max memory used for handling input lines	2048
Max size of a message	10240000	Max number of messages in the active queue	10000
Max number of in-memory recipients	10000	Min free space in the queue file system	0
Max time after which stale lock is released	500s	Time in seconds between attempts to contact a broken MDT	60s

Figure 10-6: General resource control

Max time for delivery to external commands

When delivering mail to an external command (rather than via direct mailbox delivery), Postfix will wait this amount of time for the delivery to complete. If this value is to be set to a high limit (3600s or more) the value of **Timeout for I/O on internal comm channels** in **General Options** must also be increased. This option correlates to the command_time_limit directive and defaults to 1000s.

Max number of Postfix child processes

This option limits the number of child processes that Postfix will spawn. On high load servers the default may be too low and may need to be raised to as much as 500 or more. More likely, for most environments, 50 is more than adequate and may even be overkill. For example, on dial-up or consumer broadband serving one to ten users, a more appropriate limit might be 10. If in doubt, leave it at its default unless it causes problems. This option correlates to the default_process_limit directive and defaults to 50.

Max number of addresses remembered by the duplicate filters

While expanding aliases and .forward files Postfix will remember addresses that are being delivered to and attempt to prevent duplicate deliveries to the same address. This option limits the number of recipient addresses that will be remembered. It corresponds to the duplicate_filter_limit directive and defaults to 1000. There is probably no compelling reason to increase this value.

Max attempts to acquire file lock

This option limits the number of attempts Postfix will make when attempting to obtain an exclusive lock on a mailbox or other file requiring exclusive access. It corresponds to the deliver_lock_attempts directive and defaults to 20.

Time in seconds between file lock attempts

Postfix will wait a specified time between attempts to lock a given file, after a failed lock attempt. This option configures the deliver_lock_delay directive and defaults to 1s.

Max attempts to fork a process

If Postfix attempts to fork a new process and fails, due to errors or a lack of available resources, it will try again a specified number of times. This option correlates to the fork_attempts directive and defaults to 5.

Time in seconds between fork attempts

Postfix will try to spawn a new process a specified time after a failed attempt. This option correlates to the fork_delay directive and defaults to 1s.

Max memory used for processing headers

This option limits the amount of memory in bytes that Postfix will use to process message headers. If a message header is too large to fit into the memory specified, the headers that do not fit into memory will be treated as part of the message body. This option correlates to the header_size_limit directive and defaults to 102400.

Max memory used for handling input lines

This option limits the amount of memory in bytes that Postfix will use to handle input lines. And input line is any line read from an :include: or .forward file. In order to prevent the mail server from using excessive amounts of memory, it will break up these files into chunks of this length. This option correlates to the line_length_limit directive and defaults to 2048.

Max size of a message

This option limits the size in bytes of a message that will be delivered, including the message envelope information. This limit should be set high enough to support any email messages your users will need to be able to send or receive. This option correlates to the message_size_limit directive and defaults to 10240000.

Max number of messages in the active queue

This option limits the number of messages that can exist in the message queue at any given time. It correlates to the qmgr_message_active_limit directive and defaults to 10000.

Max number of in-memory recipients

This parameter limits the number of in-memory recipient data structures. This memory contains the short-term *dead list*, which indicates a destination was unavailable when last contacted, among other things. This option correlates to the qmgr_message_recipient_limit directive and defaults to 1000.

Min free space in the queue file system

Postfix will refuse mail if the filesystem on which the queue is located has less available space in bytes than the value set in this option. This option correlates to the queue_minfree directive and defaults to 0.

Max time after which stale lock is released

This option configures how old an external lock file may be before it is forcibly removed. This option correlates to the stale_lock_time and defaults to 500s.

Time in seconds between attempts to contact a broken MDT

This option configures the time in seconds between the queue manager attempts to contact an unresponsive mail delivery transport. This option correlates to the transport_retry_time and defaults to 60s.

SMTP Server Options

This page configures the majority of the options that directly affect the behavior of the SMTP server portion of Postfix, specifically the portions of Postfix that impact how the server behaves toward an SMTP client that connects to the server.

SMTP greeting banner

When a client connects to an SMTP server a *greeting banner* will be sent to the client (note the term *client* in this context is not the end user, but rather the email software program that is being used to make the connection). This option configures the text that will follow the status code in the banner. It is possible to use a number of variable expansions, for example, to display the specific version of the server software, though Postfix does not include the version by default. If configuring this option to be other than the default, you must include $myhostname at the start of this line, as it allows Postfix to report and respond to a mailer loop rather than overloading the system with many multiple deliveries. This option correlates to the smtpd_banner directive and contains $myhostname ESMTP $mail_name by default.

NOTE *A proposed federal law in the U.S. would make it illegal to send unsolicited commercial email through a mail server if the server included in its SMTP greeting the words* NO UCE. *Because spammers are generally of a criminal mindset anyway, it is unlikely that many of them will respect the new law if it is ever passed. Nonetheless, it is worth mentioning in hopes that sometime soon, all Americans will have legal protection against the stolen resources and time that UCE represents.*

Max number of recipients accepted for delivery

This option limits the number of recipients that may be specified in a single message header. It is usually rare for legitimate messages to have an extremely large number of recipients specified in a single message header, but it is often done in UCE messages. The legitimate exception is messages to a mailing list (possibly sent by mailing list software like majordomo or mailman. This option correlates to the smtpd_recipient_limit and defaults to 1000.

Disable SMTP VRFY command

Normally, the SMTP VRFY command is used to verify the existence of a particular user. However, it is also illegitimately used by spammers to harvest live email addresses. Thus it is sometimes useful to disable this command. This option correlates to disable_vrfy_command and defaults to No.

Timeout in seconds for SMTP transactions

This option sets the timeout in seconds for a client to respond to the SMTP server's response with an SMTP request. The connection process involves the client opening a connection to the server, the server replies with a greeting, and then the client makes its request. If the client request does not come within the time specified here, the connection will be closed. This option correlates to the opts_smtpd_timeout directive and defaults to 300s.

Timeout before sending 4xx/5xx error response

When sending an error response to a client, the server will sleep a specified time. The purpose of this feature is to prevent certain buggy clients from hitting the server with repeated requests in rapid succession. This option correlates to the smtpd_error_sleep_time directive and defaults to 5s.

Error count for temporarily ignore a client

This option configures the number of errors that a client may generate before Postfix will stop responding to requests for a specified time. Some buggy mail clients may send a large number of requests, while ignoring or responding incorrectly to the error messages that result. Postfix attempts to minimize the impact of these buggy clients on normal service. This option correlates to the smtpd_soft_error_limit directive, and defaults to 10.

Error count for closing connection

If the number exceeds this limit the connection will be closed. This option correlates to the smtpd_hard_error_limit directive and defaults to 100.

HELO is required

Enabling this option causes Postfix to require clients to introduce themselves with a HELO header at the beginning of an SMTP session. This may prevent some UCE software packages from connecting, though it may also impact other legitimate clients from connecting. This option correlates to the smtpd_helo_required directive and defaults to No.

Allow untrusted routing

This option configures whether Postfix will forward messages with *sender-specified routing* from untrusted clients to destinations within the accepted relay domains. This feature closes a sneaky potential loophole in access controls that would normally prevent the server from being an open relay for spammers. If this behavior is allowed, a malicious user could possibly exploit a backup MX mail host into forwarding junk mail to a primary MX server that believes the mail has originated from a local address, and thus delivers it as the spammer intended. This option correlates to the allow_untrusted_routing directive and is disabled by default. Enabling this option should only be done with extreme caution and care to prevent turning your Postfix installation into an open relay.

Restrict ETRN command upon . . .

The SMTP ETRN command is a rather clumsy means for a client that is not always connected to the Internet to retrieve mail from the server. The usage of this command is rather outdated, and rarely used, as POP3 and IMAP are better suited to solve this problem in the general case. This option correlates to the smtpd_etrn_restrictions directive, and the default is to allow ETRN from any host. This option accepts the following directives: check_etrn_access maptype:mapname, permit_naked_ip_address, reject_invalid_hostname, check_helo_access maptype:mapname, reject_maps_rbl, reject_unknown_client, permit_mynetworks, check_client_access, permit, reject, warn_if_reject, and reject_unauth_pipelining.

This option as well as the following three **Restrictions** options accept one or all of the following values in the text field. Each is described only once here, and the specific entry will include the list of accepted directives for the option. The impact of some of these choices depends on configuration performed elsewhere and could potentially open security holes if not configured carefully.

permit_mynetworks

Permit the message if the relevant address (sender or recipient depending on the restriction) is within the local network.

reject_unknown_client

The request will be refused is the client IP has no PTR record in the DNS. This means that a client with an IP address that cannot be resolved to a host name cannot send mail to this host.

check_client_access maptype:mapname

This option requires the inclusion of an already configured map, as discussed earlier. This will restrict based on the contents of the map, allowing only clients that are allowed by the map. The map may contain networks, parent domains, or client addresses, and Postfix will strip off unnecessary information to match the client to the level of specificity needed.

check_sender_access maptype:mapname

This will restrict based on the contents of the map, allowing only senders that are allowed by the map. The map may contain networks, parent domains, or localpart@.

reject_maps_rbl

An RBL is a relay domain black hole list. By testing a reverse domain lookup against a name server that receives a domain black hole list transfer, the server can know if the mail was sent through a known open mail relay. There are a number of free and for-fee services providing black hole data. The largest and longest lasting is the service operated by MAPS [http://www.mail-abuse.org/], while two new similar services are operated by the Open Relay Database [http://ordb.org/] and by Distributed Sender Boycott List [http://dsbl.org/]. All operated on the principle of allowing administrators to choose to refuse mail sent from open mail relays. If this option is listed, the client will be checked against the available RBL domains, and if any match the mail will be refused.

NOTE *If using any of the free RBL services on the network, consider donating money, time, or resources to the project maintainers. The projects are generally run by volunteer labor, using network resources that have been paid for by the maintainers.*

reject_invalid_hostname

If the client host name is invalid, due to bad syntax, the request will be rejected.

permit_naked_ip_address

If the client HELO or EHLO command contains a naked IP address without the enclosing [ ] brackets as required by the mail RFC, the message will be rejected. Beware that some popular mail clients send a HELO greeting that is broken this way.

reject_unknown_hostname

Reject the request if the host name in the client HELO command has no A or MX record in the DNS.

reject_non_fqdn_hostname

If the client host name is not in the form of a fully qualified domain name, as required by the RFC, the message will be rejected.

check_helo_access maptype:mapname

The server will search the named access database map for the HELO host name or parent domains. If the result from the database search is REJECT or a 4xx text or 5xx text error code the message will be refused, while a response of OK or RELAY or an all numerical response will permit the message.

permit

This simply permits anything. Generally this will be at the end of a set of restrictions in order to allow anything that has not been explicitly prohibited.

reject

Rejects everything. This can be used at the end of a chain of restrictions to prohibit anything that has not been explicitly permitted.

warn_if_reject

This is a special option that changes the meaning of the following restriction, so that a message that would have been rejected will be logged but still accepted. This can be used for testing new rules on production mail servers without risk of denying mail due to a problem with the rules.

reject_unauth_pipelining

If the client sends commands ahead of time without first confirming that the server support SMTP command pipelining, the message will be rejected. This will prevent mail from some poorly written bulk email software that improperly uses pipelining to speed up mass deliveries.

Restrictions on client hostnames/addresses

This restriction applies to the client host name and/or address. By default, Postfix will allow connections from any host, but you may add additional restrictions using the following: reject_unknown_client, permit_mynetworks, check_client_access maptype:mapname, reject_maps_rbl, maps_rbl_reject_code, permit, reject, warn_if_reject, reject_unauth_pipelining.

Restrictions on sends in HELO commands

This option specifies additional restrictions on what information can be sent by client in the HELO and EHLO commands. This option correlates to the smtpd_helo_restrictions directive. By default Postfix accepts anything, and the following restrictions may be added: reject_invalid_hostname, permit_naked_ip_address, reject_unknown_hostname, reject_non_fqdn_hostname, check_helo_access maptype:mapname, reject_maps_rbl, reject_unknown_client, check_client_access maptype:mapname, permit, reject, warn_if_reject, reject_unauth_pipelining.

Restrictions on sender addresses

This option restricts what can be contained in the MAIL FROM command in a message. It may be used to prevent specific email addresses from sending mail, reject clients without a resolvable host name, and so on. This option correlates to the smtpd_sender_restrictions directive and may contain any of the following restrictions: permit_mynetworks:, reject_unknown_client, reject_maps_rbl, reject_invalid_hostname, reject_unknown_hostname, reject_unknown_sender_domain, check_sender_access maptype:mapname, check_client_access maptype:mapname, check_helo_access maptype:mapname, reject_non_fqdn_hostname, reject_non_fqdn_sender, reject, permit.

Restrictions on recipient addresses

This parameter places restrictions on the recipients that can be contained in the RCPT TO command of a sent message. It can be used to dictate where email may be sent. This option correlates to the smtpd_recipient_restrictions and may contain any of the following restrictions: permit_mynetworks, reject_unknown_client, reject_maps_rbl, reject_invalid_hostname, reject_unknown_hostname, reject_unknown_sender_domain, check_relay_domains, permit_auth_destination, reject_unauth_pipelining, permit_mx_backup, reject_unknown_recipient, check_recipient_access, check_client_access, check_helo_access, check_sender_access, reject_non_fqdn_hostname, reject_non_fqdn_sender, reject_non_fqdn_recipient, reject, permit.

DNS domains for blacklist lookups

This option configures the optional blacklist DNS servers that will be used for all RBL checks that have been specified in all access restrictions. It may contain any number of servers in a whitespace separated list. These services can be used to help prevent spam, as discussed earlier in this section, with the **Restrict ETRN command upon** parameter. This option configures the maps_rbl_domains directive and is empty by default.

Restrict mail relaying

This option specifies from which hosts, networks, domains, and so on. Postfix will relay email for. This option correlates to the relay_domains directive and defaults to $mydestination.

SMTP server response on access map violation, SMTP server response on RBL domains violation, SMTP server response on forbidden relaying, SMTP server response on unknown client reject, SMTP server response on invalid hostname reject, SMTP server response on unknown domain reject, SMTP server response on unknown hostname reject

These options configure the error result code that will be sent to the client when any of the specified restrictions are being applied. These errors have sensible default values and generally should not need to be changed. Consult with RFC 822 if you wish to understand more about the SMTP error codes or have a reason to change any of these values.

SMTP Client Options

The SMTP client options configures how Postfix will behave when dealing with other mail servers as a client, e.g., when sending mail on behalf of a user. This portion of the configuration primarily dictates how the server will respond to certain error conditions.

Action when listed as best MX server

As discussed in the BIND chapter, a mail server performs a name server query to find the MX, or mail server, record for the destination domain. If this record indicates that the local server *is* the server to which mail should be sent, it can respond in a couple of ways. The default is to bounce the message with an error indicating a mail loop. If the field is selected and local is entered, the mail will be directed to the local delivery agent instead of bouncing the mail. This option correlates to the best_mx_transport directive.

Hosts/domains to hand off mail to on invalid destination

By default, mail that cannot be delivered because the destination is invalid will be bounced with an appropriate error message. However, it is possible to configure postfix to hand off email to another server instead. This option correlates to the fallback_relay directive.

Ignore MX lookup error

If a name server query fails to provide an MX record, the server defaults to deferring the mail and trying again later. If Yes is selected instead, an A record query will be done and an attempt will be made to deliver to the resulting address. This option correlates to the ignore_mx_lookup_error directive.

Skip 4xx greeting

If a remote server responds to a connection with a 4XX status code, Postfix will, by default, select the next available mail exchanger specified by the MX records. If set to No, mail delivery will be deferred after the first mail delivery attempt, and another attempt will be made later. This option correlates to the smtp_skip_4xx_greeting directive.

Skip wait for the QUIT command

This option configures whether Postfix will wait for the receiving mail server to respond to the QUIT command. This option correlates to the smtp_skip_quit_response directive and defaults to no.

Max number of parallel deliveries to the same destination

This option specifies the maximum number of deliveries that Postfix will perform to the same destination simultaneously. This option correlates to the smtp_destination_concurrency_limit directive and defaults to the system-wide limit for parallel deliveries configured in the **Delivery Rates** page documented in the next section.

Max number of recipients per delivery

Limits the number of recipients per delivery. This option correlates to the smtp_destination_recipient_limit directive and defaults to the system-wide limit for recipients per delivery.

Timeout for completing TCP connections

Specifies the time in seconds that the Postfix delivery agent will wait before timing out a TCP connection. This option correlates to the smtp_connect_timeout directive and defaults to 0, which disables connection timeouts.

Timeout on waiting for the greeting banner

Limits how long Postfix will wait for a greeting banner to be received from the destination server. This option corresponds to the smtp_helo_timeout directive and defaults to 300 seconds.

Timeout on waiting for answer to MAIL FROM

Sets the timeout in seconds for sending the SMTP MAIL FROM command and for receiving the destination server's response. This option correlates to the smtp_mail_timeout directive and defaults to 300 seconds.

Timeout on waiting for answer to RCPT TO

Sets the timeout in seconds for sending the SMTP RCPT TO command and for receiving the destination server's response. This option correlates to the smtp_rcpt_timeout directive and defaults to 300 seconds.

Timeout on waiting for answer to DATA

Sets the timeout in seconds sending the SMTP DATA command and for receiving the destination server's response. This option correlates to the smtp_data_init_timeout directive and defaults to 120 seconds.

Timeout on waiting for answer to transmit of message content

Specifies the SMTP client timeout in seconds for sending the contents of the message. If the connection stalls for longer than this timeout, the delivery agent will terminate to transfer. This option corresponds to the smtp_data_xfer_timeout directive and defaults to 180 seconds.

Timeout on waiting for answer to ending "."

Specifies the SMTP client timeout in seconds for sending the closing SMTP "." and receiving the destination server's reply. This option correlates to the `smtp_data_done_timeout` directive and defaults to 600 seconds.

Timeout on waiting for answer to QUIT

Sets the timeout in seconds sending the SMTP QUIT command and for receiving the destination server's response. This option correlates to the `smtp_quit_timeout` directive and defaults to 300 seconds.

Delivery Rates

This page contains the options for setting the default rate and concurrency limits for all Postfix components. These rates can usually be overridden within their respective configuration sections.

Max number of parallel deliveries to the same destination

This option specifies the maximum number of deliveries that Postfix will perform to the same destination simultaneously. This option correlates to the `default_destination_concurrency_limit` directive and defaults to 10.

Max number of recipients per message delivery

Limits the number of recipients per delivery. This option correlates to the `default_destination_recipient_limit` directive and defaults to 50.

Initial concurrency level for delivery to the same destination

Specifies the initial number of simultaneous deliveries to the same destination. This limit applies to all SMTP, local, and pipe mailer deliveries. A concurrency of less than two could lead to a single problem email backing up delivery of other mail to the same destination. This option configures the `initial_destination_concurrency` directive and defaults to 5.

Max time (days) in queue before message is undeliverable

Defines the number of days a message will remain queued for delivery in the event of delivery problems before the message is sent back to the sender as undeliverable. This option configures the `maximal_queue_lifetime` directive and defaults to 5 days.

Min time (secs) between attempts to deliver a deferred message

In the event of a delivery deferral, Postfix will wait the specified amount of time before reattempting delivery. This value also specifies the time an unreachable destination will remain in the destination status cache. This option correlates to the `minimal_backoff_time` directive and defaults to 1000 seconds.

Max time (secs) between attempts to deliver a deferred message

Specifies the maximum amount of time between delivery attempts in the event of a deferred delivery. This option configures the maximal_backoff_time directive and defaults to 4000 seconds.

Time (secs) between scanning the deferred queue

Specifies the time in seconds between queue scans by the queue management task. This option correlates to the queue_run_delay and defaults to 1000 seconds.

Transports that should not be delivered

This field specifies which delivery transports, if any, of the transports defined in the **Transport Mapping** section will not have their messages sent automatically. Instead the messages for these transports will be queued and can be delivered manually using the sendmail -q command. This option correlates to the defer_transports directive and contains nothing by default.

Debugging Features

Postfix has two levels of logging. The first level is the normal maillog, which reports on all normal mail activities such as received and sent mail, server errors, shutdowns, and startups. The second level is more verbose and can be tuned to log activity relating to specific SMTP clients, host names, or addresses. This page contains the configuration for the second level of logging.

List of domain/network patterns for which verbose log is enabled

This is a list of patterns or addresses that match the clients, hosts, or addresses whose activity you would like to have more verbose logging for. Values here could be an IP address like 192.168.1.1 or a domain name like swelltech.com. This option correlates to the debug_peer_list directive and is empty by default.

Verbose logging level when matching the above list

Specifies the level of verbosity of the logging for the activity that matches the above patterns. This option correlates to the debug_peer_level directive and defaults to 2. The above field must have at least one value for this debug level to have any impact.

Postfix, Unsolicited Commercial Email, and Access Controls

Postfix offers an extremely flexible set of access controls, primarily targeted at preventing unsolicited commercial email from being delivered through the server. In order to construct a suitable set of controls it is necessary to understand the order in which rules are checked and how they interact. By default Postfix will accept mail for delivery from or to any client on your local network and any domains that are hosted by Postfix. So, by default, Postfix is not an open relay. This is a good beginning and may be all that is needed in many environments. However, because UCE is such a nuisance for users and network administrators, it may be worthwhile to implement more advanced filtering. This section will address the basics of the Postfix UCE control features.

Access Control List Order

Every message that enters the smtpd delivery daemon will be processed by a number of access control lists and checked against a number of rules to ensure that the message is one that the administrator actually wants delivered. The goal for most administrators is to prevent unsolicited commercial email from passing through these rules, yet allow every legitimate email to be delivered. This is a lofty goal and a delicate balance. No perfect solution exists, as long as people are willing to steal the resources of others for their own commercial gain and go to great lengths to overcome the protections in place to prevent such abuse. However, in most environments it is possible to develop a reasonable set of rules that prevents most spam and allows most or all legitimate mail through unharmed.

It is important to understand the order of processing if complex sets or rules are to be used, as attempting to use a particular rule too early in the chain can lead to subtle errors or strange mail client behavior. Because not all clients react exactly correctly to some types of refusals, and not all clients create correctly formed SMTP requests, it is not unlikely that a misplaced rule will lock out some or all of your clients from sending legitimate mail. It could also just as easily lead to opening a hole in your spam protections early in the rule set, which would allow illicit mail to pass.

The Postfix UCE controls begin with a couple of simple yes or no checks, called smtpd_helo_required and strict_rfc821_envelopes, both configured in the **SMTP Server Options** page. The first, if enabled, requires a connecting mail client to introduce itself fully by sending a HELO command. This can stop some poorly designed bulk email programs. The second option requires for the envelope to fit the SMTP specification precisely, thus enforcing complete headers. Though the envelope and HELO can be forged by a bulk mailer, it may stop the more hastily implemented variants (well, how many *good* programmers do you know that write tools to help spammers?).

The next stage is the four SMTP restrictions also found on the **SMTP Server Options** page. These further limit from where and to where mail will be delivered. The order of traversal for these four lists of rules is:

1. **Restrictions on client hostnames/addresses** or smtpd_client_restrictions
2. **Restrictions on sends in HELO commands** or smtpd_helo_restrictions
3. **Restrictions on sender addresses** or smtpd_sender_restrictions
4. **Restrictions on recipient addresses** or smtpd_recipient_restrictions

Each of these checks can return REJECT, OK, or DUNNO. If REJECT, the message will be refused, and no further rules will be checked. If OK, no further rules in the given restriction will be checked, and the next restriction list will be checked. If

DUNNO, the list will continue to process the current restriction until it gets another result (OK or REJECT) or until the list end is reached, which is an implicit OK. If all lists return OK, the message will be passed to the regular expressions checks, otherwise it will be rejected.

Next come the regular expression–based header_checks and body_checks. These options, if enabled, provide a means to test the actual contents of the headers and the body of the email, respectively. Both operate in the same way, though they should be used somewhat differently. Header checks can be used to prevent well-known spamming domains from sending you email or for stopping some well-known bulk-mailer software. By entering some signature of the offender, like the domain name, or the X-mailer field identifying the software, the mail can be rejected before the body is even sent. Body checks, though they use the same regular expressions and file format as header checks, should be used more sparingly, as the mail must be accepted before it can be checked. Thus bandwidth is wasted on receipt of the mail, and worse, the server will be occupied for a potentially long while with processing the entire contents of every email. In short, use header checks whenever is convenient, and use body checks only when an effective header check cannot be devised. Only REJECT or OK is permitted for the returned values.

NOTE *Webmin, as of this writing (version 1.020), does not provide access to the regular expressions–based checks,* header_checks *and* body_checks. *It is likely that a near-future version will support these features, however.*

Tutorial: Setting Up a Basic Postfix Mail Server

As with most of the server software documented here, Postfix has an intimidatingly large number of options and features. But, as we've already seen with BIND and Apache, even complex software can be easy and quick to set up if you know just what to do to get started. Postfix is no different. At the end of this short section you'll have a fully functioning mail server, capable of sending and receiving mail on behalf of one or more domains.

In most environments, only three configuration details are needed to begin providing mail service with Postfix. First, browse the **General Options** page of the module. The top two options, **What domain to use in outbound mail** and **What domains to receive mail for**, need to be configured to suit your environment.

For the first option, you will likely want to select Use domainname in order to select the domain name of your server as the source of email sent from it. For example, if my mail server is named mail.swelltech.com and I selected this option, mail will appear to originate from swelltech.com.

The second option specifies the domains for which you will receive email. The default is probably too restrictive in that it will only permit receipt of mail to $mydomainname and localhost.$mydomain, or the server itself. While this depends on your environment and needs, it is likely that you will want to at least add the $mydomain variable to the list of accepted domains.

The last step to making Postfix fully functional for sending and receiving mail is to ensure the **Local networks** parameter is set appropriately. If you only have one network block, this will already be set appropriately, as the default is to accept mail for delivery from all attached networks (i.e., all configured and active network addresses). However, if you have a public and private network interface, you'll likely want to remove to the public interface to prevent other clients of your ISP from being able to relay mail through your server.

Click the **Save and Apply** button to make your changes take effect. It is, of course, a good idea to test your changes to make sure things are working as intended. First, assuming an appropriate DNS MX record has already been configured as discussed in the BIND tutorials, you can send yourself an email at the new domain. Watch the maillog in the **System Logs** module for errors and to see if the message is delivered as expected. Next configure your mail client to send through your new mail server, to ensure it is working for sending mail, as well. The maillog will likely give clues about what is wrong in the event of problems.

Tutorial: Virtual Hosting Email with Postfix

At this point, if you've performed the configuration in the previous tutorial, you'll be able to accept mail for any number of domains. However, this is not the same as providing independent virtual hosting support with Postfix, because you can only have one user of a given name and mail sent to that username at any of the domains for which you accept mail will be delivered to that user. So, for example, if you hosted swelltech.com, penguinfeet.org, and nostarch.com on the same server, and mail was sent to user joe at each of those domains, all three mails would end up in the same mailbox. Therefore, you have to introduce another layer to solve this problem.

Postfix has two commonly used methods for solving this problem. The first is the native Postfix method, using a virtual table to direct mail to the correct destination. The second method is modeled after the way Sendmail handles the problem, and is therefore a lot more complex. Because simplicity is better than complexity, you'll learn the native Postfix mechanism exclusively. The Postfix virtual man page covers both methods in moderate detail. If you have an older Sendmail installation that is being converted to Postfix you may wish to use the second method and maintain your current virtual mail configuration. If you will be running an extremely large number of virtual domains, it is likely preferable to use the second method, as well.

The first step for setting up virtual domain delivery is for you to create a virtual map table using the **Virtual Domains** page (Figure 10-7). Enter the map type (hash, dbm, and so on), followed by the filename of the flat file that will contain the table information. For example, you could use /etc/postfix/virtual for this purpose. This is a pretty common location for this file.

Figure 10-7: The Virtual Domains table

Save and apply the change, and return to the **Virtual Domains** page. Now, you can click the **New mapping** button. You first have to create a generic map for the new domain. So, for the **Name** field, enter your virtual domain name. In the

Maps to field, you can technically enter anything you like (as long as we enter something). The custom seems to be to enter virtual in this field, as that is its purpose. Click **Save mapping** to add it to the virtual table.

Next, you'll want to add a postmaster alias, as all mail servers must have a functioning postmaster address to be compliant with the relevant RFC. So, click **New mapping** again. This time enter postmaster@virtual.domain into the **Name** field, where virtual.domain is the name of your domain. Then enter postmaster into the **Maps to** field so that mail to this address will be mapped to the local postmaster address for normal delivery.

Finally, you're ready to start adding your virtual domain users to the table. Once again, create a new mapping. Fill in your new virtual domain mail address in the **Name** field. For example, you might fill in joe@virtual.domain. In the **Maps to** section, enter the name of a local user that you would like to receive mail for this address. In this case, you would use virtual-joe or perhaps virtual.domain.joe. This new local user must exist for mail to be delivered; therefore you'll need to add the new user to the system.

Now, **Save and Apply** your changes, and test it out! The virtual maps can be handled by various database types or exported to an LDAP database. There is no reasonable limit to the number of virtual users and domains you can have.

11

SENDMAIL

Sendmail is the de facto standard mail transfer agent, or *MTA*, in use on the Internet today. While there are now several worthy contenders for the title of best or most popular MTA, including Postfix and QMail (both of which have very good Webmin modules, and Postfix is documented in the preceding chapter), more mail probably passes through Sendmail than any other single MTA.

An MTA is the software that provides mail services for a network. A client mail user agent, or *MUA*, sends email, usually via the Simple Mail Transport Protocol, or *SMTP*, to the MTA. The MTA uses one of several transport protocols, most often via SMTP, to deliver it either directly to the recipient (if the address is served by the same server) or to the mail server for the user. Clients then access the mail on the server using either POP3 or IMAP. So, Sendmail will operate on your server and provide those intermediary services, both sending and receiving mail, for clients and other MTAs on the Internet.

Configuring Sendmail

Sendmail has a reputation, not entirely undeserved, for being extremely obtuse and confusing to configure. The famously terse sendmail.cf file was designed to be easy and quick for the computer to parse, not for humans to be able to read and edit. Relatively recently, attempts have been made to remedy this problem, and the solution now provided with Sendmail is an "m4" macro–based configuration file, called sendmail.mc by default, that allows you to use much more human comprehensible configuration constructs. This configuration file is also supported by Webmin in the **Sendmail M4 Configuration** page.

Sendmail also uses a few other configuration files to dictate certain other behaviors. These include aliases, mailertable, access, and domaintable. These files are quite readable by mere mortal humans, usually containing a few (or more than a few in large networks) names, hosts, or domains, and an option or permission that applies to the name, host, or domain. Webmin provides a nice interface for these files as well, so you won't have to deal with them directly. However, it is good to know about them and what they're used for. You'll learn about them in more detail as the relevant Webmin sections are discussed.

The Sendmail Module

The Sendmail module in Webmin is thoroughly comprehensive, and it provides one-to-one access to nearly all, if not all, of Sendmail's important options and features. Opening the main Sendmail module page provides you with a number of icons that represent each type of option in the Sendmail configuration files (Figure 11-1). From here, you can edit the various global options, edit aliases, configure user mail settings, restrict access to your mail server, and even control the mail queue and read mail.

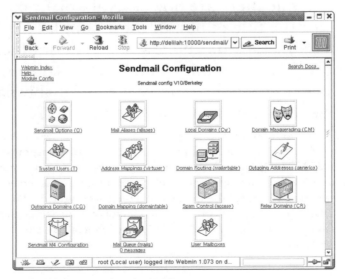

Figure 11-1: Sendmail module

Sendmail is configured in a number of files. The first, and most intimidating, is the `sendmail.cf` file. This configures all of the various limits and behaviors of Sendmail. The rest are related to users, hosts, domains, and aliases. They dictate primarily to whom mail is sent, and who and what hosts or networks have permission to send and receive mail from the server. The `sendmail.cf` file is configured on the **Options** page, discussed in the next section, while each of the other option files have their own page which are discussed in the Other Files section.

Options

The Sendmail Options page provides access to most of the relevant `sendmail.cf` directives. These options are usually "set and forget"–type options. Unless you have a problem with load, or memory, or untimely failed message delivery, you will have little reason to alter these options after first setting up your Sendmail system.

Send outgoing mail via host

This option sets whether outgoing mail will be sent directly or via another mail server. If it is to go through another mail server, it is entered here. If you are not on a permanently attached network (i.e., with a permanent IP and a domain name), then you should relay through the mail server at your ISP, as many mail servers refuse mail from hosts that cannot be resolved. This option edits the *Smart Host* macro named S in `sendmail.cf`. More on this and other common macros can be found in the macros sections of the *Administrative Details* [http://www.sendmail.org/m4/admin.html] documentation page at the Sendmail home page.

Forward unqualified usernames to host

If an email is sent by a local user that is unqualified (i.e., *joe* instead of *joe@swelltech.com*) it will by default attempt to deliver the mail locally (i.e., on the same machine that Sendmail runs on). However, if this is set, mail will be forwarded to the host selected. This is useful if you have a large organization with many Sendmail servers running, but you'd like all local mail to be delivered to a single host. This option edits the R macro, which refers to the *Relay* (for unqualified domains) configuration.

Forward mail for local users to host

Email that is received from anywhere that is destined for a user on the local host will be delivered locally, unless this option is set. This allows all mail to be collected on a single host. This option edits the R macro, which refers to the *Relay* (for unqualified domains) configuration.

Delivery mode

This option controls how messages will be scheduled for delivery. If Background is selected, Sendmail will deliver messages as soon as possible silently in the background. Queue only places mail into a queue to be delivered upon a manual or periodically scheduled flush of the queue. Interactive messages are delivered immediately synchronously. Deferred is like Queue only, except Sendmail will not attempt to resolve host names until the queue is flushed (ideal for a sporadic net connections, such as a dial-up). This option configures the DeliveryMode directive.

Max load average for sending

This option determines at what load average Sendmail will no longer continue to send messages. If this load average is crossed, Sendmail will queue messages for later delivery. This option configures the QueueLA directive and defaults to 8. If your system is becoming overloaded at times with delivering mail, it may be possible to tune this setting to help ease the load.

Max load average for receiving

This option determines at what load average Sendmail will stop accepting incoming messages via SMTP. This forces other mail servers to queue them for later delivery. While most mail servers will be polite and actually save the refused messages for later delivery, if assurance of mail service is important to your users, it is probably best to avoid refusing mail. This option configures the RefuseLA option and defaults to 12.

Max child processes

Controls how many child processes Sendmail will spawn in order to handle incoming mail. Limiting this allows you to control, somewhat, the memory footprint of Sendmail. This option configures the MaxDaemonChildren directive and defaults to 12.

Max connections/second

Configures the maximum number of new connections per second that Sendmail will accept. With this option, you may limit the CPU and memory usage of Sendmail on your system, or in high load environments allow Sendmail to receive a larger volume of mail. This option configures the ConnectionRateThrottle directive and defaults to 3.

Min time before retrying send

This sets the minimum amount of time mail will wait in the queue after a failed send attempt, before Sendmail attempts to re-send it. Values can be in seconds (e.g., 45s), minutes (30m), hours (2h), days (3d), or weeks (1w). This correlates to the MinQueueAge directive and defaults to 30m.

Maximum queue size

Determines the maximum number of queued jobs Sendmail will process in a single queue run. This correlates to the MaxQueueRunSize directive and defaults to 1000. This should remain as high as possible to avoid losing jobs that fall late in the queue.

Time before giving up

This is the amount of time that Sendmail will continue to try resending a failed message before giving up and considering it undeliverable. Non-permanent delivery failures can occur for a number of reasons, including network connectivity problems, DNS resolution failure, the recipient server not responding, and so on. When this limit is reached, a bounced message will be sent to the sender, and the message will be discarded. This option accepts times in the same format as discussed above, for seconds, minutes, hours, days, and weeks. This configures the Timeout.queuereturn directive and defaults to 5d.

Time before sending warning

In the event of a non-permanent delivery failure, as discussed in the previous option, this option configures how long Sendmail will wait before sending a warning to the sender of the message that a problem has occurred. Because these warnings usually resolve themselves shortly (either the network comes back up, DNS resolves again, the recipient server returns to service, and so on) it is often not necessary to trouble the sender with an error message until it begins to appear that a problem might become a permanent failure. This option configures the Timeout.queuewarn directive and defaults to 4h.

Mail queue directory

This sets the location of your mail queue directory where Sendmail stores queued mail. This option correlates to the QueueDirectory, and often defaults to /var/spool/mail, though on some systems this may differ. There is rarely reason to change this.

Send error messages to

In the event of a problem, such as a delivery failure, error messages will be sent to some user on the system. This is usually Postmaster, which on many systems is aliased to root. This option correlates to the PostMasterCopy directive.

User forward files

This option dictates where Sendmail will search for forwarding information for users. This is a colon-separated list (much like the shell PATH environment variable). This option allows you to use variables to include certain values, such as username ($u), user's home directory ($z), and system host name ($w). So, for example, if I wanted to search first for /var/forward/username and then in /home/joe/.forward, I could enter /var/forward/$u:$z/.forward. This option configures the ForwardPath directive and usually defaults to $z/.forward.$w:$z/.forward.

Min free disk space

If the amount of free disk space is lower than this value, Sendmail will refuse to accept messages from other systems. Allows one to prevent Sendmail from filling the disk on which the queue resides. This option correlates to the MinFreeBlocks directive and often defaults to 100.

Max message size

This option sets the maximum size of a message that will be accepted by Sendmail. Any message over this size, either received from a local user or a remote mail server, will be bounced. This option configures the MaxMessageSize directive and defaults to 1000000.

Log level

This option sets the logging behavior of Sendmail. Logging levels 0-10 are, by convention, used for useful information that is probably worth logging on any system. The default logging level is 9 and is a good middle ground, wherein Sendmail usually only logs things that an administrator would want to be aware of. Higher log levels between 10 and 64 will provide much more information, while levels over 64 are reserved for extremely verbose debugging output. The normal log levels are documented in the *The System Log* [http://www. sendmail. org/~ca/email/doc8.10/op-sh-2.html#sh-2.1] section of the *Installation and Operation Guide* [http://www.sendmail.org/~ca/email/doc8.10/op.html]. This option configures the LogLevel directive.

MIME-encode bounce messages?

This option configures whether Sendmail will encode bounce messages in multi-part MIME format or as a plain-text message. Most mail clients today support MIME encoded messages, but if your client base has problems with this you may turn it off. This correlates to the SendMimeErrors directive and defaults to True. More on MIME can be found in *RFC 2045* [http://www.ietf.org/rfc/ rfc2045.txt?number=2045] and *RFC 1344* [http://www.ietf.org/rfc/ rfc1344.txt?number=1344].

File security options

In order to avoid cracking attempts, Sendmail checks most of its support files. If these files are in group writable directories, or some other risky configuration, Sendmail will ordinarily refuse to run. This option allows you to turn off this checking in the ways described by the options available. This option configures the DontBlameSendmail directive and defaults to Safe. For obvious reasons, it is strongly suggested that you solve the permissions problem(s) you may have, rather than turning off any of these checks.

Other Support Files

The other side of configuring Sendmail is setting up how it will deliver mail and who it will allow to use its services. The rest of the Sendmail module is devoted to these options, and you are likely to spend more time on these pages than on the Options page. These pages configure all of the other files that Sendmail relies on to tell it how to do its job, including the aliases, access, domaintable, mailertable, relay-domains, and virtusertable files.

Mail Aliases

Sendmail provides a means to direct mail to a given recipient under an *alias*. For example, it is possible to have mail sent to Postmaster delivered to root. It is also possible to direct mail, to several addresses, into a file, to feed it to a program, or provide an automatic reply. These aliases are stored in a file called aliases that is usually located in /etc.

Address

This is simply the address that will be the alias. When mail is sent to this address, the action defined in Alias to option below will be performed. The alias does not contain the domain name. For example, joesalias instead of joesalias@swelltech.com.

Enabled

Here you may mark an alias as enabled or disabled. A disabled address will be preceded by a # in the aliases and will appear in *italics* in the list of aliases in the Webmin display.

Alias to

Here you define what Sendmail does when it receives a message for this aliased address. There are several options for this, and they are selected from the drop-down list. Email address is simply another email address to deliver the mail to. Addresses in a file causes the mail to be sent to every address named in the file provided in the text entry field — this allows you to more easily allow users to create their own aliases without giving them access to the /etc/aliases file. Write to file will cause Sendmail to write every mail sent to the address to a file chosen in the text entry field. Feed to program is interesting, in that it allows you to direct mail to any program on your system, thus you could write a script or a program (or find one already written) to provide any number of services based on the email received. Or it could file your mail in a database, or customer service system, or any number of other useful things. Finally, Autoreply from file simply sends a mail automatically back to the sender containing whatever is in the file listed in the text field.

The rest of the page is devoted to a listing of existing aliases. As mentioned above, enabled entries are in plain text, while disabled entries are in *italics*. Clicking an alias allows you to edit, delete, or add destinations to an alias. Clicking Manually edit /etc/aliased provides a simple text editor field wherein you can manually edit or view your aliases file. Be careful, as the format and entries will not be checked by Webmin for correctness. If you make a mistake your Sendmail may complain loudly (in the logs) and stop working.

Local Domains

This page configures the sendmail.cw file and allows you to choose what domains Sendmail will accept local mail delivery for. By default Sendmail only accepts delivery for the local host. In order to accept mail for a whole domain, or a number of domains, they must be listed here. Also, the domains must have a DNS MX record that points to the server where your Sendmail is running. Sendmail can handle mail for any number of domains; however, setting up virtual hosting with Sendmail is a little tricky. A good document that describes the technique can be found on the *Virtual Hosting With Sendmail* [http://www.sendmail.org/virtual-hosting.html] page. Virtual hosting is also discussed briefly in the tutorial section of this chapter.

NOTE *For virtual hosting in Sendmail, you will also need to perform some configuration in* **Address Mapping** *and possibly in* **Outgoing Addresses (generics)**.

Domain Masquerading

The Domain Masquerading page provides access to the domain masquerading features of Sendmail. This allows you to make all outgoing messages appear to be from the same domain. When a domain masquerading rule is in place, Sendmail will replace the From address of all outgoing mail to appear to come from the domain to be masqueraded as. Also see the **Local Domains** page for more as well as a helpful link regarding virtual hosting in Sendmail.

Trusted Users

Ordinarily, Sendmail will not allow a user to claim to be a different user. However, if listed here, users will be trusted to claim they are another user or from another domain. Care should be taken when using this option, as it is one of the safeguards against *spoofed* email addresses.

Address Mapping

An Address mapping is similar to an alias, except they are able to handle domain information, as needed by virtual domains. To create an address mapping, all you must do is enter the address or domain to act upon. And a send to action to perform on each message as it is received by Sendmail. For example, if I host the domain penguinfeet.org on my swelltech.com server, then I must set up a method for mail sent to sysadmin@penguinfeet.org to make it into my mailbox at joe. So, I would create a map wherein the **Mail for** address is sysadmin@penguinfeet.org and the **Send to** address is joe.

Domain Routing

This option provides a special type of gateway in which your server accepts mail for a domain or host, but then passes it on to another specific mail server. This can be of use in environments where one or more subdomains have their own mail server that is behind a firewall and cannot directly deliver or receive mail on its own. Also, this allows Sendmail to provide gateway/proxy/translation services, if the other mail server does not support common transports and protocols. This use is in decline, as the vast majority of mail servers (even the few not running Sendmail) now speak the common protocols. These domains should not be listed in **Local Domains**, as then the server would accept the mail for local delivery, which is not what is desired in this case. You should still have a DNS MX record that points to the Sendmail server for each of the domains listed here, so that mail will be sent first to this system, where it then will handle it in whatever way is defined.

Mail for

This field allows you to enter a host or domain for which Sendmail will accept mail. It will not deliver the mail locally, but will instead pass it on to another server.

Delivery

Here you select how Sendmail will deliver the mail for the selected domain. The most common method is SMTP; however, Sendmail supports a wide range of delivery methods.

Send to

This should be the mail server where mail for this domain should be forwarded to. Checking the **Ignore MX for SMTP delivery** box will cause Sendmail to ignore MX entries in the DNS server for the domain and send to an explicitly selected server.

Outgoing Addresses (Generics)

Here you define mappings that Sendmail will use to modify the From addresses of outgoing mail (either from local users or from other hosts for delivery to other servers). This can be useful if you host multiple domains on the same mail server and want mail from some users to be addressed as though coming from those other domains. You must also include any domains to be remapped on the **Outgoing Domains** page, before Sendmail will perform any remappings on an address. Also, this mapping will not affect mail delivered to local users unless your .cf contains support for FEATURE('always_add_domain').

NOTE *This option is not enabled by default in most Linux distributions and other operating systems, nor in a default Sendmail installation. You must add the* genericstable *feature to your* sendmail.mc *file and regenerate the* .cf *file. The procedure for regenerating a* .cf *is documented later in this guide.*

Mail from

Here you enter a username or full email address for a user to remap.

Change to

Here you enter the address to change the above address into.

Manually edit /etc/mail/genericstable

Clicking this provides a simple text entry field, where all genericstable mappings are listed. You may edit them manually here. Take care, however, as manually edited entries are not checked by Webmin for grammatical correctness.

Outgoing Domains

By default Sendmail only performs **Outgoing Address** translations on mail from local users (users in the same domain as the Sendmail server). Any outside domains to be remapped must be entered here.

Domain Mapping

This feature allows you to remap all To and From addresses for a domain to another domain. This is useful if, for example, your company changes names and you'd like all mail to be changed from mailuser@oldname.com to mailuser@newname.com. This change will affect all mail that is delivered to, relayed through, or sent out from your server. Use of this should be limited to *your domains*.

Spam Control

On this page, you may configure any number of rules, with the purpose of preventing spammers from using your system and network resources for their evil purposes. Though this is just the tip of the iceberg for the spam control features provided by recent Sendmail versions, it does provide you with a very good means of preventing spam on your network. The first and primary goal is to prevent anyone from outside of your network from using your server as a relay for spam. Luckily, in recent versions of Sendmail, the default is to refuse to relay from any host not on your local network. This makes your job a little easier, because all you must do is allow mail relaying from your trusted hosts and domains. Here also, you can add rules to explicitly disallow mail from some known spammers. For example, if your users began receiving large batches of unsolicited commercial email (*UCE*, affectionately known as spam) from the big-dumbspammers.com (not a real domain at the time of this writing) and the administrators of this domain either don't care or are active participants in the spamming, you could simply block them from sending mail to any of our clients. You would enter the domain name and select Reject or provide an error message by using the Error code.

  For more on spam control topics in Sendmail, the *Allowing controlled SMTP relaying in Sendmail* [http://www.sendmail.org/tips/relaying.html] page provides more documentation for several of the new Sendmail features to prevent spam, such as using *The Realtime Blackhole List* [http://mail-abuse.org/rbl/], which provides a blacklist of known spammers and open relays. Also, it may be worthwhile to visit *The Mail Abuse Prevention System* [http://mail-abuse.org/] for more on ways to fight spam.

Relay Domains

Any local domains that you would like to allow relaying to should be listed here. Any incoming mail that is not for a local user and not for one of these listed domains will be rejected by Sendmail. If your Sendmail is providing mail service for several domains in a virtual hosting fashion, those domains should be listed here also.

Mail Queue

This page provides access to the mail queue. Depending on your configuration, your queue may be a fleeting thing, or it may fill until it is flushed periodically or manually. Usually, if you have full-time Net access and a full-time DNS server, you will use the background mode of delivering mail. In this case, mail will only be in the queue for a few seconds or minutes before being sent out to the recipient servers. However, in the event of a transient delivery failure (a non-permanent error), the message will remain in the queue until the message is discarded (due to permanent error) or successfully sent. Any message in the queue may be viewed by clicking the message ID. Also, messages may be deleted from the queue. Finally, it is possible to manually flush the queue, and Sendmail will attempt to deliver all messages in the queue immediately.

User Mailboxes

A great feature of the Webmin Sendmail module is the ability to read mail via a Web interface. While not a full-featured mail client (even as web-based clients go), it is a quick and easy way to check messages for accounts that ordinarily do not get checked by a user. For example, on my system, I receive daily backup reports from my backup system, so I check them periodically via the Webmin interface just to look out for problems.

To check mail for root simply click the name. From there you'll be presented with a list of all of that user's emails. Clicking the message will display it. From the **User Email** page it is also possible to delete messages and to compose a new message (Figure 11-2).

Editing the m4 Configuration File

Sendmail on your system probably has a pretty good feature set included in the default sendmail.cf. But as has been discussed, some features are often left out, such as genericstable. Usually, these features are not needed, but if they are, you must add them to your configuration file. Manually editing the sendmail.cf is generally regarded as not being an option for mere mortals like you and I (Eric Allman, the creator of Sendmail, *might* be able to do it). However, recent versions of Sendmail provide a novel method of adding features to the sendmail.cf, which uses a macro file named sendmail.mc and the **m4** macro processor.

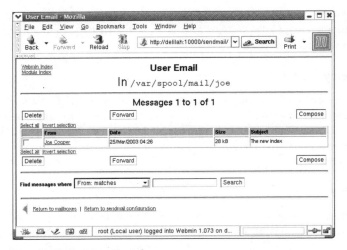

Figure 11-2: User Email

Adding a Feature

Unlike directly editing the .cf, adding a feature using the **m4** macro file is actually pretty easy.

After opening the **M4 Configuration** page, you'll see a file that looks something like the page shown in Figure 11-3.

Each line, with the exception of the dnl comment lines and the divert(-1) line, are of the form macro-type(value list). In this example, you're going to add a new feature called genericstable. So you'll insert a line like this into the FEATURE list:

```
FEATURE(`genericstable',`hash -o /etc/mail/genericstable')
```

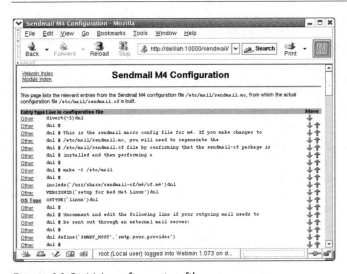

Figure 11-3: M4 configuration file

To do this, select Feature from the drop-down list at the bottom of the page, and click the **Add new entry of type** button. Then, select genericstable (Outgoing Addresses). Next in the parameters field you specify the type and location of the table file, hash -o /etc/mail/genericstable. The single quote marks are not required, as Webmin will insert them for you. For later convenience it is probably wise to use the arrow buttons on the right of the page to raise the new entry to be just below the other FEATURE lines in your file. It isn't strictly necessary, but it is nice to have neat configuration files, even if Webmin hides them from you most of the time.

After saving the changed file, you will generate the new sendmail.cf (don't forget to back up the old one to another file if you've already set up your Sendmail). To create a new sendmail.cf based on your .mc file, click the **Rebuild Sendmail Configuration** button. You'll then be able to open the **Outgoing Domains** page, and create the new genericstable file and edit it normally. A restart of Sendmail will be required to apply the changes you've made.

Tutorial: Setting Up Sendmail

When first installed Sendmail will only need a few small changes in order to begin providing service for sending and receiving mail. The first step is to specify for whom mail will be accepted, which you will specify in the **Local Domains** page, while the second step will be to permit local network users to send, or relay, email through the server, which will be specified in the **Spam Control** page.

NOTE   *This tutorial assumes you have already configured DNS service for your network, including an MX record for your domain. If you haven't already done so, refer back to the BIND chapter, and configure name resolution before attempting the steps in this tutorial.*

Configuring Domains to Receive Mail For

By default, Sendmail is not configured to receive mail for any host or network other than the machine on which it is running. So you must first configure Sendmail to permit anyone to send mail for delivery to your domain through your server. Open the **Local Domains** page, and enter the domains for which your server will accept mail. In my case, I would enter swelltech.com. Any number of domains can be entered here, as can host names, so I could also enter www.swelltech.com if ever I expected mail to be delivered to that address.

Click the Save button to update the sendmail.cf file. This will add new Cw lines to include your specified domains.

Permitting Local Users to Relay

The next step to achieving a simple mail server is to permit your local users to send mail through your server. Click the **Spam Control** icon, and create one or more rules matching your local networks. To create a new rule, first select a **Mail source** of Network, and specify the IP of the network you'd like to relay for. For example, on a local network using private IP addresses, one might enter 192.168.1 to specify all of the hosts in the 192.168.1.0/24 network. Then, select Allow relaying, and click **Create** to add the new rule to the access file.

Finally, return to the primary Sendmail page, and click the **Start Sendmail** button. It is usually useful to keep an eye on the logs when starting a daemon so that problems will be immediately obvious. Sendmail logs to the `maillog` on most systems, which is likely located in `/var/log` directory. You can use the Webmin **System Logs** module to view this log.

Tutorial: Virtual Hosting Email with Sendmail

Virtual hosting is a rather broad term applied to many network services to specify that the server in question provides service to two or more network domains with some degree of separation. Specifically, in the case of a mail server, it means that the mail server will deliver to a unique local user based on the username *and* the domain in the to field of the received email. For example, an email to `joe@swelltech.com` would be treated differently from an email sent to `joe@notswelltech.com` and would be delivered to a different mailbox.

As with most Open Source software there are many ways to accomplish our goal, but here you'll learn the simplest method provided by Sendmail. Configuring Sendmail for virtual mail hosting is a three-step process. First, DNS must be appropriately configured for each domain being served including an MX record, as documented in the BIND chapter of this book. Second, the new domain is added to the **Local Domains** table. Finally, one or more entries are added to the **Address Mapping** table. As DNS has its own chapter, and adding an entry to the **Local Domains** table was covered in the preceding tutorial, you'll only learn the final step here.

Adding Address Mapping Entries

Click on the **Address Mapping** icon, and create new mappings as appropriate for your environment. To create a new entry, select Address and fill in the address on which mail will be received in the **Mail for** field. This will include the name and domain name of the recipient, so for example, I might enter `joe@virtualhost.com` in this field. Next, select the Address option and enter the destination mailbox for this user in the, which needs to be an existing user, into the **Send to** field. For example, I might enter a username of `virtualhost-joe` here. The username must be created on the system, as well, which can be done using the section called "Users and Groups" in Chapter 5.

Click the **Create** button, and test your work by sending mail to your newly created virtual user.

12

SQUID

Squid is a feature-rich and extremely flexible web-caching proxy daemon. Most configuration is performed by editing a simple configuration file called `squid.conf`, which is usually located in `/usr/local/squid/etc/squid.conf` or, on systems derived from Red Hat Linux, `/etc/squid/squid.conf`. Each behavior is set by a directive followed by one or more options. The Webmin interface provides access to most of the directives available for configuring Squid. Because Squid is a quite complex package, the Webmin interface opens with a series of icons to represent the different types of configuration options. Figure 12-1 shows the Squid main page.

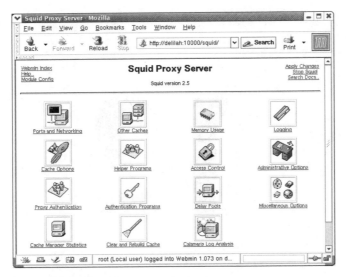

Figure 12-1: Squid proxy main page

These options are pretty self-explanatory, though a couple of them are worth discussing. The **Cache Manager Statistics** icon, when clicked, will open the Squid **cachemgr.cgi** program to provide direct access to all of Squid's various runtime values and statistics. The program provides real-time information about hit ratios, request rates, storage capacity, number of users, system load, and more. The **Calamaris Log Analysis** icon is only present if the **calamaris** access.log analyzer is present on your system. Calamaris is a nice Perl script that will parse your access log files and provide a nice overview of the type of usage your cache is seeing. Note that by default the **Calamaris** Webmin tool will only parse the last 50,000 lines of your access log. This number can be raised in the **Squid** module configuration, but is not recommended on heavily loaded caches. The parsing of the access logs is a very system-intensive task that could interfere with your system's ability to continue answering requests.

Ports and Networking

The **Ports and Networking** page provides you with the ability to configure most of the network level options of Squid. Squid has a number of options to define what ports Squid operates on, what IP addresses it uses for client traffic and intercache traffic, and multicast options. Usually, on dedicated caching systems these options will not be useful. But in some cases you may need to adjust these to prevent the Squid daemon from interfering with other services on the system or on your network.

Proxy port

Sets the network port on which Squid operates. This option is usually 3128 by default and can almost always be left on this address, except when multiple Squids are running on the same system, which is usually ill-advised. This option corresponds to the http_port option in squid.conf.

ICP port

This is the port on which Squid listens for Internet Cache Protocol, or *ICP*, messages. ICP is a protocol used by web caches to communicate and share data. Using ICP it is possible for multiple web caches to share cached entries so that if any one local cache has an object, the distant origin server will not have to be queried for the object. Further, *cache hierarchies* can be constructed of multiple caches at multiple privately interconnected sites to provide improved hit rates and higher-quality web response for all sites. More on this in later sections. This option correlates to the icp_port directive.

Incoming TCP address

The address on which Squid opens an HTTP socket that listens for client connections and connections from other caches. By default Squid does not bind to any particular address and will answer on any address that is active on the system. This option is not usually used, but can provide some additional level of security, if you wish to disallow any outside network users from proxying through your web cache. This option correlates to the tcp_incoming_address directive.

Outgoing TCP address

Defines the address on which Squid sends out packets via HTTP to clients and other caches. Again, this option is rarely used. It refers to the tcp_outgoing_address directive.

Incoming UDP address

Sets the address on which Squid will listen for ICP packets from other web caches. This option allows you to restrict which subnets will be allowed to connect to your cache on a *multi-homed*, or containing multiple subnets, Squid host. This option correlates to the udp_incoming_address directive.

Outgoing UDP address

The address on which Squid will send out ICP packets to other web caches. This option correlates to the udp_outgoing_address.

Multicast groups

The multicast groups that Squid will join to receive multicast ICP requests. This option should be used with great care, as it is used to configure your Squid to listen for multicast ICP queries. Clearly if your server is not on the MBone, this option is useless. And even if it is, this may not be an ideal choice. Refer to the *Squid FAQ* [http://www.squid-cache.org/Doc/FAQ/FAQ-13.html] on this subject for a more complete discussion. This option refers to the `mcast_groups` directive.

TCP receive buffer

The size of the buffer used for TCP packets being received. By default Squid uses whatever the default buffer size for your operating system is. This should probably not be changed unless you know what you're doing, and there is little to be gained by changing it in most cases. This correlates to the `tcp_recv_bufsize` directive.

Other Caches

The **Other Caches** page provides an interface to one of Squid's most interesting, but also widely misunderstood, features. Squid is the reference implementation of ICP, a simple but effective means for multiple caches to communicate with each other regarding the content that is available on each. This opens the door for many interesting possibilities when one is designing a caching infrastructure.

Internet Cache Protocol

It is probably useful to discuss how ICP works and some common usages for ICP within Squid, in order to quickly make it clear what it is good for, and perhaps even more importantly, what it is *not* good for. The most popular uses for ICP are discussed, and more good ideas will probably arise in the future as the Internet becomes even more global in scope and the web-caching infrastructure must grow with it.

Parent and Sibling Relationships

The ICP protocol specifies that a web cache can act as either a parent or a sibling. A *parent cache* is simply an ICP capable cache that will answer both hits and misses for child caches, while a *sibling* will only answer hits for other siblings. This subtle distinction means simply that a parent cache can proxy for caches that have no direct route to the Internet. A sibling cache, on the other hand, cannot be relied upon to answer all requests, and your cache must have another method to retrieve requests that cannot come from the sibling. This usually means that in sibling relationships, your cache will also have a direct connection to the Internet or a parent proxy that can retrieve misses from the origin servers. ICP is a somewhat chatty protocol, in that an ICP request will be sent to every neighbor cache each time a cache miss occurs. By default, whichever cache replies with an ICP hit first will be the cache used to request the object.

When to Use ICP

ICP is often used in situations wherein one has multiple Internet connections, or several types of paths to Internet content. Other possibilities include having a *cache mesh* such as the *IRCache Hierarchy* [http://www.ircache.net/Cache/] in the

U.S. or *The National Janet Web Caching Service* [http://wwwcache.ja.net/] in the UK, which can utilize lower-cost non-backbone links to connect several remote caches in order to lower costs and raise performance. Finally, it is possible, though usually not recommended, to implement a rudimentary form of load balancing through the use of multiple parents and multiple child web caches. All of these options are discussed in some detail, but this document should not be considered the complete reference to ICP. Other good sources of information include the two RFCs on the subject, *RFC 2186* [http://www.ircache.net/Cache/ICP/rfc2186.txt], which discusses the protocol itself, and *RFC 2187* [http://www.ircache.net/Cache/ICP/rfc2187.txt], which describes the application of ICP.

One common ICP-based solution in use today is satellite cache pre-population services. In this case, there are at least two caches at a site, one of which is connected to a satellite Internet uplink. The satellite-connected cache is provided by the service provider, and it is automatically filled with popular content via the satellite link. The other cache uses the satellite-connected cache as a sibling, which it queries for every cache miss that it has. If the satellite connected sibling has the content it will be served from the sibling cache; if not the primary cache will fetch the content from the origin server or a parent cache. ICP is a pretty effective, if somewhat bandwidth and processor intensive, means of accomplishing this task. A refinement of this process would be to use Cache-Digests for the satellite connected sibling in order to reduce traffic between the sibling caches. Nonetheless, ICP is a quite good method of implementing this idea.

Another common use is cache meshes. A cache mesh is, in short, a number of web caches at remote sites interconnected using ICP. The web caches could be in different cities, or they could be in different buildings of the same university or different floors in the same office building. This type of hierarchy allows a large number of caches to benefit from a larger client population than is directly available to it. All other things being equal, a cache that is not overloaded will perform better (with regard to hit ratio) with a larger number of clients. Simply put, a larger client population leads to a higher quality of cache content, which in turn leads to higher hit ratios and improved bandwidth savings. So, whenever it is possible to increase the client population without overloading the cache, such as in the case of a cache mesh, it may be worth considering. Again, this type of hierarchy can be improved upon by the use of Cache Digests, but ICP is usually simpler to implement and is a widely supported standard, even on non-Squid caches.

Finally, ICP is also sometimes used for load balancing multiple caches at the same site. ICP, or even Cache Digests for that matter, are almost *never* the best way to implement load balancing. However, for completeness, I'll discuss it briefly. Using ICP for load balancing can be achieved in a few ways. One common method is to have several local siblings, which can each provide hits to the others' clients, while the client load is evenly divided across the number of caches. Another option is to have a very fast but low-capacity web cache in front of two or more lower-cost, but higher-capacity, parent web caches. The parents will then provide the requests in a roughly equal amount. As mentioned, there are much better options for balancing web caches, the most popular being WCCP (version 1 is fully supported by Squid), and L4 or L7 switches.

Other Proxy Cache Servers

This section of the **Other Caches** page provides a list of currently configured sibling and parent caches, and also allows one to add more neighbor caches. Clicking the name of a neighbor cache will allow you to edit it. This section also provides the vital information about the neighbor caches, such as the type (parent, sibling, multicast), the proxy or HTTP port, and the ICP or UDP port of the caches. Note that Proxy port is the port where the neighbor cache normally listens for client traffic, which defaults to 3128.

Edit Cache Host

Clicking a cache peer name or clicking *Add another cache* on the primary **Other Caches** page brings you to this page, which allows you to edit most of the relevant details about neighbor caches (Figure 12-2).

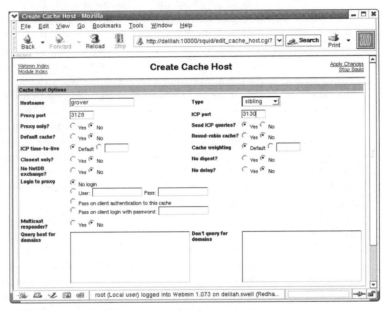

Figure 12-2: Edit Cache Host page

Hostname

The name or IP address of the neighbor cache you want your cache to communicate with. Note that this will be one-way traffic. Access Control Lists, or ACLs, are used to allow ICP requests from other caches. ACLs are covered later. This option plus most of the rest of the options on this page correspond to cache_peer lines in squid.conf.

Type

The type of relationship you want your cache to have with the neighbor cache. If the cache is upstream, and you have no control over it, you will need to consult with the administrator to find out what kind of relationship you should set up. If it is configured wrong, cache misses will likely result in errors for your users. The options here are sibling, parent, and multicast.

Proxy port

The port on which the neighbor cache is listening for standard HTTP requests. Even though the caches transmit availability data via ICP, actual web objects are still transmitted via HTTP on the port usually used for standard client traffic. If your neighbor cache is a Squid-based cache, then it is likely to be listening on the default port of 3128. Other common ports used by cache servers include 8000, 8888, 8080, and even 80 in some circumstances.

ICP port

The port on which the neighbor cache is configured to listen for ICP traffic. If your neighbor cache is a Squid-based proxy, this value can be found by checking the icp_port directive in the squid.conf file on the neighbor cache. Generally, however, the neighbor cache will listen on the default port 3130.

Proxy only?

A simple yes or no question to tell whether objects fetched from the neighbor cache should be cached locally. This can be used when all caches are operating well below their client capacity, but disk space is at a premium or hit ratio is of prime importance.

Send ICP queries?

Tells your cache whether or not to send ICP queries to a neighbor. The default is Yes, and it should probably stay that way. ICP queries is the method by which Squid knows which caches are responding and which caches are closest or best able to quickly answer a request.

Default cache

This be switched to Yes if this neighbor cache is to be the *last-resort* parent cache to be used in the event that no other neighbor cache is present as determined by ICP queries. Note that this does not prevent it from being used normally while other caches are responding as expected. Also, if this neighbor is the sole parent proxy, and no other route to the Internet exists, this should be enabled.

Round-robin cache?

Chooses whether to use round-robin scheduling between multiple parent caches in the absence of ICP queries. This should be set on all parents that you would like to schedule in this way.

ICP time-to-live

Defines the multicast TTL for ICP packets. When using multicast ICP, it is usually wise for security and bandwidth reasons to use the minimum tty suitable for your network.

Cache weighting

Sets the *weight* for a parent cache. When using this option it is possible to set higher numbers for preferred caches. The default value is 1, and if left unset for all parent caches, whichever cache responds positively first to an ICP query will be sent a request to fetch that object.

Closest only

Allows you to specify that your cache wants only CLOSEST_PARENT_MISS replies from parent caches. This allows your cache to then request the object from the parent cache *closest* to the origin server.

No digest?

Chooses whether this neighbor cache should send cache digests.

No NetDB exchange

When using ICP, it is possible for Squid to keep a database of network information about the neighbor caches, including availability and RTT, or *Round Trip Time*, information. This usually allows Squid to choose more wisely which caches to make requests to when multiple caches have the requested object.

No delay?

Prevents accesses to this neighbor cache from affecting delay pools. Delay pools, discussed in more detail later, are a means by which Squid can regulate bandwidth usage. If a neighbor cache is on the local network, and bandwidth usage between the caches does not need to be restricted, then this option can be used.

Login to proxy

Select this if you need to send authentication information when challenged by the neighbor cache. On local networks, this type of security is unlikely to be necessary.

Multicast responder

Allows Squid to know where to accept multicast ICP replies. Because multicast is fed on a single IP to many caches, Squid must have some way of determining which caches to listen to and what options apply to that particular cache. Selecting Yes here configures Squid to listen for multicast replies from the IP of this neighbor cache.

Query host for domains, Don't query for domains

These two options are the only options on this page to configure a directive other than cache_peer in Squid. In this case it sets the cache_peer_domain option. This allows you to configure whether requests for certain domains can be queried via ICP and which should not. It is often used to configure caches not to query other caches for content within the local domain. Another common usage, such as in the national web hierarchies discussed above, is to define which web cache is used for requests destined for different TLDs. So, for example, if one has a low cost satellite link to the U.S. backbone from another country that is preferred for web traffic over the much more expensive land line, one can configure the satellite-connected cache as the cache to query for all .com, .edu, .org, net, .us, and .gov addresses.

Cache Selection Options

This section provides configuration options for general ICP configuration (Figure 12-3). These options affect all of the other neighbor caches that you define.

Figure 12-3: Some global ICP options

Directly fetch URLs containing

Allows you to configure a match list of items to always fetch directly rather than query a neighbor cache. The default here is *cgi-bin ?* and should continue to be included unless you know what you're doing. This helps prevent wasting inter-cache bandwidth on lots of requests that are usually never considered cacheable, and so will never return hits from your neighbor caches. This option sets the hierarchy_stoplist directive.

ICP query timeout

The time in milliseconds that Squid will wait before timing out ICP requests. The default allows Squid to calculate an optimum value based on average RTT of the neighbor caches. Usually, it is wise to leave this unchanged. However, for reference, the default value in the distant past was 2000, or 2 seconds. This option edits the icp_query_timeout directive.

Multicast ICP timeout

Timeout in milliseconds for *multicast probes*, which are sent out to discover the number of active multicast peers listening on a given multicast address. This configures the mcast_icp_query_timeout directive and defaults to 2000 ms, or 2 seconds.

Dead peer timeout

Controls how long Squid waits to declare a peer cache *dead*. If there are no ICP replies received in this amount of time, Squid will declare the peer dead and will not expect to receive any further ICP replies. However, it continues to send ICP queries for the peer and will mark it active again on receipt of a reply. This timeout also affects when Squid expects to receive ICP replies from peers. If more than this number of seconds have passed since the last ICP reply was received, Squid will not expect to receive an ICP reply on the next query. Thus, if your time between requests is greater than this timeout, your cache will send more requests DIRECT rather than through the neighbor caches.

Memory Usage

This page provides access to most of the options available for configuring the way Squid uses memory and disks (Figure 12-4). Most values on this page can remain unchanged, except in very high load or low resource environments, where tuning can make a measurable difference in how well Squid performs.

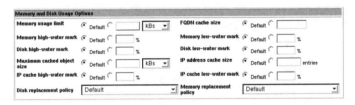

Figure 12-4: Memory and disk usage

Memory usage limit

The limit on how much memory Squid will use for *some parts* of its core data. Note that this does not restrict or limit Squid's total process size. What it does do is set aside a portion of RAM for use in storing in-transit and hot objects, as well as negative cached objects. Generally, the default value of 8MB is suitable for most situations, though it is safe to lower it to 4 or 2MB in extremely low load situations. It can also be raised significantly on high-memory systems to increase performance by a small margin. Keep in mind that large cache directories increase the memory usage of Squid by a large amount, and even a machine with a lot of memory can run out of memory and go into swap if cache memory and disk size are not appropriately balanced. This option edits the cache_mem directive. See the section on cache directories for more complete discussion of balancing memory and storage.

CAUTION *If Squid is using what you consider to be too much memory, do not look here for a solution. It defaults to a modest 8MB, and only when you have configured a very small amount of cache storage will this 8MB be a significant portion of the memory Squid allocates. If you do find yourself running out of memory, you can lower the size of your configured cache directories for a more noticeable decrease in memory used.*

FQDN cache size

Size of the in-memory cache of *fully qualified domain names*. This configures the fqdncache_size parameter and defaults to 1024, which is usually a safe value. In environments where DNS queries are slow, raising this may help.

Memory high water mark, Memory low water mark

Sets the points at which Squid begins to remove objects from memory. As memory usage climbs past the low water mark, Squid more aggressively tries to free memory. Note this applies to the memory usage limit defined above, *not* the total process size of Squid. If you have a system that is doing double or triple duty and providing more than cache services, it may be wise to set the low water mark at a low number, like 50%, and the high mark at a high number like 95%. In such a case, Squid will mostly keep its usage at 50%, but if it begins to get overloaded, or a particularly large object comes through the cache, it can briefly go over that point. This option configures the cache_mem_low and cache_mem_high options, which default to 90% and 95%, respectively.

Disk high-water mark, Disk low-water mark

Provide a mechanism for disk usage similar to the memory water marks above. To maximize hit ratio and provide most efficient use of disk space, leave this at the default values of 90% and 95%. Or to maximize performance and minimize fragmentation on disk, set them to a higher spread, such as 85% and 100%. Note that these settings are not where the amount of disk space to use is configured, they only define the percent of the allotted cache space at which Squid should begin to prune out old data to make room for incoming new objects. These options correlate to the cache_swap_high and cache_swap_low directives.

Maximum cached object size

The size of the largest object that Squid will attempt to cache. Objects larger than this will never be written to disk for later use. Refers to the maximum_object_size directive.

IP address cache size, IP cache high-water mark, IP address low-water mark

The size of the cache used for IP addresses and the high and low water marks for the cache, respectively. This option configures the ipcache_size, ipcache_high, and ipcache_low directives, which default to 1024 entries, 95%, and 90%.

Logging

Squid provides a number of logs that can be used when debugging problems and when measuring the effectiveness and identifying users and the sites they visit (Figure 12-5). Because Squid can be used to "snoop" on user's browsing habits, one should carefully consider privacy laws in your region and, more importantly, be considerate to your users. That being said, logs can be very valuable tools in ensuring that your users get the best service possible from your cache.

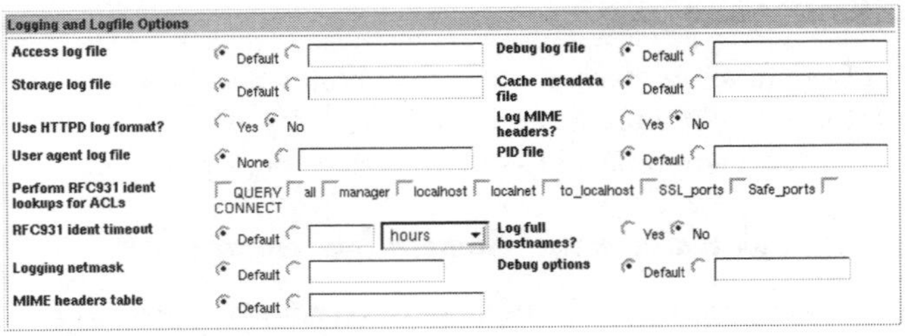

Figure 12-5: Logging configuration

Access log file

The location of the cache access.log. The Squid access.log is the file in which Squid writes a small one-line entry for every request served by the cache. This option correlates to the cache_access_log directive and usually defaults to /usr/local/squid/log/access.log or on some RPM-based systems /var/log/squid/access.log. The format of the standard log file looks like this:

```
973421337.543  11801 192.168.1.1 TCP_MISS/200 1999 GET http://www.google.com/ -
DIRECT/64.208.34.100 text/html
```

In the preceding line, each field represents some piece of information that may be of interest to an administrator:

1. *System time* in standard UNIX format. The time in seconds since 1970. There are many tools to convert this to human readable time, including this simple Perl script:

```
#! /usr/bin/perl -p
s/^\d+\.\d+/localtime $&/e;
```

2. *Duration* or the elapsed time in milliseconds the transaction required.

3. *Client address* or the IP address of the requesting browser. Some configurations may lead to a masked entry here, so that this field is not specific to one IP, but instead reports a whole network IP.

4. *Result codes* provides two entries separated by a slash. The first position is one of several *result codes* [http://www.squid-cache.org/Doc/FAQ/FAQ-6.html#cache-result-codes], which provide information about how the request was resolved or wasn't resolved if there was a problem. The second field contains the *status code* [http://www.squid-cache.org/Doc/FAQ/FAQ-6.html#http-status-codes], which comes from a subset of the standard HTTP status codes.

5. *Bytes* is the size of the data delivered to the client in bytes. Headers and object data are counted toward this total. Failed requests will deliver and error page, the size of which will also be counted.

6. *Request method* is the HTTP *request method* [http://www.squid-cache.org/Doc/
    FAQ/FAQ-6.html#request-methods] used to obtain an object. The most
    common method is, of course, GET, which is the standard method web
    browsers use to fetch objects.

7. *URL* is the complete Uniform Resource Locator requested by the client.

8. *RFC931* is the ident lookup information for the requesting client, if ident
    lookups are enabled in your Squid. Because of the performance impact,
    ident lookups are not used by default, in which case this field will always con-
    tain "-".

9. *Hierarchy code* consists of three items. The first is simply a prefix of
    TIMEOUT_ if all ICP requests timeout. The second (first if there is not
    TIMEOUT_ prepended) is the code that explains how the request was
    handled. This portion will be one of several *hierarchy codes* [http://
    www.squid-cache.org/Doc/FAQ/FAQ-6.html#hier-codes]. This result is
    informative regardless of whether your cache is part of a cache hierarchy,
    and will explain how the request was served. The final portion of this field
    contains the name or IP of the host from which the object was retrieved.
    This could be the origin server, a parent, or any other peer.

10. *Type* is simply the type of object that was requested. This will usually be a rec-
    ognizable MIME type, but some objects have no type or are listed as ":".

There are two other optional fields for cases when MIME header logging has
been turned on for debugging purposes. The full HTTP request and reply headers will be included enclosed in [and] square brackets.

Debug log file

The location for Squids cache.log file. This file contains startup configuration
information, as well as assorted error information during Squids operation. This
file is a good place to look when a website is found to have problems running
through the web cache. Entries here may point towards a potential solution. This
option correlates to the cache_log directive and usually defaults to either
/usr/local/squid/log/cache.log or /var/log/squid/cache.log on RPM-based systems.

Storage log file

Location of the cache's store log file. This file contains a transaction log of all
objects that are stored in the object store, as well as the time when they get
deleted. This file really doesn't have very much use on a production cache, and it
is primarily recommended for use in debugging. Therefore, it can be turned off
by entering none in the entry field. The default location is either /usr/local/squid/
log/store.log or /var/log/squid/store.log.

Cache metadata file

Filename used in each store directory to store the web cache meta data, which is a sort of index for the web cache object store. This is not a human-readable log, and it is strongly recommended that you leave it in its default location on each store directory, unless you really know what you're doing. This option correlates to the cache_swap_log directive.

Use HTTPD log format

Allows you to specify that Squid should write its access.log in HTTPD common log file format, such as that used by Apache and many other web servers. This allows you to parse the log and generate reports using a wider array of tools. However, this format does not provide several types of information specific to caches and is generally less useful when tracking cache usage and solving problems. Because there are several effective tools for parsing and generating reports from the Squid standard access logs, it is usually preferable to leave this at its default of being off. This option configures the emulate_httpd_log directive. The **Calamaris** cache access log analyzer does not work if this option is enabled.

Log MIME headers

Provides a means to log extra information about your requests in the access log. This causes Squid to also write the request and response MIME headers for every request. These will appear in brackets at the end of each access.log entry. This option correlates to the log_mime_hdrs directive.

Perform RFC931 ident lookups for ACLs

Indicates which of the Access Control Lists that are defined should have ident lookups performed for each request in the access log. Because of the performance impact of using this option, it is not on by default. This option configures the ident_lookup_access directive.

RFC931 ident timeout

The timeout, usually in seconds, for ident lookups. If this is set too high, you may be susceptible to denial of service from having too many outstanding ident requests. The default for this is 10 seconds, and it applies to the ident_timeout directive.

Log full hostnames

Configures whether Squid will attempt to resolve the host name, so the fully qualified domain name can be logged. This can, in some cases, increase latency of requests. This option correlates to the log_fqdn directive.

Logging netmask

Defines what portion of the requesting client IP is logged in the access.log. For privacy reasons it is often preferred to only log the network or subnet IP of the client. For example, a netmask of 255.255.255.0 will log the first three octets of the IP and fill the last octet with a zero. This option configures the client_netmask directive.

Debug options

Provides a means to configure all of Squid's various debug sections. Squid's debugging code has been divided into a number of sections. If there is a problem in one part of Squid, debug logging can be made more verbose for just that section. For example, to increase debugging for just the Storage Manager in Squid to its highest level of 9 while leaving the rest at the default of 1, the entry would look like Figure 12-6.

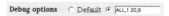

Figure 12-6: Setting Squid debug levels

There is a *complete list of debug sections* [http://www.swelltech.com/support/docs/squid/debug-sections.txt] at the Swell Technology website and in the Squid source distribution in the doc directory. More information can be found in the *Squid FAQ* [http://www.squid-cache.org/Doc/FAQ/FAQ-11.html#ss11.20].

MIME headers table

The pathname to Squid's MIME table. This usually should remain at the default value. This option configures the mime_table directive and defaults to /usr/local /squid/etc/mime.conf or /etc/squid/mime.conf.

Cache Options

The **Cache Options** page provides access to some important parts of the Squid configuration file. This is where the cache directories are configured as well as several timeouts and object size options.

Cache Directories

The **Cache directories** option sets the cache directories and the amount of space Squid is allowed to use on the device. The first example displays an example cache_dir line in the squid.conf file, while Figure 12-7 shows the **Cache Options** screen in Webmin where the same options can be configured.

```
cache_dir ufs /cache0 1500 8 256
```

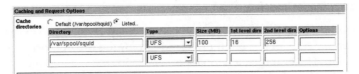

Figure 12-7: Configuring Squid's cache directories

The directive is cache_dir, while the options are the type of filesystem, the path to the cache directory, the size allotted to Squid, the number of top-level directories, and, finally, the number of second level directories. In the example, I've chosen the filesystem type ufs, which is a name for all standard UNIX filesystems. This type includes the standard Linux ext2 filesystem as well. Other possibilities for this option include aufs and diskd.

The next field is simply the space, in megabytes, of the disk that you want to allow Squid to use. Finally, the directory fields define the upper- and lower-level directories for Squid to use. Calculating the L1 number precisely is tricky, but not difficult if you use this formula:

```
x=Size of cache dir in KB (i.e., 6GB=~6,000,000KB)
y=Average object size (just use 13KB)
z=Number of directories per first level directory

(((x / y) / 256) / 256) * 2 = # of directories
```

As an example, if your cache used 6GB of each of two 13GB drives:

```
6,000,000 / 13 = 461538.5 / 256 = 1802.9 / 256 = 7 * 2 = 14
```

Your cache_dir line would look like this:

```
cache_dir ufs /cache0 6000 14 256
```

Other Cache Options

The rest of the **Cache Options** page is a bit of a hodgepodge of other general options (Figure 12-8). Generally most configuration will take place on this page, as it addresses many of the tunable items in Squid that can make a difference in performance.

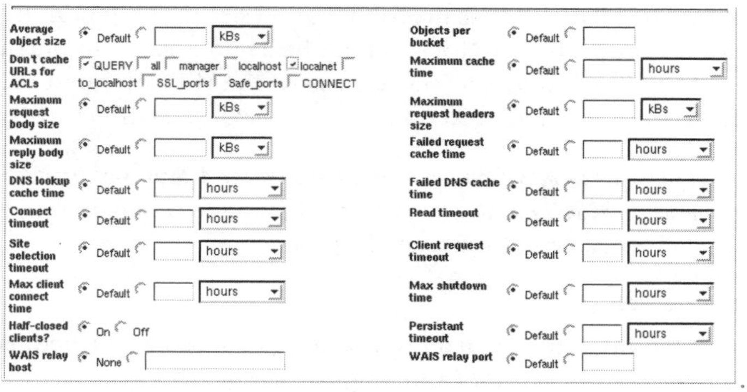

Figure 12-8: Other cache options

Average object size

The average size of objects expected in your cache. This item is generally safe at its default value of 13KB. In older versions of Squid (prior to 2.3) this option affected the number of filemap bits set aside by Squid at runtime. In newer Squids filemap bits are configured dynamically, as needed, and so configuration of this option is unnecessary and arguably pointless. This option will go away in some future version of Squid. Until then, it correlates to the store_avg_object_size directive.

Objects per bucket

The number of objects in each store hash table. Again, it is not worth bothering to change it, as its default value is probably a good safe value, and changing it provides little or nothing in the way of performance or efficiency improvements. This option corresponds to the store_objects_per_bucket directive.

Don't cache URLs for ACLs

Allows you to easily pick which ACL matches will not be cached. Requests that match the selected ACLs will always be answered from the origin server. This option correlates to the always_direct directive.

Maximum cache time

The maximum time an object will be allowed to remain in the cache. This time limit is rarely reached, because objects have so many occasions to be purged via the normal replacement of the cache object store. However, if object freshness is of prime importance, then it may be worthwhile to lower this from its default of 1 year to something much shorter, such as 1 week, though it is probably counterproductive to do so for most users. This option configures the reference_age parameter.

Maximum request size

The maximum size of request that will be accepted by Squid from the client. The default is 100KB, however, in environments where the POST method may be used to send larger files to web servers, or web mail is used for sending attachments, it will probably be necessary to raise this limit to something more reasonable. 8 or 16MB is probably a good size that will permit most uploads without any problems. Note that this bears no relation to the size of object that is being retrieved; it only affects the size of the HTTP request being sent from the client. This option corresponds to the request_size directive.

NOTE *Squid versions from 2.5 onward have removed the default size limit, and requests can be unlimited in size. Thus if you rely on the default limit being in place, you will need to modify your configuration when upgrading.*

Failed request cache time

The amount of time that a request error condition is cached. For example, some types of *connection refused* and *404 Not Found* errors are negatively cached.

DNS lookup cache time

The length of time that DNS lookups are cached. Squid provides functionality as a basic caching name server, in order to further accelerate web service through the proxy. This value defaults to 6 hours and correlates to the positive_dns_ttl directive. If rapid updates of cache DNS data are required, such as to keep up with dynamic DNS systems or to avoid load balance problems with local network sites in a website acceleration environment, it may be wise to reduce this value significantly. Ensuring you have reliable and suitably fast DNS service on the local network is mandatory, however, if you do reduce this value by a large amount.

Failed DNS cache time

The time period for which failed DNS requests are cached. This option corresponds to the negative_dns_ttl directive and defaults to 5 minutes. This option rarely needs tuning.

Connect timeout

An option to force Squid to close connections after a specified time. Some systems (notably older Linux versions) cannot be relied upon to time out connect requests. For this reason, this option specifies the timeout for how long Squid should wait for the connection to complete. This value defaults to 120 seconds (2 minutes) and correlates to the connect_timeout directive.

Read timeout

The timeout for server-side connections. Each successful read() request the timeout is reset to this amount. If no data is read within this period of time, the request is aborted and logged with ERR_READ_TIMEOUT. This option corresponds to read_timeout and defaults to 15 minutes.

Site selection timeout

The timeout for URN to multiple URLs selection. URN is a protocol designed for location-independent name resolution, specified in *RFC 2169* [http://www.ietf.org/rfc/rfc2169.txt]. This option configures the siteselect_timeout directive and defaults to 4 seconds. There is probably no need to change this.

Client request timeout

The timeout for HTTP requests from clients. By default the value is 5 minutes, and it correlates to the `request_timeout` directive.

Max client connect time

The time limit Squid sets for a client to remain connected to the cache process. This is merely a safeguard against clients that disappear without properly shutting down. It is designed to prevent a large number of sockets from being tied up in a CLOSE_WAIT state. The default for this option is 1440 minutes, or 1 day. This correlates to the `client_lifetime`.

Max shutdown time

The time Squid allows for existing connections to continue after it has received a shutdown signal. It will stop accepting new connections immediately, but connections already in progress will continue to be served for this amount of time. This option corresponds to the `shutdown_lifetime` configuration directive and defaults to 30 seconds, which is a good safe value. If rapid down->up time is more important than being polite to current clients, it can be lowered.

Half-closed clients

Defines Squid's behavior toward some types of clients that close the sending side of a connection while leaving the receiving side open. Turning this option off will cause Squid to immediately close connections when a read(2) returns "no more data to read". It's usually safe to leave this at the default value of yes. It corresponds to the `half_close_clients` directive.

Persistent timeout

The timeout value for persistent connections. Squid will close persistent connections if they are idle for this amount of time. Persistent connections will be disable entirely if this option is set to a value less than 10 seconds. The default is 120 seconds and likely doesn't need to be changed. This option configures the `pconn_timeout` directive.

WAIS relay host, WAIS relay port

The WAIS host and port to relay WAIS requests. *WAIS*, or Wide Area Information System, is a system to catalog and search large amounts of data via a WAIS or WWW browser. WAIS is a mostly deprecated protocol, but some sites probably do still exist, though this author has been unable to locate any to satiate his curiosity about the subject. These options correspond to the `wais_relay_host` and `wais_relay_port` directives and default to `localhost` and `8000`.

Helper Programs

Squid uses *helper programs* to provide extra functionality or to provide greater performance. Squid provides a standard API for several types of programs that provide extra services that do not fit well into the Squid core. Helper programs could be viewed as a simple means of modular design, allowing third parties to write modules to improve the features of Squid (Figure 12-9). That being said, some of Squid's standard functionality is also provided by helper programs. The standard helper programs include dnsserver, pinger, and several authentication modules. Third-party modules include redirectors, ad blockers, and additional authentication modules.

NOTE *Squid versions from 2.3 onward do not use the dnsserver helper program by default, replacing it with an internal non-blocking DNS resolver. This new internal DNS resolver is more memory and processor efficient, so is preferred. But in some circumstances, the older helper program is the better choice. If your Squid must be able to resolve based on any source other than a DNS server, such as via a hosts file or NIS, then you may need to use the external dnsserver helper.*

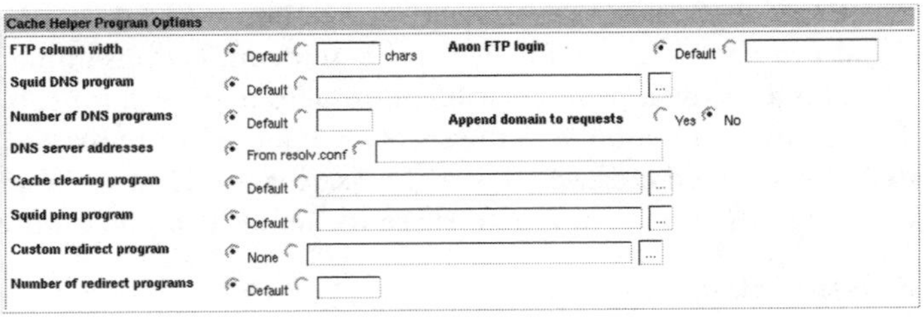

Figure 12-9: Cache helper program

FTP column width

The column width for auto-generated web pages of FTP sites queried through Squid when Squid is in forward proxy mode. Squid provides limited FTP proxy features to allow browsers (even older, non–FTP aware browsers) to communicate with FTP servers. This option gives some control over how Squid formats the resulting file lists. This option correlates to the `ftp_list_width` and defaults to 32.

NOTE *Squid only provides FTP proxy and caching services when acting as a traditional proxy, not when acting transparently. Squid does not currently provide FTP caching or proxying for standard FTP clients. The clients must be HTTP clients, for which Squid can provide gateway services.*

Anon FTP login

The email address Squid uses to log in to remote FTP servers anonymously. This can simply be a username followed by an @ symbol, which your domain name can be automatically attached to. Or it can be a full email address. This should be something reasonable for your domain, such as `wwwuser@mydomain.com`, or in the domainless case first mentioned, `Squid@`, which happens to be the default for this option. This corresponds to the `ftp_user` directive.

Squid DNS program

The helper program to use for DNS resolution. Because Squid requires a non-blocking resolver for its queries, an external program called **dnsserver** is included in the standard distribution. In Squid versions prior to 2.3, this program is the only standard choice for resolution, and the path to the file can be entered here. In Squid versions later than 2.3, there is a new default option, which is an internal non-blocking resolver that is more memory and CPU efficient. This option rarely needs to be changed from its default value. This option configures cache_dns_program directive.

Number of DNS programs

The number of external DNS resolver processes that will be started in order to serve requests. The default value of five is enough for many networks, however, if your Squid serves a large number of users, this value may need to be increased to avoid errors. However, increasing the number of processes also increases the load on system resources and may actually hinder performance if set too high. More than 10 is probably overkill. This option correlates to the dns_children directive.

Append domain to requests

When enabled, causes the dnsserver to add the local domain name to single component host names. It is normally disabled to prevent caches in a hierarchy from interpreting single component host names locally. This option configures the dns_defnames directive.

DNS server addresses

Normally defaults to From resolv.conf, which simply means that Squid's parent DNS servers will be drawn from the /etc/resolv.conf file found on the system Squid runs on. It is possible to select other DNS servers if needed—for example, to choose a more local caching DNS server or a remote Internet connected server. This option corresponds to the dns_nameservers directive.

Cache clearing program

The name of the helper program that deletes, or unlinks, old files in the cache to make room for newer objects. In all current versions of Squid, this helper is known as **unlinkd** and should probably not be changed from this unless you know what you're doing. This option configures the unlinkd_program directive.

Squid ping program

An external program that provides Squid with ICMP RTT information so that it can more effectively choose between multiple remote parent caches for request fulfillment. There are special cases when this option is required, and your Squid must have been compiled with the --enable-icmp configure option in order for it to work. This option should only be used on caches that have multiple parent caches on different networks that it must choose between. The default program to use for this task is called **pinger**. This option configures the `pinger_program` directive.

Custom redirect program, Number of redirect programs

Provides access to the redirector interface in Squid, so a redirector can be selected and the number of redirector processes needed configured. A redirector is, in short, just what it sounds like: a program that, when given a URL that matches some circumstances, redirects Squid to another URL. To be a little less brief and perhaps more complete, a redirector provides a method to export a request to an external program and then to import that program's response and act as though the client sent the resulting request. This allows for interesting functionality with Squid and an external redirector. To configure a redirector, enter the path to the redirector and the redirector filename, as shown in Figure 12-10. You should also enter any options to be passed to the redirector in the same field, as in the example shown.

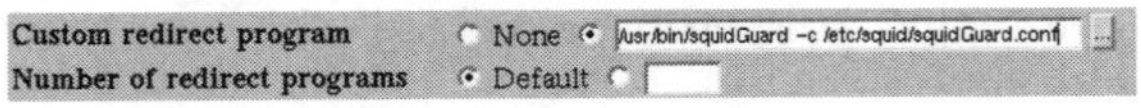

| Custom redirect program | ◯ None ⦿ | /usr/bin/squidGuard –c /etc/squid/squidGuard.conf | |
| Number of redirect programs | ⦿ Default ◯ | | |

Figure 12-10: Configuring a redirector

One common usage is to block objectionable content using a tool like *SquidGuard* [http://www.squidguard.org/]. Another popular use is to block advertising banners using the simple but effective *Ad Zapper* [http://www.zip.com.au/~cs/adzap/index.html]. The Ad Zapper not only allows one to block ads, it can also remove those pesky flashing New images and moving line images used in place of standard horizontal rules. Several other general-purpose redirectors exist that provide URL remapping for many different purposes. Two popular and well-supported general redirectors are *Squirm* [http://www.senet.com.au/squirm/] and *JesRed* [http://ivs.cs.uni-magdeburg.de/~elkner/webtools/jesred]. Finally, it is possible to write a custom redirector to provide any kind of functionality needed from your Squid. While it is not possible to use the redirector interface to alter a web page's content it is possible to perform in-line editing of some or all URLs to force many different types of results. The two redirect options configure the `redirect_program` and `redirect_children` directives.

Custom Authentication program, Number of authentication programs

Provides an interface to the external authentication interface within Squid. There are a large number of authentication modules for use with Squid, allowing users to be authenticated in a number of ways. The simplest authentication type is known as **ncsa_auth**, which uses a standard htpasswd-style password file to check for login name and password. More advanced options include a new NTLM module that allows authentication against a Windows NT domain controller, and LDAP authentication that allows use of Lightweight Directory Access Protocol servers. Most authentication modules work the same way and quite similarly to a redirector as discussed above. In Figure 12-11, you'll see the standard ncsa_auth authenticator and the location of the passwd file it should use for authenticating users. You'll notice the number of authenticator child processes has been increased from the default of 5 to 10, in order to handle quite heavy loads. These options edit the `authenticate_program` and `authenticate_children` directives, respectively.

Figure 1-11: Authentication configuration

NOTE *Authentication has been enhanced significantly in Squid 2.5 and above, adding new types of authentication (NTLM and Digest), as well as more flexible configuration options. If you are using one of these Squid versions, read the following section, "Authentication Programs," for more complete information.*

Authentication Programs

In version 2.5.STABLE1 and above, Squid has a wealth of new authentication features and options. Webmin has been expanded to account for the changes, and in the change, authentication configuration received its own section (Figure 12-12).

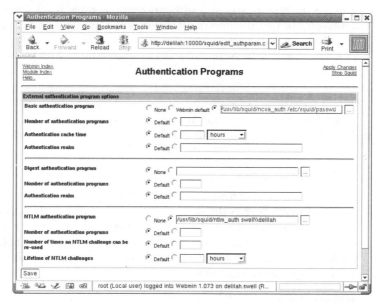

Figure 1-12: Authentication Programs

Squid 2.5 and above supports client authentication of three distinct types: Basic, Digest, and NTLM. Older Squids supported only Basic authentication, which is a simple, unencrypted authentication method documented originally. The two new methods, Digest and NTLM, support both plain-text and encrypted authentication mechanisms. Which method to use depends on your client population. Basic authentication works for all browser clients that fully support proxies. Digest authentication is a standard method of authenticating web clients securely, supported by all browsers that are fully HTTP/1.1 compliant (including modern versions of IE, Netscape, and Mozilla). NTLM is a proprietary mechanism developed by Microsoft and currently only supported by Microsoft client software.

Basic and Digest Authentication Options

Basic authentication is the simplest to use, because it is the most widely accessible and the simplest in implementation. Digest authentication is a secure authentication method documented in RFC 2617, providing encrypted authentication of proxy and web server users. The only configuration detail really required is the location of the authentication program and any command-line arguments to pass to the program, though a couple of additional parameters are available.

Basic authentication program, Digest authentication program

This is the only required option, if you wish to use Basic or Digest authentication with Squid. You may specify one of several authentication programs provided with Squid, like `ncsa_auth` to authenticate against a standalone `htpasswd`-style password file, `pam_auth` to authenticate against the local PAM system, or `smb_auth` to authenticate against a remote or local SMB server. Another, even simpler choice is to use the built-in Webmin authentication module. It is a simple NCSA-style authenticator that ties into the Webmin Squid user and password management tools without any additional configuration. This option correlates to the `auth_param basic program` directive or `auth_param digest program` and is disabled by default.

Number of authentication programs

This option correlates to the `auth_param basic children` or `auth_param digest children` directive and defaults to 5. If your Squid supports a very large number of users, you may need to raise this to 10 or 20.

Authentication cache time

This is the amount of time that Squid will cache authentication credentials. Squid normally queries the authentication program periodically and stores the result of the test in its own memory so it doesn't need to query the external authenticator frequently. This improves performance, but if rapidly changing credentials are required, you may wish to lower this value. This option correlates to the `auth_param basic credentialsttl`.

Authentication realm

When a client browser receives a basic authentication request, it includes a short string identifying the requester of the data. This information will usually be displayed to the user in the popup box where credentials are entered. This option correlates to the `auth_param basic realm` or `auth_param digest realm` directive and has no default.

NTLM authentication options

Like Digest authentication, NTLM authentication provides an encrypted connection to a network server. Beware that it is not an HTTP authentication scheme, however. It is a connection authentication scheme that cannot be proxied (though a proxy can use it to authenticate its own clients). NTLM is also less secure than Digest authentication and has a history of vulnerabilities. That said, it is quite popular, because Windows supports a sort of network "single sign-on", in which users only need to log on once to the local network, and they can be automatically authenticated to the proxy server using the same credentials.

NTLM authentication program

As in Basic and Digest authentication above, this will contain a path to the authentication program and any command-line arguments. Often the arguments will specify the domain or workgroup and the server to authenticate against. This option correlates to the `auth_param ntlm program` directive and is disabled by default.

Number of times an NTLM challenge can be re-used

This option configures the number of times that a particular NTLM challenge can be reused. Increasing this number may reduce latency and load on the server slightly, but can also increase the risk of replay attacks (where a challenge response is recorded and played back to imitate the connection of a legitimate user). This option correlates to the `auth_param ntlm max_challenge_reuses` directive and defaults to 0.

Lifetime of NTLM challenges

This option corresponds to the `auth_param ntlm max_challenge_lifetime` directive and defaults to 2 minutes. It is used to specify the length of time that a challenge can be reused. If a challenge is newer than this value *and* the challenge has been reused fewer than the previous value, a challenge will be reused.

Access Control

The access control functionality of Squid is perhaps its most complex set of features, but also among its most powerful. In fact, many use Squid primarily for these features. Because of its complexity, you will learn about it in steps, examining the process of creating and implementing an access control list. Access control lists in Squid has two meanings within the configuration file and within the Webmin interface. First, it signifies the whole *concept* of access control lists and all of the logic that can be applied to those lists. Second, it applies to the lists themselves, which are simply lists of some type of data to be matched against when some type of access rule is in place. For example, forcing a particular site or set of sites to not be cached requires a list of sites to not cache and then a separate rule to define what to do with that list (in this case, don't cache them). There is also a third type of option for configuring ICP access control. These three types of definition are separated in the Webmin panel into three sections. The first is labeled **Access control lists**, which lists existing ACLs and provides a simple interface for generating and editing lists of match criteria (Figure 12-13). The second is labeled **Proxy restrictions** and lists the current restrictions in place and the ACLs they affect. Finally, the **ICP restrictions** section lists the existing access rules regarding ICP messages from other web caches.

Access control lists

Name	Type	Matching...
QUERY	URL Path Regexp	cgi-bin \?
all	Client Address	0.0.0.0/0.0.0.0
manager	URL Protocol	cache_object
localhost	Client Address	127.0.0.1/255.255.255.255
localnet	Client Address	192.168.1.0/255.255.255.0
to_localhost	Web Server Address	127.0.0.0/8
SSL_ports	URL Port	443 563
Safe_ports	URL Port	80
Safe_ports	URL Port	21
Safe_ports	URL Port	443 563
Safe_ports	URL Port	70
Safe_ports	URL Port	210
Safe_ports	URL Port	1025-65535
Safe_ports	URL Port	280
Safe_ports	URL Port	488
Safe_ports	URL Port	591
Safe_ports	URL Port	777
CONNECT	Request Method	CONNECT
Create new ACL	Browser Regexp	

Figure 12-13: Access control lists

Access Control Lists

This section provides a list of existing ACLs and provides a means to create new ones (Figure 12-14). The first field in the table represents the name of the ACL, which is simply an assigned name, that can be just about anything the user chooses. The second field is the type of the ACL, which can be one of a number of choices that indicate to Squid what part of a request should be matched against for this ACL. The possible types include the requesting clients address, the web server address or host name, a regular expression matching the URL, and many more. The final field is the actual string to match. Depending on what the ACL type is, this may be an IP address, a series of IP addresses, a URL, a host name, and so on.

To edit an existing ACL, simply click the highlighted name. You will then be presented with a screen containing all relevant information about the ACL. Depending on the type of the ACL, you will be shown different data entry fields. The operation of each type is very similar, so for this example, you'll step through editing of the localhost ACL. Clicking the localhost button presents the page that's shown in Figure 12-15.

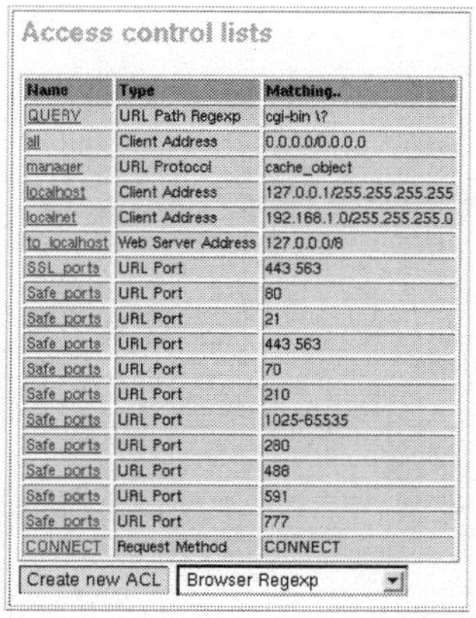
Access control lists
Name | Type | Matching..
QUERY | URL Path Regexp | cgi-bin \?
all | Client Address | 0.0.0.0/0.0.0.0
manager | URL Protocol | cache_object
localhost | Client Address | 127.0.0.1/255.255.255.255
localnet | Client Address | 192.168.1.0/255.255.255.0
to_localhost | Web Server Address | 127.0.0.0/8
SSL_ports | URL Port | 443 563
Safe_ports | URL Port | 80
Safe_ports | URL Port | 21
Safe_ports | URL Port | 443 563
Safe_ports | URL Port | 70
Safe_ports | URL Port | 210
Safe_ports | URL Port | 1025-65535
Safe_ports | URL Port | 280
Safe_ports | URL Port | 488
Safe_ports | URL Port | 591
Safe_ports | URL Port | 777
CONNECT | Request Method | CONNECT
Create new ACL
Browser Regexp

Figure 12-14: ACL section

The title of the table is **Client Address ACL**, which means the ACL is of the `Client Address` type and tells Squid to compare the incoming IP address with the IP address in the ACL. It is possible to select an IP based on the originating IP or the destination IP. The netmask can also be used to indicate whether the ACL matches a whole network of addresses or only a single IP. It is possible to include a number of addresses or ranges of addresses in these fields. Finally, the **Failure URL** is the address to send clients to if they have been denied access due to matching this particular ACL. Note that the ACL by itself does nothing; there must also be a proxy restriction or ICP restriction rule that uses the ACL for Squid to use the ACL.

Client Address ACL
ACL Name
localnet
From IP
To IP
Netmask
192.168.1.0
255.255.255.0
Failure URL

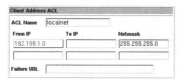

Figure 12-15: Edit an ACL

Creating a new ACL is equally simple (Figure 12-16). From the ACL page, in the **Access control lists** section, select the type of ACL you'd like to create. Then click **Create new ACL**. From there, as shown, you can enter any number of ACLs for the list. In my case, I've created a list called `SitesThatSuck`, which contains the websites of the Recording Industry Association of America and the Motion Picture Association of America. From there, I can add a proxy restriction to deny all accesses through my proxy to those two websites.

Figure 12-16: Creating an ACL

Available ACL Types

Browser Regexp

A *regular expression* that matches the client's browser type based on the *user agent* header. This allows for ACLs to operate based on the browser type in use. For example, using this ACL type, one could create an ACL for Netscape users and another for Internet Explorer users. This could then be used to redirect Netscape users to a Navigator-enhanced page, and IE users to an Explorer-enhanced page. This is probably not the wisest use of an administrator's time, but it does indicate the unmatched flexibility of Squid. This ACL type correlates to the browser ACL type.

Client IP Address

The IP address of the requesting client, or the client's IP address. This option refers to the src ACL in the Squid configuration file. An IP address and netmask are expected. Address ranges are also accepted.

Client Hostname

Matches against the client domain name. This option correlates to the srcdomain ACL and can be either a single domain name or a list of domain names, or the path to a file that contains a list of domain names. If a path to a file, it must be surrounded by parentheses. This ACL type can increase the latency and decrease throughput significantly on a loaded cache, as it must perform an address-to-name lookup for each request, so it is usually preferable to use the Client IP Address type.

Client Hostname Regexp

Matches against the client domain name. This option correlates to the srcdom_regex ACL, and can be either a single domain name, or a list of domain names, or a path to a file that contains a list of domain names. If a path to a file, it must be surrounded by parentheses.

Date and Time

This type is just what it sounds like, providing a means to create ACLs that are active during certain times of the day or certain days of the week. This feature is often used to block some types of content or some sections of the Internet during business or class hours. Many companies block pornography, entertainment, sports, and other clearly non–work-related sites during business hours, but then unblock them after hours. This might improve workplace efficiency in some situations (or it might just offend the employees). This ACL type allows you to enter days of the week and a time range or select all hours of the selected days. This ACL type is the same as the time ACL type directive.

Dest AS Number

The Destination *Autonomous System* number is the AS number of the server being queried. The autonomous system number ACL types are generally only used in Cache Peer, or ICP, access restrictions. Autonomous System numbers are used in organizations that have multiple Internet links and routers operating under a single administrative authority using the same *gateway protocol*. Routing decisions are then based on knowledge of the AS in addition to other possible data. If you are unfamiliar with the term autonomous system, it is usually safe to say you don't need to use ACLs based on AS. Even if you are familiar with the term, and have a local AS, you still probably have little use for the AS number ACL types, unless you have cache peers in other autonomous systems and need to regulate access based on that information. This type correlates to the dest_as ACL type.

Source AS Number

The Source Autonomous System number is another AS-related ACL type, and matches on the AS number of the source of the request. Equates to the src_as ACL type directive.

Ethernet Address

The Ethernet or *MAC* address of the requesting client. This option only works for clients on the same local subnet and only for certain platforms. Linux, Solaris, and some BSD variants are the supported operating systems for this type of ACL. This ACL can provide a somewhat secure method of access control, because MAC addresses are usually harder to spoof than IP addresses, and you can guarantee that your clients are on the local network (otherwise no ARP resolution can take place).

External Auth

This ACL type calls an external authenticator process to decide whether the request will be allowed. Many authenticator helper programs are available for Squid, including PAM, NCSA, UNIX passwd, SMB, NTLM (only in Squid 2.4), and so on. Note that authentication *cannot* work on a transparent proxy or HTTP accelerator. The HTTP protocol does not provide for two authentication stages (one local and one on remote websites). So in order to use an authenticator, your proxy must operate as a traditional proxy, where a client will respond appropriately to a proxy authentication request as well as external web server authentication requests. This correlates to the proxy_auth directive.

External Auth Regex

As above, this ACL calls an external authenticator process, but allows regex pattern or case insensitive matches. This option correlates to the proxy_auth_regex directive.

Proxy IP Address

The local IP address on which the client connection exists. This allows ACLs to be constructed that only match one physical network, if multiple interfaces are present on the proxy, among other things. This option configures the myip directive.

RFC931 User

The username as given by an ident daemon running on the client machine. This requires that ident be running on any client machines to be authenticated in this way. Ident should not be considered secure except on private networks where security doesn't matter much. You can find free ident servers for the following operating systems: Win NT [http://info.ost.eltele.no/freeware/identd/], Win 95/Win 98 [http://identd.sourceforge.net/], and UNIX [http://www2.lysator. liu.se/~pen/pidentd/]. Most UNIX systems, including Linux and BSD distributions, include an ident server.

Request Method

This ACL type matches on the HTTP method in the request headers. This includes the methods GET, PUT, and so on. This corresponds to the method ACL type directive.

URL Path Regex

This ACL matches on the URL path minus any protocol, port, and host name information. It does not include, for example, the "http://www.swelltech.com" portion of a request, leaving only the actual path to the object. This option correlates to the urlpath_regex directive.

URL Port

This ACL matches on the destination port for the request and configures the port ACL directive.

URL Protocol

This ACL matches on the protocol of the request, such as FTP, HTTP, ICP, and so on.

URL Regexp

Matches using a regular expression on the complete URL. This ACL can be used to provide access control based on parts of the URL or a case-insensitive match of the URL, and much more. The regular expressions used in Squid are provided by the GNU Regex library, which is documented in the section 7 and 3 regex man pages. Regular expressions are also discussed briefly in a nice article by Guido Socher [http://www.linuxfocus.org/English/July1998/article53.html] at LinuxFocus. This option is equivalent to the url_regex ACL type directive.

Web Server Address

This ACL matches based on the destination web server's IP address. Squid a single IP, a network IP with netmask, as well as a range of addresses in the form "192.168.1.1-192.168.1.25". This option correlates to the dst ACL type directive.

Web Server Hostname

This ACL matches on the host name of the destination web server.

Web Server Regexp

Matches using a regular expression on the host name of the destination web server.

More information on Access Control Lists in Squid can be found in [*Section 10* [http://www.squid-cache.org/Doc/FAQ/FAQ-10.html]] of the Squid FAQ. Authentication information can be found in [*Section 23* [http://www.squid-cache.org/Doc/FAQ/FAQ-23.html]] of the Squid FAQ.

Administrative Options

Administrative Options provides access to several of the behind-the-scenes options of Squid. This page allows you to configure a diverse set of options, including the user ID and group ID of the Squid process, cache hierarchy announce settings, and the authentication realm (Figure 12-17).

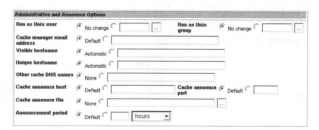

Figure 12-17: Administrative Options

Run as Unix user and group

The username and group name Squid will operate as. Squid is designed to start as root but very soon after drop to the user/group specified here. This allows you to restrict, for security reasons, the permissions that Squid will have when operating. Although Squid has proven itself to be quite secure through several years of use on thousands of sites, it is never a bad thing to take extra precautions to avoid problems. By default, Squid will operate as either nobody user and the nogroup group, or in the case of some Squids installed from RPM, as squid user and group. These options correlate to the cache_effective_user and cache_effective_group directives.

Proxy authentication realm

The realm that will be reported to clients when performing authentication. This option usually defaults to Squid proxy-caching web server, and correlates to the `proxy_auth_realm` directive. This name will likely appear in the browser popup window when the client is asked for authentication information.

Cache manager email address

The email address of the administrator of this cache. This option corresponds to the `cache_mgr` directive and defaults to either *webmaster* or *root* on RPM-based systems. This address will be added to any error pages that are displayed to clients.

Visible hostname

The host name that Squid will advertise itself on. This effects the host name that Squid uses when serving error messages. This option may need to be configured in cache clusters if you receive IP-forwarding errors. This option configures the `visible_hostname`.

Unique hostname

Configures the `unique_hostname` directive, and sets a unique host name for Squid to report in cache clusters in order to allow detection of forwarding loops. Use this if you have multiple machines in a cluster with the same visible hostname.

Cache announce host, port, and file

The host address and port that Squid will use to announce its availability to participate in a cache hierarchy. The cache announce file is simply a file containing a message to be sent with announcements. These options correspond to the `announce_host`, `announce_port`, and `announce_file` directives.

Announcement period

Configures the `announce_period` directive, and refers to the frequency at which Squid will send announcement messages to the announce host.

Miscellaneous Options

Miscellaneous Options is just what it sounds like: a hodgepodge of options that don't seem to fit anywhere else. Here you'll find several memory-related options, options regarding headers and user agent settings, and the powerful HTTP accelerator options (Figure 12-18).

Startup DNS test addresses

This should point to a number of hosts that Squid can use to test whether DNS service is working properly on your network. If DNS isn't working properly, Squid will not be able to service requests, so it will refuse to start, with a brief message regarding why in the cache.log. It is recommended that you select two or more host names on the Internet and one or two host names on your intranet, assuming you have one and Squid is expected to service it. By default, the dns_testnames directive checks a few well-known and popular sites: netscape.com, internic.net, nlanr.net, and microsoft.com.

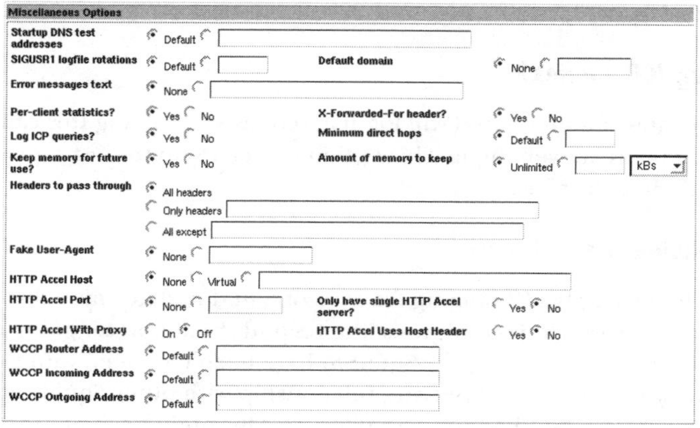

Figure 1-18: Miscellaneous Options

SIGUSR1 logfile rotations

The number of old rotated log files Squid will keep. On Red Hat systems, this option defaults to zero, as logs are rotated via the system standard *logrotate* program. On other systems, this defaults to 10, which means Squid will keep 10 old log files before overwriting the oldest. This option corresponds to the logfile_rotate directive.

Default domain

The domain that Squid will append to requests that are not possibly fully qualified domain names (more precisely, those that have no dots in them). This option correlates to the append_domain directive.

Error messages text

Provides a means to automatically add some extra information to Squid's error pages. You can add HTML or plain-text comments or links here, which will be added to the error messages displayed to clients. This option correlates to the err_html_text directive.

Per-client statistics?

Allows you to choose whether Squid will keep statistics regarding each individual client. This option configures the client_db directive and defaults to on.

X-Forwarded-For header?

This option allows you to choose whether Squid will report the host name of the system that originally made the request to the origin server. For example, if this option is disabled every request through your cache will be reported as originating from the cache. Usually, this should remain enabled. This correlates to the forwarded_for directive and defaults to on.

Log ICP queries?

Dictates whether Squid will log ICP requests. Disabling this can be a good idea if ICP loads are very high. This option correlates to the log_icp_queries directive and defaults to on.

Minimum direct hops

When using ICMP pinging features of Squid to determine distance to peers and origin servers, this configures when Squid should prefer going direct over a peer. This option requires your Squid to have been compiled with the --enable-icmp, and you must be in a peering relationship with other Squid caches, also with the appropriate build option compiled in. This option correlates to the minimum_direct_hops directive.

Keep memory for future use?

This option turns on memory_pools and allows Squid to keep memory that it has allocated (but no longer needs), so that it will not need to reallocate memory in the future. This can improve performance by a small margin, but may need to be turned off if memory is at a premium on your system. This option defaults to on and should generally be left on, unless you know what you're doing.

Amount of memory to keep

The amount of memory Squid will keep allocated, assuming the **Keep memory for future use** option is turned on. This option configures the memory_pools_limit directive and defaults to unlimited. Any non-zero value will instruct Squid not to keep more than that amount allocated, and if Squid requires more memory than that to fulfill a request, it will use your system's malloc library. Squid does not pre-allocate memory, so it is safe to set this reasonably high. If your Squid runs on a dedicated host, it is probably wisest to leave it to its default of unlimited. If it must share the system with other server processes (like Apache or Sendmail) then it might be appropriate to limit it somewhat.

Headers to pass through

Configures the anonymizing features of Squid. This option allows you to dictate what kinds of request headers are allowed to pass through Squid. For example, to prevent origin servers from being able to detect the type of browser your clients are using you would choose to allow all except User-Agent. This option has mostly obscure uses and usually doesn't need to be changed from its default of allowing all headers to pass through. There is a relevant *Squid FAQ* section [http://www.

squid-cache.org/Doc/FAQ/FAQ-4.html#ss4.18] that describes in more detail what can be accomplished with this option. This option corresponds to the `anonymize_headers` directive and defaults to allow `All headers`.

CAUTION *Indiscriminate use of Squid's anonymizing features can cause websites to behave incorrectly. Because modern websites often rely on the contents of cookies or other headers to know the right JavaScript and HTML code to serve for everything to look and act correctly, many sites could be confused into serving the wrong content or refusing to serve any content to the user.*

Fake User-Agent

Acts as an addition to the above option, in that it allows you to configure Squid to report a fake User-Agent header. For example, using this option you could have your Squid report that every client being served is named *Mozilla/42.2 (Atari 2600; 8-bit)*. That would be lying, but perhaps the person looking over the logs at origin servers will find it amusing. If you are using the anonymize headers features to hide your client's User-Agent headers, it is probably wise to include a fake User-Agent header because some servers will not be happy with requests without one. Further, this *will* cause problems with some web pages for your users, as the User-Agent header is sometimes used to decide which of a number of pages to send based on the features available within a particular browser. The server will usually end up choosing the least interesting page for your clients (e.g., text only, or no JavaScript/Java/etc.).

HTTP Accel Host and Port

The options you will use to configure Squid to act as an accelerator, or as a transparent proxy. When using your Squid as an accelerator, you must configure these two options to point to the IP and port of the web server you are accelerating. If you are using Squid to accelerate a number of virtual hosts, you must choose virtual as the Accel Host. Note that this opens potential security problems, in that your Squid will then be open to users outside of your network as a proxy. This can be avoided via proper firewall rules on your router or on the Squid system itself. Finally, if you are operating your Squid transparently, you would also configure the Accel Host to be virtual and the Accel Port to be 80. Outgoing port 80 traffic will then need to be redirected to your Squid process in order for it to work. This is discussed in much greater detail in the tutorial on transparent proxying. These options configure the `httpd_accel_host` and `httpd_accel_port` directives.

HTTP Accel with Proxy

Allows you to operate your cache as both an accelerator and a caching proxy. This option tells Squid to accept both traditional proxy connections and requests intended for an origin web server. This option correlates to the `httpd_accel_with_proxy` directive.

HTTP Accel Uses Host Header

Configures Squid to use the host header information as described in the HTTP 1.1 specification. This option must be turned on for transparent operation, in order for virtual servers to be cached properly. This option correlates to the httpd_uses_host_header directive.

WCCP Router Address, WCCP Incoming Address, WCCP Outgoing Address

The *Web Cache Coordination Protocol* is a standard method of implementing an interception proxy. Routers that support WCCP can be configured to direct traffic to one or more web caches using an efficient load balancing mechanism. WCCP also provides for automatic bypassing of an unavailable cache in the event of a failure. Usually, configuring Squid to use WCCP is as simple as configuring it for interception proxying, using the steps discussed later in the Interception Caching tutorial and then entering the address of the router in the WCCP Router Address field. The other two options are very rarely needed, but can be used in some complex network environments where incoming and outgoing data must travel via different routes or from different addresses. These options correspond to the wccp_router, wccp_incoming_address, and wccp_outgoing_address directives and are disabled by default.

Tutorial: A Basic Squid Proxy Configuration

Squid is almost entirely preconfigured for traditional proxying as soon as it is installed from source distribution or from a binary package. It can be up and running in just a few minutes, if your needs are simple. This tutorial covers the first changes you'll need to make to get your caching proxy up and running quickly.

NOTE   *This tutorial assumes you have already installed Squid and have configured Webmin to know where to find all of the appropriate Squid files. If you've installed from a vendor-supplied package, Webmin will probably already know where to find everything.*

Opening Access to Local Clients

The only change that *must* be made before using your Squid installation is to open access for your local users. By default Squid denies access to all users from any source. This is to prevent your proxy from being used for illicit purposes by users outside of your local network (and you'd be amazed at how many nasty things someone can do with an open proxy).

Click the **Access Control** icon to edit the access control lists and access rules for your proxy. First, create a new ACL by selecting Client Address from the drop-down list and then clicking **Create new ACL**. This will open a new page where you can define your ACL. First, enter a name, like localnet, in the **Name** field. Next, specify your network either in terms of a network range, or by specifying a network and netmask. If you have only 10 addresses, for example, that you would like to be permitted to use your proxy you could enter, for example, a **From IP** of

192.168.1.20 and a **To IP** of 192.168.1.30. Or if you have a whole network to which you would like to allow proxy access, you could enter a **From IP** of 192.168.1.0 and a **Netmask** of 255.255.255.0. Click Save.

Next, you need to add a proxy restriction to permit the clients matched by the localnet ACL to use the proxy. So click the **Add proxy restriction link**. On the proxy selection page, choose the Allow option for the **Action**, and select localnet in the **Match ACLs** selection box. Click Save.

Then use the arrow icons to the right of the list of proxy restrictions to move the rule you've just created above the **Deny all** rule.

Initializing the Cache Directory

You may have noticed, on the front page of the Webmin Squid module, there is a warning that the configured cache directory has not been initialized. Before starting Squid, you'll want to make sure it gets initialized. Webmin, of course, will do this for us. Just click the **Initialize Cache** button. If you plan to alter your cache directories to something other than the default, you'll likely want to do so in the **Cache Options** page before initializing the directories. Details are covered earlier in this chapter.

Starting Squid and Testing

To start Squid, click the **Start Squid** link in the upper right corner of the main module page. It is worthwhile to then check the information provided by Squid during its startup in the cache.log. You can use the Webmin file manager, or you can add this log to the **System Logs** module for viewing there (read the section covering that module for information on adding non-syslog log files to make them viewable). Squid is usually quite forthcoming about problems that might prevent it from starting or operating correctly.

To test your new Squid, configure a browser on your local network to use the Squid server as its proxy. Doing this is browser dependent. In Netscape and Mozilla, the proxy options are located under the **Advanced:Proxy Settings** preferences category, while in Internet Explorer, they are located under **Internet Options:Connections**. Squid can act as a proxy for HTTP, HTTPS, FTP, Gopher, and WAIS protocols. Socks is not supported by Squid, though there are a few good Open Source Socks proxies available.

Now, just browse for a bit to be sure your caching proxy is working. Take a look in the access.log for information about whether a request was served with a cache hit or a cache miss. If Calamaris is installed on your system, Webmin will generate an access report on demand whenever you click the **Calamaris** icon on the Squid module main page.

Tutorial: Interception Proxying

Ordinarily, when using Squid on a network to cache web traffic, browsers must be configured to use the Squid system as a *proxy*. This type of configuration is known as *traditional proxying*. In many environments, this is simply not an acceptable method of implementation. Therefore Squid provides a method to operate as an interception proxy, or *transparently*, which means users do not even need to be aware that a proxy is in place. Web traffic is redirected from port 80 to the port where Squid resides, and Squid acts like a standard web server for the browser.

Using Squid transparently is a two-part process, requiring first that Squid be configured properly to accept non-proxy requests, and second that web traffic gets redirected to the Squid port. The first part of configuration is performed in the Squid module, while the second part can be performed in the **Linux Firewall** module. That is, assuming you are using Linux, otherwise you should consult the *Squid FAQ Transparent Caching/Proxying* [http://www.squid-cache.org/Doc/FAQ/FAQ-17.html] entry.

Configuring Squid for Transparency

In order for Squid to operate as a transparent proxy, it must be configured to accept normal web requests rather than (or in addition to) proxy requests. Here, you'll learn about this part of the process, examining both the console configuration and the Webmin configuration. Console configuration is explained, and Webmin configuration is shown in the figure below.

As root, open the `squid.conf` file in your favorite text editor. This file will be located in one of a few different locations depending on your operating system and the method of installation. Usually it is found in either `/usr/local/squid/etc`, when installed from source, or `/etc/squid` on Red Hat–style systems. First you'll notice the `http_port` option. This tells you what port Squid will listen on. By default, this is port 3128, but you may change it if you need to for some reason. Next you should configure the following options, as shown in Figure 12-19.

Figure 12-19: Transparent configuration of Squid

```
httpd_accel_host virtual
httpd_accel_port 80
httpd_accel_with_proxy   on
httpd_accel_uses_host_header on
```

These options, as described in the Miscellaneous Options section of this document, configure Squid as follows. `httpd_accel_host virtual` causes Squid to act as an accelerator for any number of web servers, meaning that Squid will use the request header information to figure out what server the user wants to access, and that Squid will behave as a web server when dealing with the client. `httpd_accel_port 80` configures Squid to send out requests to origin servers on port 80, even though it may be receiving requests on another port, 3128 for example. `httpd_accel_with_proxy on` allows you to continue using Squid as a traditional proxy as well as a transparent proxy. This isn't always necessary, but it does make testing a lot easier when you are trying to get transparency working, which is discussed a bit more later in the troubleshooting section. Finally, `httpd_accel_uses_host_header` on tells Squid that it should figure out what server to fetch content from based on the host name found in the header. This option must be configured this way for transparency.

Linux Firewall Configuration for Transparent Proxying

The `iptables` portion of your transparent configuration is equally simple. The goal is to *hijack* all outgoing network traffic that is on the HTTP port (that's port 80, to be numerical about it). `iptables`, in its incredible power and flexibility, allows you to do this with a single command line or a single rule. Again, the configuration is shown and discussed for both the Webmin interface and the console configuration.

NOTE *The Linux Firewall module is new in Webmin version 1.00. All previous revisions lack this module, so to follow these steps, you'll need to have a recent Webmin revision.*

When first entering the **Linux Firewall** module, the `Packet filtering rules` will be displayed. For your purposes you need to edit the `Network address translation` rules. So, select it from the drop-down list beside the **Showing IPtable** button, and click the button to display the NAT rules.

Now, add a new rule to the **PREROUTING** chain by clicking the **Add rule** button to the right of the **PREROUTING** section of the page.

Fill in the following fields. The **Action to take** should be `Redirect` and the **Target ports for redirect** set to `3128`. Next you'll need to specify what clients should be redirected to the Squid port. If you know all port 80 traffic on a single interface should be redirected, it is simplest to specify an **Incoming interface**, but you could instead specify a **Source address or network**. Next, set the **Network protocol** to `Equals TCP`. Finally, set the **Destination TCP or UDP port** to `80`. Click **Create** to add the new rule to the configuration. Once on the main page again, click the **Apply Configuration** button to make the new rule take effect. Finally, set the firewall to be activated at boot so that redirection will continue to be in effect on reboots.

```
# iptables -t nat -I PREROUTING 1 -i eth0 -p tcp --dport 80 -j REDIRECT --to-port
3128
```

While a detailed description of the **iptables** tool is beyond the scope of this section, it should briefly be explained what is happening in this configuration. First, you are inserting a rule into the first `PREROUTING` chain of the NAT routing path, with the `-t nat -I PREROUTING 1` portion of the command. Next you're defining whose requests will be acted upon; in this case iptables will work on all packets originating from the network attached to device `eth0`. This is defined by the `-i eth0` portion of the rule. Then comes the choice of protocol to act upon; here you've chosen TCP with the `-p tcp` section. Then, the last match rule specifies the destination port you would like for your redirect to act upon with the `--dport 80` section. Finally, iptables is told *what to do* with packets that match the prior defined criteria; specifically, it will `REDIRECT` the packets `--to-port 3128`.

13

NETWORKING CONFIGURATION

The fourth category tab in Webmin is for **Networking**-related configuration. Specifically, this is where you'll find the modules to configure inetd or xinetd, iptables, NFS exports, NIS client and server, and network interfaces. The **Networking** category was introduced in Webmin version 1.0, so if for some reason you are using an earlier Webmin revision (upgrade already; it's free!), these modules will be found under other category tabs.

NFS Exports

The **NFS Exports** module lists all exported directories. Clicking **Add a new export** will bring you to the **Create Export** page, as shown in Figure 13-1.

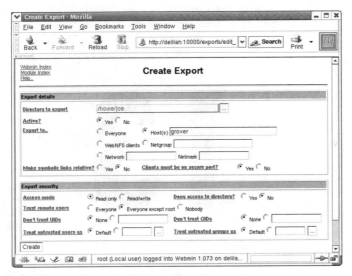

Figure 1-1: Create NFS export

In the preceding figure, you can see that the module allows you to select a directory to export, and choose a number of options for that directory and to whom the directory should be exported.

Export Details

The following options configure the location, type, and permissions of the directory to be exported:

Directory to export

This is simply the full path to the directory you would like to export.

Active?

An export may be disabled when it is not needed by selecting no. Otherwise the export will always be active and available as long as the NFS server is running.

In the next few fields it is possible to select access controls to dictate which machines or users on the network will be permitted to mount the exported directory.

Everyone

Specifies that anyone may mount the directory. This is similar to an anonymous FTP server.

CAUTION *Use extreme caution when exporting a directory to everyone. If your local network is not protected by a very good firewall, it will be possible for outsiders to mount your exported directory. It may also be possible for outsiders to stage a denial-of-service attack against your server, as NFS is not renowned for its reliability in the face of determined attackers. It is always a good idea to restrict NFS exports to just those machines that need access, and additionally to implement a firewall to block anyone outside of your local network from even attempting to connect to your NFS server.*

Host(s)

Allows you to specify a host name or IP that may mount the directory. Wild cards are accepted in this field as well, so that names of the form *.company.com can be entered to match all hosts in the company.com domain.

WebNFS clients

WebNFS is a relatively new protocol that has been developed by Sun, who also created NFS, and is designed for file sharing across the Internet. It allows users to browse exported directories using a familiar web browser as the interface. It has largely been ignored by the mass market in favor of WebDAV, but it may have its uses in some environments. If you will be supporting WebNFS clients with this export, select this option. Not all operating system variants support this option, or if support is provided it may not be complete or stable.

Netgroup

If your local network uses NIS services, you may use netgroups to specify access to exports. Any existing group name may be specified here.

Network

To export to all hosts on a given network, enter the network number and netmask. This may be a full network class, or it may be a smaller subnet.

Make symbolic links relative?

On NFS mounted directories, symbolic links can pose a problem, due to the change in where a directory might be mounted on the client machine. For example, a directory located on /home/nfsusers on the NFS server may be mounted on the client on /home. If a symbolic link on the server points to /home/nfsusers/joe/work, the link will be broken on the client machine if the link is not converted to a relative link. If made relative, the link will become joe/work and will work fine on the client machine. This option corresponds to the link_relative switch.

Clients must be on secure port?

The effect of turning this option on is that NFS will insist upon a connection on ports below 1024. This does improve security in some circumstances, but may interfere with Windows clients mounting the exported directory. In reality, security of most current NFS variants in use is relatively weak, providing only mediocre authentication methods and no data encryption.

NOTE *In UNIX systems, software run by a normal user is not permitted to bind to a port below 1024. This means that only the root user on a multi-user system can start services that run on ports below 1024. The security implication of this is that when you connect to a UNIX server on a port below 1024 (such as making an NFS connection when this option is enabled) you may have some assurance that the NFS server is one being operated by the administrator of the server. If the NFS server has normal users, and NFS connections are not forced to be made on low ports, it might be possible for a malicious user to operate an*

illicit NFS server whose only purpose is to obtain access to parts of the network he should not
have access to. As discussed earlier, Webmin is often run on port 1000 or some other sub-
1024 port in order to avoid this risk for the Webmin server.

Export Security

In the *Export Security* section you can specify several other security options,
including the ability to treat some UIDs and/or GIDs as untrusted users. This
section also provides fields for declaring what user and group name will be used
for the untrusted users' permissions.

Access mode

The exported directory may be mounted for reading and writing, or just for
reading. This option correlates to the ro and rw switches in the exports file.

Deny access to directory?

Normally, when a directory is exported, all of its subdirectories will be exported
with the same access rules. This is usually exactly what is desired, as in the case of
exporting home directories to users via NFS. Obviously, the users will need to
access everything in their own home directory, including subdirectories thereof.
This option explicitly denies access to a directory, when the connecting client
matches the export rules in this export. This can be useful to explicitly disallow
access to a subdirectory of a directory that is exported in another rule. This
option corresponds to the noaccess directive.

Trust remote users

NFS provides a simple trust model, wherein some users will be trusted, all users
will be trusted, or no users will be trusted. To be more explicit, when another
computer on the network connects to your NFS server, the UID of the user
attempting to access the exported directory is included in the negotiation
process. Depending on the configuration of this option, the user may be able to
use files with the same permissions as if he were working on the local machine,
assuming other configuration details don't prevent it. If either Everyone or
Everyone except root are selected, all normal users will be able to use the files on
the NFS export as though they are working on the local machine. The root user
will have this same ability only if the Everyone option is selected. In the case of
exporting user home directories, it makes sense to enable the Everyone except root
option. The Nobody option means that the connecting user will always be treated
as the untrusted user. This option sets the no_root_squash and all_squash
directives. The default is Everyone except root, which correlates to the implicit
root_squash directive.

The untrusted user is a user that is used specifically for NFS, but it is very
similar in function to an anonymous user on an FTP server. This can be useful for
many situations where some or all client machines are not directly under the
control of the administrator of the NFS server. A common use for such exports is
system boot images and anonymous access to file or document repositories.

Don't trust UIDs, Don't trust GIDs

If there are specific user IDs or group IDs that should be treated as the untrusted user, they may be specified here. The IDs may be specified as a range, such as 0-500, or as a comma-separated list or a combination of both. Most UNIX variants reserve some subset of UIDs and GIDs for system-specific users and groups, like nobody and lp. It may be useful to distrust a user claiming to be one of these system users or groups. This option correlates to the squash_uids and the squash_gids directives, respectively.

Treat untrusted users as, Treat untrusted groups as

This option specifies the user ID and group ID to which an untrusted user or group is mapped to. If unspecified, the untrusted UID or GID will be set to the default of the NFS server. This varies somewhat between NFS versions, but it is safe to assume the default is a user or group with very limited permissions, and is usually an appropriate choice for the system on which it is running.

Network Configuration

The **Network Configuration** module provides a nice, clean interface to most of the important network configuration details on your system (Figure 13-2). It is possible to set IP addresses, create IP aliases, define routing and gateway information, configure DNS clients, and edit the /etc/hosts file.

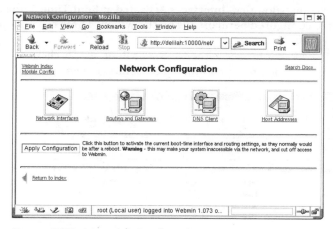

Figure 13-2: Network Configuration

Network Interfaces

Clicking the **Network Interfaces** icon will open a page similar to Figure 13-3, which allows you to configure the currently active interfaces as well as interfaces that are brought up at boot time (usually these will be the same).

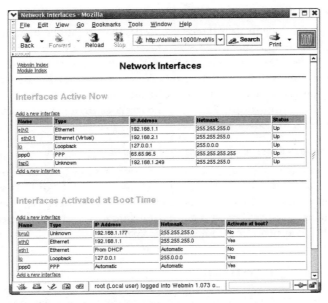

Figure 13-3: Network Interfaces

The **Interfaces Active Now** section is a list of interfaces that are currently *up*. The same data could be gathered by running **ifconfig -a** from the command line. The section below that, **Interfaces Activated at Boot Time**, is the list of interfaces that are configured permanently on the system. These can optionally be brought up on boot.

To edit an interface, either **Active** or **Boot**, simply click the name of the interface. You will be presented with a page similar to Figure 13-4.

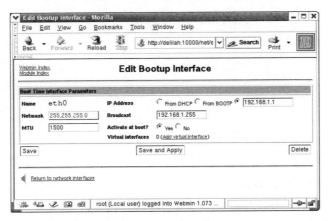

Figure 13-4: Editing a bootup interface

Here it is possible to specify the **IP address** for the system or to choose DHCP or BOOTP to auto-configure the IP. Also editable from this page are **Netmask** and **Broadcast** settings.

Adding a new interface is equally simple. From the main page, click the **Create new interface** under either **Interface Active Now** for a temporary interface or **Interfaces Activated at Boot Time** for a permanent interface. Then on the configuration page, choose a name for the interface. Manually enter the IP, or choose DHCP or BOOTP for automatic IP configuration. If manually entering the IP, also enter the **Netmask** and **Broadcast** settings, or select **Automatic** for these settings, if preferred and available (Automatic is only available when creating an **Active** interface.

Note when editing a just-created **Boot** interface it is possible to activate it immediately by clicking **Save and Apply** rather than simply **Save**.

Routing and Gateways

Routing is an encompassing term that basically refers to the paths that your system should take to reach certain hosts and networks. In the simplest configuration, you will only have one route, known as the *default router* or *gateway*. This simply means the all packets that are bound for a network that *is not local* will be sent to the address defined by the default route setting.

In Figure 13-5 the **Default router** is blank, because on the example machine, the route is set automatically by DHCP. It could contain an IP or a host name, if a router did need to be defined. **Default route device** simply defines which device, on systems with more than one device, will be considered the *default* device. This device name could be any active device on your system, such as eth0. The **Act as router** option turns on packet forwarding on some Linux systems. On Red Hat Linux systems this is done in /etc/sysconfig/network or /etc/sysctl.conf on versions from 6.2 onward.

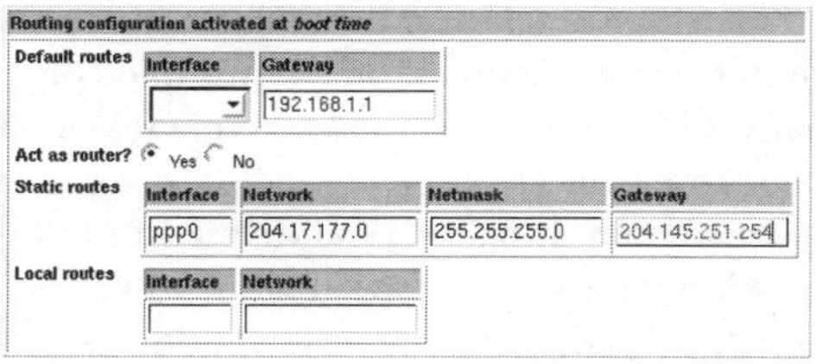

Figure 13-5: Routing and gateways

Static routes provide a means for some traffic to choose another route to some known host or network, rather than going through the default route. This is commonly used for accessing local networks on different subnets through a single *multi-homed* host, or a host having more than one network interface. For example, if my system were on the 192.168.1.0/24 local subnet, and I had a second subnet on 172.16.1.0/24. I could provide a static route with the **interface** value of eth0 and a **Network** of 172.16.1.0, a **Netmask** of 255.255.255.0, and finally, a **Gateway** of 192.168.1.23, assuming the host at 192.168.1.23 also had an active interface on the 172.16.1.0 network.

DNS Client

The **DNS Client** module allows you to configure your system's resolver settings (Figure 13-6). Usually, all you need to do is add your name server's IPs to this list. In the case shown in the following figure, there is a local caching name server running on IP 127.0.0.1, as well as two remote name servers as backups. **Resolution order** allows you to select the order in which the system will try to resolved host names. In the example in the figure, DNS will be checked first, followed by the /etc/hosts file. Other available resolution options are NIS and NIS+. Finally, the **Search domains** field usually contains the domain name where your computer is located, and possibly others. Search domains will be searched first if a fully qualified domain name is not entered. For example, if I tried to **ping** a host named *gigi* on the machine shown in the example, the name *gigi.swell* would be looked up first, and then if there was no such system in DNS or /etc/hosts it would try to resolve just the name *gigi*.

Figure 13-6: DNS Client

Host Addresses

The /etc/hosts file is another common resolution method on UNIX systems. It is a very simple way to deal with a small number of host addresses. However, because host files are not easily shared amongst multiple computers, its usage is limited. Nonetheless, Webmin does provide a nice means of editing your hosts file, so I'm going to document it.

In Figure 13-7 there are a number of IP addresses and the host names they are associated with. Clicking any of the IPs will allow you to edit the entry. Creating a new entry is done by clicking **Add a new host address**. If you only have a very small network, a host file on each machine may be all you need; otherwise, use DNS for most resolution tasks.

IP Address	Hostnames
127.0.0.1	delilah.swell delilah localhost.localdomain localhost
192.168.0.11	grover grover.swell
192.168.1.170	mini mini.swell
192.168.1.79	printer laser brokenlex
192.168.1.177	tsunami

Figure 13-7: Host addresses

TIP   *When testing Apache virtual hosts that are not yet ready for production use, it can be useful to configure the address and host name here, so that you can browse your test server on the host name where it will eventually live. Of course, you can do the same thing by running a local DNS server, but the* hosts *file is a simpler way to achieve the same task.*

14

HARDWARE CONFIGURATION

The **Hardware** configuration tab presents several options for hardware level settings (Figure 14-1). This includes disk partitions, boot loader, printer administration, system time and date, and more. The exact options available vary greatly depending on platform.

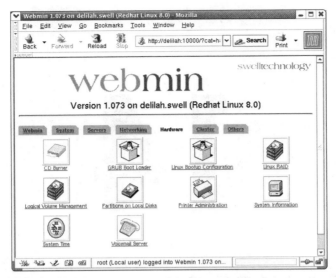

Figure 14-1: Hardware configuration

Linux Boot Configuration

If you are running Linux, Webmin provides module for editing the /etc/lilo.conf file that the *LInux LOader*, or LILO for short, uses. LILO is the boot manager most commonly used with Linux. It works by writing a small boot sector to the MBR on your boot disk. This boot sector contains the code needed to first present a prompt:

LILO:

This allows you to select the kernel or operating system to boot. LILO can boot multiple operating systems and multiple versions of the Linux kernel. When you open the **Linux Bootup Configuration** page (Figure 14-2), you should see at least one *boot kernel* or *boot partition*. Boot kernels are for Linux kernels, while boot partitions are for other operating systems.

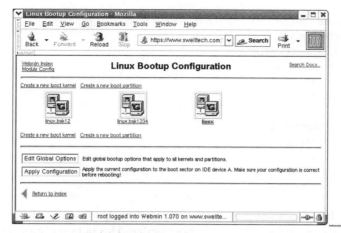

Figure 14-2: Linux Bootup Configuration

Clicking one of the boot kernel or boot partition icons will allow you to edit that boot kernel or partition (Figure 14-3).

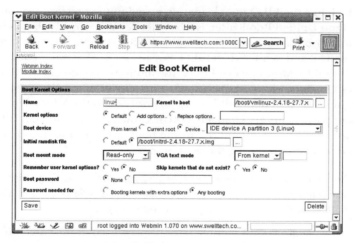

Figure 14-3: Edit Boot Kernel

Here the **name** is an identifier for the kernel and it translates to **label** in the /etc/lilo.conf file. The **Kernel to boot** is the path to the Linux kernel boot image to load.

Kernel options

This field can be used to enter any arguments you need to pass to your kernel on boot. It is often used for specifying the amount of memory in a machine when Linux doesn't recognize it all. For example, to specify 127MB of RAM, one could select **Add options** and add the line mem=127MB in the text field. This will be translated in the /etc/lilo.conf file to:

```
boot=/dev/hda
map=/boot/map
install=/boot/boot.b
prompt
timeout=50
default=linux

image=/boot/vmlinuz-2.2.16-11.0
label=linux
read-only
root=/dev/hda5
append="mem=127MB"
```

It is always necessary to click **Apply Changes** from the main page in order to write a new boot sector to the boot device. This button simply runs /sbin/lilo.

GRUB Boot Loader

Much like the LILO boot loader discussed in the previous section, GRUB, or the GRand Unified Bootloader, is a boot loader that provides boot selection for any number of Linux kernel revisions and other operating system variants. It is more powerful and flexible than LILO, but also somewhat more complex in operation than LILO. Most modern Linux distributions provide both GRUB and LILO boot loaders, with GRUB being the default. GRUB operates slightly differently than LILO, as it does not have to be rewritten to the MBR anytime the kernel or boot parameters are changed. GRUB knows how to read many filesystem types, and therefore can mount the system boot disk and read in its configuration files and new kernels during the boot process.

TIP *GRUB is extensively documented in the grub info pages. Simply type* info grub *on the command line to browse the GRUB documentation. More information can also be found on the GRUB home page [http://www.gnu.org/software/grub/].*

The main GRUB module page displays each of the currently configured kernels and operating systems that GRUB will list in its boot menu (Figure 14-4). Clicking a kernel will open a new page displaying all of the configured options for that kernel, where they can be edited. Clicking the **Edit Global Options** button will allow you to configure options that will apply to all bootable kernels and operating systems.

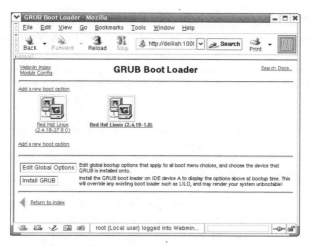

Figure 14-4: GRUB Boot Loader

NOTE   *When you click a kernel or OS icon or the* **Edit Global Options** *button, Webmin runs GRUB to obtain the details for that kernel or the global configuration details. This process can take 30 seconds or more, because GRUB scans the system for disks and reads in the current boot configuration details.*

Global Options

The **Global Options** page provides access to the options that will apply to all bootable kernels and operating systems, including the kernel to boot by default, password options, and boot timeout (Figure 14-5).

Figure 14-5: Global Options

Default boot option

This option allows you to specify the kernel or operating system that will be booted by default, if nothing is selected by the user from the boot menu. This option corresponds to the `default` directive in the `grub.conf` configuration file.

Fallback boot option

If the user-selected or default boot option fails because GRUB cannot locate the necessary file, this specifies the kernel or OS that GRUB should attempt to boot. This option correlates to the `fallback` directive.

Timeout before loading default

When booting, GRUB normally displays a menu of bootable items and waits for a few seconds for the user to select an option. If nothing is selected, the default item will be booted. This timeout is usually ten seconds, but can be made shorter or longer with this option. This option correlates to the timeout directive.

Boot password

If the system will be located in an unsecured environment, and may contain sensitive data, it can be password protected so that even during booting the installed system cannot easily be compromised. This option correlates to the password directive and defaults to none.

CAUTION   *Even if GRUB is configured to require a password, and the operating system has been locked down appropriately, it may still be possible to compromise a system by someone who has physical access to the hardware on which the system is running. If the hardware provides alternate methods of booting, like CD, floppy disk, or USB disks, it may be possible for an attacker reboot the system into their own OS from which they can mount the system disks containing your data. Or, even without the ability to boot directly from another external medium, an attacker could install a hard disk of his own into the system and boot from it instead of your boot. This isn't likely to be a problem in traditional office environments, but if you operate a public kiosk that gathers user data, or some other publicly available system, it is worth devoting some time to considering the many ways in which an attacker could obtain access to your data.*

Install GRUB on disk/partition

This option allows you to specify the disk, and the location on the disk, for where the first stage GRUB boot loader will be installed. The first stage contains only the code needed to read the later stages and configuration details off of the system disks. Normally, it will reside on the Master Boot Record, or MBR, of the first disk in the system, though it can reside on a specific partition (where GRUB itself must be booted by another boot loader) or on other disks. This option corresponds to the directive.

Edit Boot Option

Clicking on a kernel or operating system icon will open the **Edit Boot Option** page (Figure 14-6), which allows you to configure the boot options for the kernel or operating system specified. Here you may specify the title that will be display on the boot menu and the location of the item to be loaded, and enable password protection.

Option title

When GRUB is first loaded, it will display a menu of items that can be booted. This option specifies the title of the item. It is usually used to indicate the name and version of the operating system, but may contain any information you would like to present to the user. This option correlates to the title directive.

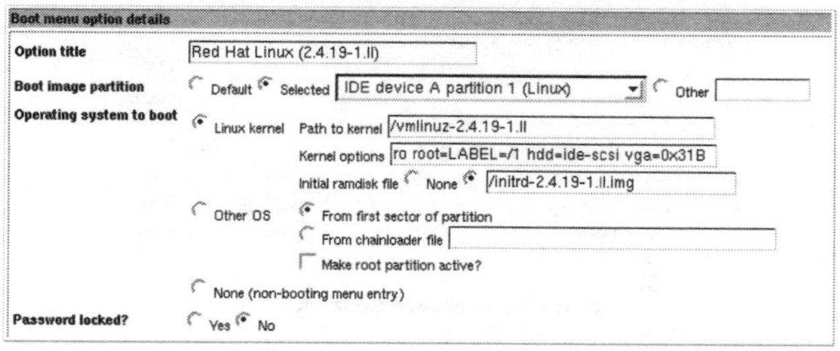

Figure 14-6: Edit boot option

Boot image partition

This option allows you to specify the location of the item to be booted. It is not required to be on the same disk or partition as the GRUB boot loader, but it must be contained on a disk and filesystem type that GRUB is able to access. This option corresponds to the root directive.

Operating system to boot

Here you may specify the type of operating system to boot and the filename of the specific kernel to boot if booting a Linux kernel. GRUB supports most operating systems that have their own boot loader, in addition to booting Linux directly. Thus, it is possible to boot Windows operating systems, multiple Linux versions, or BSD operating systems, using the same GRUB menu. Kernel options may be passed to a Linux kernel, by specifying them in the Kernel options field of this section. For example, you may wish to have a menu item entitled **Single User** that boots your system into single user mode, for emergency maintenance (or resetting the root password, if it is lost). Doing this simply requires you to copy an existing boot entry and add the word single to the end of the list of existing kernel options.

Password locked?

GRUB has relatively fine-grained access control (for a boot loader, anyway), in that you can specify which boot menu items will require a password to boot. This option corresponds to the lock directive. Password protection must be enabled in the **Global Options** page for this directive to work.

Partition Manager

The partition manager provides a graphical interface to both the fdisk partition editing command and the /etc/fstab file on your system (Figure 14-7). fdisk is commonly used to create and remove partitions on a disk, while the /etc/fstab file is where the mounting information for the system is configured.

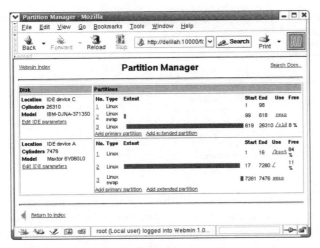

Figure 14-7: Partition Manager

The partition manager page provides a list of currently accessible disks and the partitions on it. In the first column there is the type and location of the disk, the number of cylinders reported by the BIOS (this isn't necessarily the actual number of physical cylinders; it depends on the type of CHS structure that is reported by the BIOS), and model number reported by the drive. The other larger row contains the drive partition structure. The red bars represent primary or secondary partitions. If you have secondary partitions, the *Extended* partition that contains them will fill the whole portion of the drive occupied by all of the secondary partitions.

To edit the parameters of a partition, click the number of the partition to edit. Note that mounted partitions cannot be edited. To edit the mount information for a partition click the mount point listed under **Use**. Clicking this will take you out of the **Partition Manager** and into the **Disk and Network Filesystems** module.

To create a new partition on a disk with space available, click either **Add primary partition** or **Add logical partition**. Choose the type of partition to create (usually Linux or Linux swap) and then the size of the partition in the **Extent** field. This is the range of cylinders to use for this partition, so take care to correctly identify the cylinders and to not overwrite any existing partitions. Finally, click **Create**.

Printer Administration

The **Printer Administration** module (Figure 14-8) may behave somewhat differently under different operating systems, as printer driver details and configuration often varies between systems and even between Linux distributions. Nonetheless, Webmin minimizes the differences between systems, and these directions work more or less unchanged.

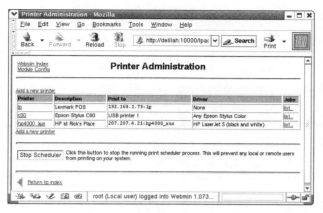

Figure 14-8: Printer Administration

When entering the **Printer Administration** page, you will see a list of currently configured printers, a link to **Add a new printer** and a button to **Stop Scheduler** or **Start Scheduler** depending on the current status of the print scheduler.

Clicking the **Add a new printer** link opens a page where you can configure a new printer. The **Name** field is an arbitrary name for the printer. Conventionally, lp or lp0 are often used for the first printer, but you can name it anything. The **Description** can be a longer description of the printer. **Accepting requests** simply sets whether the printer should be available, and **Printing enabled** defines whether it is enabled for printing (the queue can still receive requests with this turned off if the previous option is still on). **Max print job size** is the maximum size request that will be accepted. This shouldn't be too small, as many PostScript files are quite large.

The next section is **Print Destination**, where you define the device type (local, file, remote UNIX, or remote Windows). Many standalone network printers support standard UNIX lp functionality in addition to Windows printer sharing. If your printer is local, choose the physical device to use, and if it is a remote printer, enter the IP or host name for the host where the print queue is located. If using a Windows shared printer, enter the **User**, **Password**, and **Workgroup** for the printer share (Figure 14-9).

Finally, the third section of the page is for configuring the driver for your printer (Figure 14-10). If your printer is a simple text printer or a PostScript printer, the top selection is probably right for you. The second option is for a program to handle printer control. This could be a custom print driver for your printer or one of a couple of competing commercial and non-commercial printer packages. Finally, if your system provides them, there will be a list of available drivers. This section, on Red Hat systems, is a front end to the GhostScript printer drivers that come standard with Red Hat. It's quite likely that your system will have its own set of drivers, or a front end, much like that of Red Hat.

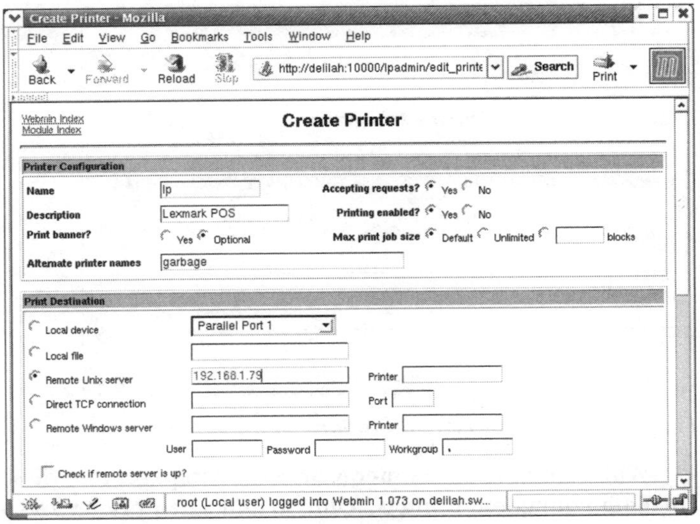

Figure 14-9: Adding a new printer

The **Send EOF** option is for some printers that require an explicit EOF to be sent after every page before they will print. If your printer acts as though it is preparing to print, but never does (for example, if the busy light flashes), try turning this option on. **Paper size** is just what it seems: the size of the paper you print from this printer. Keep in mind that this doesn't limit programs to only print on this paper size. It merely configures the standard system printing tools to print on whatever paper size is selected by default.

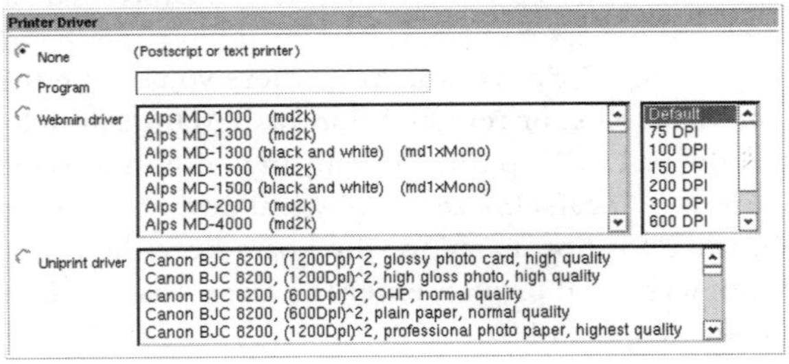

Figure 14-10: Adding a new printer (cont'd)

Pages per output page is the number of pages that will be printed per paper page. This allows you to conserve paper by printing multiple pages on a single page of paper. This option will arrange the text in rows and columns. These rows and columns can be further configured, as well as numerous other options (too many to begin to discuss here), in the next field, **Additional GS options**. You may wish to consult the man pages for GhostScript, as well as those for lp, lpd, and lpr, to find out more about the printer capabilities of your system. You can, of course, view these man pages in the Webmin **Manual Pages** module. Another good source of information regarding printing includes the *Printing HOWTO* [http://www.tldp.org/HOWTO/Printing-HOWTO/index.html] at the *Linux Documentation Project* [http://www.tldp.org/].

15

OTHERS CATEGORY

Clicking the **Others** category tab will take you to a page of tools that don't really fit anywhere else. This includes a small module that allows you to run any system command from a button, a Java file manager much like Windows Explorer or the Gnome File Manager tool, a Perl modules manager, a system and server status module, and a Java-based telnet client.

Command Shell

The **Command Shell** is a simple HTML-based shell, allowing you to execute arbitrary commands by entering them into a text entry field (Figure 15-1). The page reloads with the output from the command displayed. This module can be extremely useful if you must perform some command-line tasks, but cannot access a SSH or telnet session to the machine. Because the **Command Shell** is entirely web-based, it can be used on any machine that Webmin can be used on.

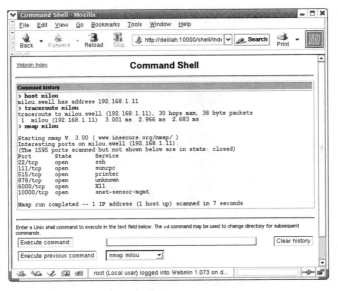

Figure 15-1: Command Shell

Custom Commands

The **Custom Commands** module provides a simple interface to every single command on your server at the press of a button. It sounds pretty impressive. Unfortunately, you actually have to create those command buttons before you can use them. The simplest way to document it is to create an example custom command and demonstrate how it works (Figure 15-2).

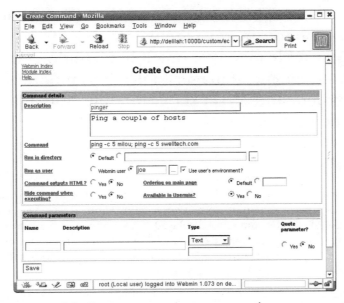

Figure 15-2: Create a new custom command

As you can see in the preceding figure, there is a command called *pinger*, which runs ping three times in succession for each of three computers on my network. The -c 5 sets **ping** to try to ping the host five times and then exit. The output of this command looks similar to Figure 15-3.

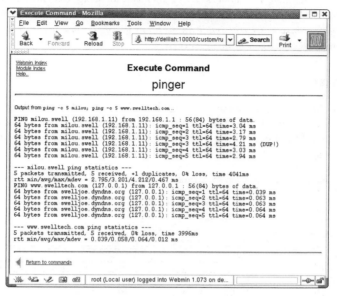

Figure 15-3: Output from pinger custom command

It is also possible to accept options for your commands by choosing a type of input and naming it in the **Command Parameters** section of the **Create Command** page (Figure 15-4). To make the above example more flexible, you can change it so that any host may be pinged by the user of the command.

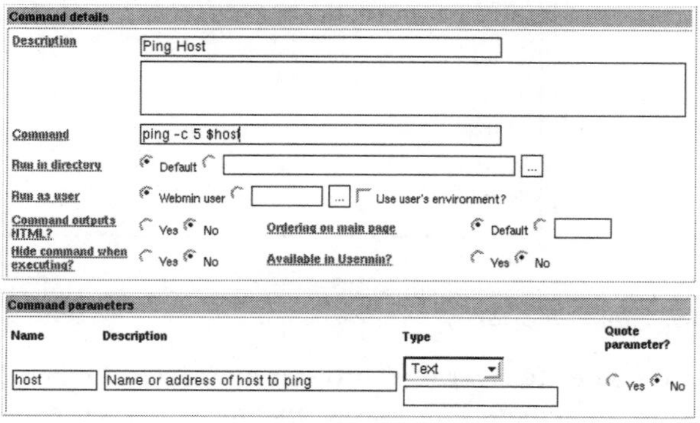

Figure 15-4: Ping Host custom command

In the preceding figure, you'll see that a variable named $host has been added to the command. I've still chosen to force -c 5 to be included in the command, although it could also be made into a variable option. Now, the user can choose to enter any host name they wish to ping in the text entry field provided.

The way this feature works is that a variable name is assigned to each entry field you create in the **Command Parameters** section. You can then insert those variables contents into the command that is executed.

NOTE *Beware that there have been security issues with allowing user-entered data on custom commands in the past. All known exploits have been fixed, but it is still probably a wise idea to carefully consider security implications before giving a normally untrusted user access to commands that allow arbitrary text entry.*

File Manager

The **File Manager** is a complete tool similar to the Windows Explorer or Nautilus. It is a Java applet that runs within your browser and provides most of the features one would expect from a traditional GUI-based file manager, including file copies, moves, deletions, editing, viewing, and more (Figure 15-5).

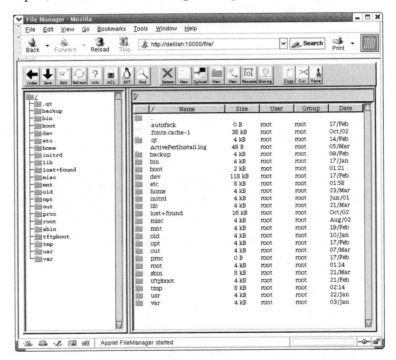

Figure 15-5: File Manager

To run the **File Manager** your browser must have the Java JVM plug-in. Its use is probably immediately obvious to anyone who has used Windows Explorer, Nautilus, or any other graphical file manager.

Editing

Clicking the Edit button while a text file is selected in the File Manager will open a simple text editor, similar in function to the Windows Notepad (Figure 15-6). The text editor supports cut and paste and simple search and replace. While not nearly as powerful or flexible as the traditional UNIX text editors, like vi and emacs, it can be useful to have an entirely web-based platform for editing text files on your Webmin server.

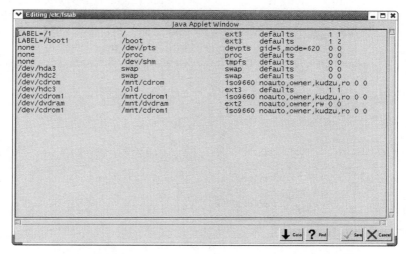

Figure 15-6: Editing

Info

Clicking the Info button with a filename selected in the File Manager will open a window containing some useful meta data about the file (Figure 15-7). This window provides information about the file ownership, permissions, setuid status, last modified date, and file size.

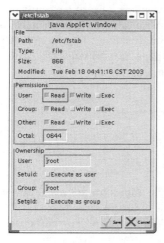

Figure 15-7: Info

EXT

On Linux, clicking the EXT button while a file is selected will open a new window listing the attributes of the file (Figure 15-8). File attributes can be used to make certain files behave differently than they ordinarily would. For example, selecting the "Do not allow modification" check box will *lock* the file, so that even the root user cannot change it without first unsetting this bit. To find out more about attributes in the Linux ext2 and ext3 filesystem, read the chattr man page.

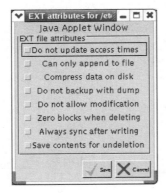

Figure 15-8: EXT

Perl Modules

The **Perl Modules** module provides an interface for browsing installed Perl modules, installing new Perl modules from CPAN, and uninstalling Perl modules.

The upper section of the page displays a list of currently installed modules, the number of submodules within the module, the description of the module, and the date on which the module was installed (Figure 15-9). Clicking the name of a module opens an information page that provides the names of the submodules and displays the module documentation.

Module	Submodules	Description	Installed on
Apache::DBI	1	Initiate a persistent database connection	Fri Jan 31 07:02:08 2003
Chronos	14		Fri Jan 31 07:04:39 2003
RPM::Specfile	0	Perl extension for creating RPM Specfiles	Mon Oct 14 04:27:55 2002
URI::Find	1	Find URIs in arbitrary text	Fri Jan 31 07:02:32 2003

Figure 15-9: Installed Perl modules

The lower portion of the module allows you to install new modules from a variety of sources. The first choice is to install directly from CPAN. If you know the name of the module you would like to install, you can enter it into the text field and click Install. Or, if you don't know the precise name, you can click the ... browse button to the right of the text entry field and browse the categorized CPAN archive. You can also install Perl modules from files, located on the local machine, your client machine, or on an FTP or HTTP server.

When installing a new module, you will be able to select the install actions Webmin will take (so you can test an install before actually doing it, if you like). You can also enter additional build and installation arguments and configure environment variables that will be active during the configuration and installation of the module.

System and Server Status

The **System and Server Status** module is a simple but flexible service monitor that provides emailed alerts, scheduled checks, and a status GUI (Figure 15-10). With this module, it is possible to monitor a server and its software to ensure it is operating as expected. The module provides tests for server daemon status, disk usage, CPU load, memory usage, ping response time, file modification, network traffic, and more.

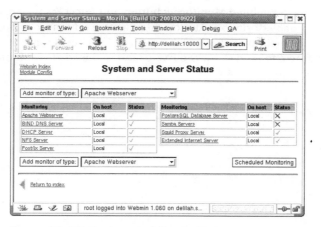

Figure 15-10: System and Server Status

Adding a Monitor

To add a new monitor, select a type of monitor from the drop-down list, and click **Add monitor of type**. This will open the **Create Monitor** page (Figure 15-11).

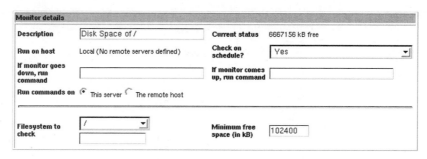

Figure 15-11: Create Monitor

In the preceding figure, you can see that the **Description** field has been set to Disk Space of /. This is the title that will be displayed on the main page of the module and will be used in any emailed status alerts regarding this monitor. **Run on host** is set to Local, but if any remote Webmin servers existed in my configuration, it could also check a remote system. **Check on schedule?** is set to Yes so that if automatic checks are enabled in the module configuration, this monitor will be tested. It is possible to specify commands to be run when the monitor goes down or comes back up, as well as specify on which host the commands will be run. For the **Filesystem to check** I've selected / and specified a minimum free space of 100MB.

Scheduled Monitoring

In order for status checks to be performed regularly (rather than only when you view the module main page), you must enable scheduled monitoring. To do this click on the **Scheduled Monitoring** button and select Yes for the **Scheduled checking enabled?** option. Also on this page are options to choose how often checks are performed, days and hours in which checks will be performed, an email address to send status reports to, and under what circumstances an email should be sent.

INDEX

BIND, *continued*
> server, 83, 99, 120–24, 126, 128–35, 137, 139–47, 149–53, 155–57, 205, 227
> slave zone, 133, 139
> stacksize, 127
> stub zone, 133, 139
> template records, 131, 135
> transfer format, 122, 126
> TXT record, 138
> WKS record, 138
> zone transfers, 122, 125–26, 132, 139

bootup, 51, 52, 252, 256–57

C

Cache Hierarchy, 219, 237, 238
cachemgr.cgi, 208
caching name server, 140, 224, 254
categories, 21, 63, 123, 124
certificate authority, 22, 23, 95
changepass.pl, 6
CNAME record, 137, 142
CPAN, 32, 39
cron, 35, 38, 47–48, 51, 61–62, 67
csh, 78

D

datasize, 137, 16
default shell, 72
device files, 55, 57
DHCP, 252, 253
dig, 144, 146–47
disk filesystems, 43
DNS client, 254
DNS keys, 122, 129
documentation, 32, 35, 54, 58–59, 64, 85, 89, 91, 93, 100, 104–05, 111, 114, 160, 195, 202, 258, 264
domain name system, 119, 138

E

environment variables, 68–70, 94, 98, 176
errata, xxv, 21

F

fdisk, 261
filesystems
> disk, 52, 56, 57, 133, 139, 258, 260–62
> Linux, 53–57, 61, 63, 67–68, 71–72, 75, 80, 114, 120, 127, 164, 167, 201, 207, 222, 224, 253, 256–58, 261–262, 264
> network, 52, 60, 83, 86, 89–91, 93, 96, 119–120, 125–29, 131, 133, 134, 135, 137–40, 142, 149, 153–54, 156, 165, 181, 182, 190, 191, 193, 195,.197, 202, 247, 262
> Solaris, 52, 53, 56–58, 63, 64, 72, 80, 114
finger, 74, 75, 77
firewall, 6, 16, 21, 26, 31, 34, 126, 133, 140, 162, 172–73, 201, 241, 244–245, 248
fstab, 54, 55
FTP, 16–17, 32, 72, 104, 112, 138, 149–58, 226, 236, 243, 248, 250
ftpd, 149, 150, 151, 153–56

G

gateway, 58, 97, 162, 168–69, 201, 226, 235, 251, 253
GhostScript, 263–64
GID, 56–57, 69, 71, 76, 79–81, 151, 251
GnuPG, 38, 41
group
> primary, 68, 71–73, 75, 80, 125, 135–36, 138, 140, 142–43, 147, 202
> secondary, 68–69, 72, 80

THE BOOK OF OPENOFFICE.ORG
Your Guide to the Free Microsoft Compatible Office Suite

author tba

This book is the complete guide to using this remarkably powerful and stable office suite. Practical and task-based, it includes coverage of installation, working with documents and spreadsheets, creating presentations and databases, using the draw utility, and much more. Clear and straightforward examples make it easy to switch from MS Office to OpenOffice.org.

2003, 432 PP., $34.95 ($52.95 CDN)
ISBN 1-886411-98-0

ABSOLUTE OPENBSD
UNIX for the Practical Paranoid

by MICHAEL W. LUCAS

This practical guide to mastering the powerful and complex OpenBSD operating system is for the experienced UNIX user who wants to add OpenBSD to his or her repertoire. It takes you through the intricacies of the platform and teaches how to manage your system, offering friendly explanations, background information, troubleshooting suggestions, and copious examples throughout.

2003, 600 PP., $39.95 ($61.95 CDN)
ISBN 1-886411-99-9

THE LINUX COOKBOOK
Tips and Techniques for Everyday Use

by MICHAEL STUTZ

Over 1,500 step-by-step Linux "recipes" cover hundreds of day-to-day issues, including printing; managing files; editing and formatting text; working with digital audio; creating and manipulating graphics; and connecting to the Internet.

Winner of the Outstanding Academic Title Award from Choice Magazine

2001, 402 PP., $29.95 ($44.95 CDN)
ISBN 1-886411-48-4

STEAL THIS COMPUTER BOOK 3
What They Won't Tell You About the Internet

by WALLACE WANG

This offbeat, non-technical book looks at what hackers do, how they do it, and how readers can protect themselves. The third edition of this bestseller adopts the same informative, irreverent, and entertaining style that made the first two editions a huge success. Thoroughly updated, this edition also covers rootkits, spyware, web bugs, identity theft, hacktivism, wireless hacking (wardriving), biometrics, and firewalls.

"If this book had a soundtrack, it'd be Lou Reed's Walk on the Wild Side.*"*
— InfoWorld

2003, 348 PP, $24.95 ($37.95 CDN)
ISBN 1-59327-000-3

ABSOLUTE BSD
The Ultimate Guide to FreeBSD

by MICHAEL W. LUCAS

FreeBSD, the powerful, flexible, and free UNIX-based operating system, is the preferred server for many enterprises. This definitive guide covers installation, networking, security, network services, system performance, kernel tweaking, file systems, SMP, upgrading, crash debugging, and much more.

"One of the Top Ten Books of 2002." — ;login

2002, 616 PP., $39.95 ($61.95 CDN)
ISBN 1-886411-74-3

PHONE:

1 (800) 420-7240 OR
(415) 863-9900
MONDAY THROUGH FRIDAY,
9 A.M. TO 5 P.M. (PST)

FAX:

(415) 863-9950
24 HOURS A DAY,
7 DAYS A WEEK

EMAIL:

SALES@NOSTARCH.COM

WEB:

HTTP://WWW.NOSTARCH.COM

MAIL:

NO STARCH PRESS
555 DE HARO STREET, SUITE 250
SAN FRANCISCO, CA 94107
USA

UPDATES

Visit **http://www.nostarch.com/webmin.htm** for updates, errata, and other information.